D1555230

FAMILIES AND SOCIETIES
SURVIVAL OR EXTINCTION?

To my mother

Contents

Preface to the
Revised Edition

Major changes have taken place in family life since the publication of the first edition of this book—some anticipated, some not anticipated.

It is now even more imperative than when the first edition of this book was written to make clear the connection between the economic and political characteristics of the wider society and family structure, functions, problems, and conflicts. This connection must be drawn for families and societies in the distant and not so distant past, and in the present, especially in the United States, where we have more data, but also in other parts of our one world.

As in the first edition, I will present a well-documented portrait of changes in family life in major types of societies and in the United States today. These changes will be explained largely as consequences of developments in technology, science, and in the amount, distribution, and control of economic resources within societies and within families. But the policy implications of current research data and the direct effects of inadequate government subsidized family support systems, especially in the United States, will be made more explicit in this edition.

An added section in the first chapter will make clear the distinction between sociological and psychological approaches to understanding family life and family problems. The chapter on the biological basis of family roles now includes additional research information on sex differences in personality—on sexual behavior as well as differences in aggressive behavior and other aspects of temperament. The present edition also contains more demographic data on contemporary family life in the United States.

Most sociologists in the United States are quite aware that knowledge is not power and that power corrupts. But we continue to hope for the emergence of a more distant vision on the part of the hereditary upper classes in capitalist societies. The politically active members of these classes court disaster as they promote economic disaster, among individuals and within families and societies, in the United States and elsewhere.

The pen is not mightier than the latest technological and scientific inventions for monitoring, controlling, and destroying dissatisfied and disenchanted populations. But we continue to write. We know and can document the effects of economic stress and deprivation, absolute and relative, on family relationships. We continue to write so that others can also know.

BETTY YORBURG

Preface to the

Original Edition

It has become very difficult, as scientific knowledge accumulates, to select, organize within a theoretical framework, and present to students and general readers a comprehensive, carefully documented synthesis of a specialized field of study. A short, general source that brings together the basic ideas of a sociological perspective on the family is rare in an age of specialization.

Introductory textbooks on this topic are usually massive and encyclopedic. They lack the integration of a unified theoretical perspective and they burden the student with summaries of countless numbers of discrete and fragmented studies whose relevance to major issues and problems in contemporary American family life is often lost. The statistics that are dutifully reported in such sources are soon outdated and even sooner forgotten.

Popularized accounts of topics such as divorce, marital infidelity, adolescence, and the so-called sexual revolution are interesting and relevant but may contain generalizations that are oversimplified or untrue. I feel it is an important obligation of social scientists to make available to others their information and their understanding of the nature of our society, carefully and in a language that communicates and does not alienate or frustrate the reader. Because my goal is a broad synthesis of accumulated social scientific knowledge about family life, rather than a detailed analysis, many subtleties and qualifications of the accumulated evidence will necessarily be omitted. I feel this is legitimate as long as the standard of accuracy is respected and pursued.

Whatever the variations in the structure and functioning of the family at different times and in different places, it is the basic group in human societies. It provides newborn members with their initial experiences of other human beings and with their earliest definitions of themselves and the world in which they are destined to live.

Knowledge of the roles people have played in family dramas through time and in different societies, the new roles and values that are emerging or becoming more widespread, and the societal sources and consequences of these changes in roles and values is a first step for individuals who want a basis for making choices in family life. We live in an era of unprecedented searching for meaning and guidance. Never before in Western societies has there been so much freedom for so many people to choose varying solutions to the problems of living.

Students in my classes at the City College of New York have been actively engaged in this search and in making these choices. Their refusal, at times, to accept the traditional wisdom has taught me, through the years, to avoid oversimplification, to go back, search the literature, reexamine the evidence on family life, and to come up with new answers—and new questions.

BETTY YORBURG

FAMILIES AND SOCIETIES

SURVIVAL OR EXTINCTION?

ONE

The Sociological Mandate

We live in a time when certain traditonal values are being challenged. Increasingly we are opting for new values or an insistence that old values be more effectively promoted. In family life, the formerly dominant values of loyalty, duty, obedience, and self-sacrifice are slowly being displaced by the standards of personal fulfillment, companionship, sexual gratification for both sexes, equalitarianism, and compatibility, at least among the upper classes in advanced industrial countries.

Critical questioning of the family, the economy, government, religion, and education arises whenever there is mobility: geographic (within and between countries), social (up and down the class structure), and psychological (in aspirations and expectations). In modern societies, these kinds of mobility are commonplace. Social change in the material and nonmaterial spheres is accelerated by developments in mass transportation and mass communication. Few people can avoid contact with what is new in thought and technology. The remotest village is subject to the step-by-step invasion of modern technology: first a road and a bus, then an electric power line, then a radio, and finally, television and the world.

Human expectations not only rise, they change or they become confused and uncertain. Modern humans have far greater possibilities of choice and unprecedented availability of alternatives. They tend to feel, increasingly, that these choices should be made rationally, although they may have grave doubts that this is possible.

In the past, during periods of rapid change and the breakdown of tradition, philosophers and religious and political leaders have arisen to provide alternatives and solutions. In modern times, social scientists are drawn into this arena, willingly or not. They are the new and the latest arrivals in the history of science. Objects farthest removed from humans (the stars and the planets) were the first to be withdrawn from the realm of the sacred and defined as proper subjects for study by the experimental method. The social sciences were the last to achieve the status of sciences, as the human animal came to be viewed as a legitimate object of empirical study and rational change. The social scientists first task is to provide accurate and reliable information about social life—information based on observation rather than impression, intuition, or speculation. The existence of social science is a logical outgrowth of trends toward secularism and rationalism in urban, industrial societies.

Religion declines in its influence over people's minds as the realm of the uncertain, the unknown, and the uncontrollable is narrowed by developments in science and technology. The belief in supernatural intervention in human affairs is supplemented, increasingly, by rational techniques for influencing these affairs. Ancient humans prayed to the gods for rain; modern humans seed the clouds and irrigate the land. Faith and fatalism decline together—often to be replaced by pessimism, however, in recent times.

Rationalism implies a means-ends orientation in action: a choice of the most efficient, logically and empirically effective means for realizing one's goals. Values determine goals. They are the intervening variables that may deflect behavior from the most rational course. Force, for example, or violence, may be the most effective means for obtaining or maintaining power in a particular situation. Yet it is rejected as a possible means where humanistic values prevail.

Rationalism and secularism proceed together to change the

quality of human life. To give an example from contemporary social life, traditional beliefs and ethics in the realm of sexual behavior are losing their hold on the populace. Empirical investigations by William Masters, Virginia Johnson, and others seek new prescriptions for sexual behavior on the basis of the scientific study of the sexual act.[1] For these scientists, the standards for determining sexual norms are rational rather than traditional or religious. The new value underlying their investigations is sexual gratification, a value that is consistent with the general decline in self-denial that is characteristic of industrialized societies.

This is only one example of the widespread tendency in modern societies to seek guidance for personal behavior from experts and from scientific knowledge. The psychotherapist, the doctor, and the social worker replace the priest, faithhealer, and extended family as a source of advice, support, and designs for living as individuals become increasingly aware of the possibility of thinking about and changing their personal destinies.

The Role of Sociology

Auguste Comte, the French social philosopher who gave sociology its name in the 1830s, defined the field as the scientific study of society. Its purpose, as in all science, was "to know in order to predict, to predict in order to control." When it is human beings, groups, or societies that one is studying, questions of control become problematic, however. Control involves a conception of desired goals. These goals depend, ultimately, on the values in a society, and in complex, heterogeneous societies, many values are not shared by all. The implementation of goals will depend on the allocation of societal resources by national decision-makers, based on priorities as they define them. Sociologists have been involved in these decisions only as consultants. They can, however, provide the raw material of rational choices. Their work can provide new awareness, understanding, implications, and guidelines for action.

Knowledge and understanding of human needs and how they

are met or not met in various social settings can provide a basis for action in social affairs, just as basic research in medicine guides the clinician's work and research in physics is applied by engineers. Inequalities in the distribution of power, wealth, and prestige and the existence of values and emotions in human beings undermine the possibility of unbridled human engineering, but the analogy is not entirely false.

Sociological knowledge cannot directly help people in making choices. Sociology is an academic discipline. It is not a helping profession. It can, however, help individuals understand that what they may regard as unique and idiosyncratic frustrations or dissatisfactions are a common response to common life conditions. People are rarely alone in their suffering. Accurate information about society may reveal this fact to them in a way that is more convincing, if not more dramatic, than a novel or play.

Human beings, especially in individualistic America, dislike being pegged and classified. Nevertheless, there are certain regularities, recurrences, and typicalities in social life. And while there are few unvarying laws in human social relationships, generalizations can be made. Individuals can make choices more critically if they are more aware of the constraints, the necessities, and the accidents of human existence.

Sociological knowledge can also dispel common-sense notions that are untrue. Impressions are often a poor guide to what is actually going on in large, complex, rapidly changing societies. In the area of family life, for example, sociological research has revealed that large families frequently are not happy families. Reported marital happiness declines, typically, with each additional child.[2] Children, especially in the United States, are an enormous economic burden for most families. A small income tax deduction does not compensate for the lack of free health care, monetary allowances, free higher education, and other support services provided by governments in most other industrial societies. In the United States, children are a psychological burden to parents, who blame themselves rather than the gods, the genes, or the government for their children's problems, accomplishments, successes, and failures. Children also interfere with the freedom, privacy, intimacy, and companionship that are highly valued in contemporary American marriages.

Sociologists have also discovered that with the widespread use of increasingly sophisticated labor-saving appliances in the home, wives and mothers in the United States who are employed full time spend about the same amount of time on combined job and homemaking activities as rural women spent on homemaking activities alone in the 1900's.[3] This is true despite the fact that standards of cleanliness, nutrition, and child care are higher now.

Comparisons of children reared in day care centers with those reared at home by their mothers have indicated that day care children tend to be more outgoing and self-reliant. They score lower on IQ tests, however, probaby because they experience less one-to-one contact and teaching from parents. But these differences diminish with time, and day care children are not, typically, more depressed, anxious, hostile, or tense than children reared at home.[4] The full-time physical availability of a mother in the home does not guarantee her emotional availability to the child, especially if she resents being at home.

Contradictory adages such as "absence makes the heart grow fonder" and "out of sight, out of mind" are both part of the folk wisdom of our society. Which is true? Only the painstaking, careful accumulation of evidence on the effects of separation on marriage can answer this question. The answer is that both are true. Short separations make the heart grow fonder; prolonged and repeated separations wreck marriages. Societal myths, whatever their reason for being, crumble in the face of hard evidence and an open mind.

Sociology and Psychology

How do sociological and psychological approaches to family life differ? To what extent are these differing approaches complementary? To what extent are they contradictory?

Psychologists in the past have focused on specific parent-child relationships as these result, typically, in specific personality traits in children: confidence or lack of confidence, high or low self-esteem, dependence or independence, aggression or passivity, dominance or submissiveness, cheerfulness or depression. They have given the greatest weight to parental child-rearing practices in explaining the behavior, emotions, attitudes, and values, success or failure, happiness or discontent of children.

Sociologists are also interested in the typical ways of thinking, acting, and feeling of parents and children. But we locate families in time and in geographic and cultural or subcultural space. We are primarily interested in how social locations such as prehistorical or historical era, generation, class, nationality, religion, race, gender, or urban-rural residence affect personality, experience, achievements, and destinies.

Psychologists have focused on specific parent-child relationships, such as those that lead to high or low levels of achievement motivation. Sociologists have focused on external factors such as economic resources, power, and opportunities as these have varied in major types of societies, at different times, and for different categories of people. We give these factors more weight in explaining differences in levels of achievement motivation among large numbers of people—males, females, blacks, whites, young, old, Catholics, Protestants, and Jews. We are more concerned with how parent-child relationships vary, typically, within major segments of society, primarily in response to changing political and economic circumstances.

The basic differences in the focus and emphasis of psychologists and sociologists in explaining human development and family life have political and economic implications that have been spelled out by social critics.[5] Psychological solutions are ideologically conservative. They divert attention from social reform to individual reform.

In the United States, home of the American Dream, which assumes that success is possible for everyone and failure is a matter of individual responsibility, psychological theories of success and failure have been more popular, perhaps, than in any other industrial society. Blame and guilt have been thrust upon parents and their offspring, especially as genetic explanations for crime, poverty, and psychological problems became outmoded and unpopular, at least until recently.

In the United States, social scientists, philosophers, mass media commentators, and other citizens have been especially attracted to noneconomic explanations and nonpolitical solutions for persisting economic, familial, and personal problems. In this country, a handful of families and individuals (one half of one percent of the population) owns almost half of all corporate stocks, over half of all bonds, and approximately 20 percent of the national wealth.[6] At the same time, compared to other industrial societies, the United States has the highest rates of delinquency, crime, and violence, the highest divorce rates, and the highest percentage of people living in absolute or borderline poverty, as defined by official government standards. But the federal government spends less than half the amount spent for public services by other industrial societies, on a per capita basis. In the land of the free, the additional funds to provide these services remain concentrated in the hands of the few.

Preferred solutions to family stresses and conflicts in the United States have focused on familial Home Start programs rather than federally funded Head Start programs, on parenthood training rather than job training, on individual shortcomings rather than group entitlement, on good neighbors rather than big government.

In recent years, a few prominent psychologists and psychiatrists, among them Kenneth Keniston,[7] Robert Coles,[8] and Urie Bronfenbrenner[9] have crossed over to an increasing awareness of the political and economic sources of family problems, especially as these vary, typically, for the classes, the races, and the sexes in the United States. But psychologists, as helping professionals, have usually been more concerned with diagnosis and symptomatic treatment than with radical cure. This cure will have to involve a basic and profound redistribution of economic resources and political power, away from the dominant, hereditary upper class in the United States. Nothing less can work, economically, if the standard is the greatest good of the greatest number.

This alternative, not necessarily revolutionary, could be implemented through the taxation and law enforcement prerogatives of the federal and local governments, to counteract current policies that benefit the extremely rich at the expense of the poor and the middle class. It is a realistic and rational alternative, and it is imperative if our children and our children's children are to survive, as a people and as a nation. In an increasingly interdependent world, a policy aimed primarily at redistributing the enormous wealth of the hereditary upper classes in the United States and elsewhere is essential to world survival and to international programs to control famine, contamination, exhaustion of natural resources, and, above all, nuclear warfare.

Theoretical Models

Philosophers, theologians, and literary observers have speculated about the family, its problems, and its destiny since the beginning of written history. Empirical study of the family, however, did not begin until the last half of the nineteenth century in Europe. The incentive was the need for reform that followed the confusion and disorganization of the Industrial Revolution: the increase in poverty, prostitution, illegitimacy, and divorce and the rise of movements to emancipate serfs, slaves, workers, and women.

The methods used in these early studies were; 1) historical—the collection and interpretation of data about the family from surviving firsthand accounts in letters, diaries, and official records; 2) survey research—the use of questionnaires and interviews to obtain contemporary information about large numbers of families separated by class, ethnic origin, religion, nationality, urban-rural residence; and 3) case study and participant observation—the intensive study by individual researchers of small numbers of families, in nonliterate societies by anthropologists who lived in the community or with the families they studied, and in industrial societies by other researchers who collected and wrote down life histories of families.

These methods, increasingly refined to eliminate sources of bias and error, are still the most popular in family study. Modern technology, such as the use of the tape recorder and video tape for data collecting and computers for data processing, has improved the accuracy and the efficiency of both quantitative and qualitative, large-scale and small-scale social scientific research on the family.

The experimental method has also become popular, especially since World War II.[10] Face-to-face interaction in the family is observed, under controlled conditions, for a limited period of time. The purpose is to record the effects of changes, such as a task to perform, on family communication patterns, decision-making processes, dominance of one member over others, and so on.

Science requires not only the accumulation of facts but the interpretation and explanation of these facts. This is what sociological theory is: statements of association or cause and effect that attempt to answer the question "Why?" These statements are formulated with the help of concepts and models. All sciences have models, or frames of reference, that define their particular windows on the world. These models consist of concepts that sensitize and guide observation, although they may also distort it. Concepts are abstract terms that classify or categorize people, places, things, and events. They are useful for summarizing complex aspects of reality in shorthand words or phrases, or for pointing to aspects not readily apparent to the casual observer.

In the Marxian economic model of society, for example, class struggle, exploitation, and, currently, alienation are central concepts. The concept of class is a succinct way of referring to a large category of people who possess similar amounts of prestige, power, and wealth. Given this concept of class, one can investigate the relationship between class and values, class and child-rearing practices, and class and personality. Without this concept, a possible source of explanation of similarities or typical differences that exist in a society would be impossible.

Fads in the use of specific concepts in the social sciences reflect changing concerns about different aspects of social or personal reality during any particular historical era. Currently, the concepts of alienation, identity, power structure, charisma, counterculture, and life style have moved out of the realm of social science analysis and become adopted as part of the popular culture.

For interpreting patterns in social life, models that have been influential in the social sciences are Social Darwinism,[11] Marxism,[12] and structural functionalism.[13] Other models that have been employed, particularly in studying the family, have been useful primarily as frameworks for organizing descriptive information about the family. The family life cycle or life span model, for example, helps organize research data about the family on a time perspective from the beginning of a marriage that remains intact to its end, with the death of one of the marital partners. The concepts in this model, concepts such as development or developmental tasks, are descriptive rather than explanatory. They provide rubrics under which can be placed descriptions of role changes that occur in typical family groups through time, as children are born, or leave after growing up, and as parents age. The model has little usefulness in explaining long-range historical changes in family functioning, however.[14]

Social Darwinism, Marxism, and structural functionalism, on the other hand, contain concepts that embody built-in explanatory assumptions. In the Marxist model of society, class struggle is a concept that has intrinsic explanatory implications. It is a principle that is used to explain the course of world history. Class, on the other hand, is a descriptive concept.

One model may include both types of concepts. In the psychoanalytic model, the concept of psychosexual stages is descriptive and helps organize data on personality development. Other concepts, the unconscious, defense mechanisms, oedipal conflict, are more closely linked to the problem of interpreting and explaining the particular course that personality development takes in an individual's life history.

Social Darwinism

Social Darwinism is an evolutionary model of societies and social change that had its greatest vogue at the end of the nineteenth century. Darwin's theory of organic evolution, in which the human species was the ultimate product of a unilinear and progressive selective breeding process, was applied to different populations and to the evolution of their technologies and cultures. The principles of struggle for existence and natural selection were used to explain the inequality of nations, races, classes, and men and women. Social Darwinists added the concept of the survival of the fittest to Darwin's model. The assumption was that those at the top belong there by virtue of better biological equipment—intelligence, constitution, and temperament—opportunity and other factors having always been equal.

Historically, the model served to legitimate colonialism and as an argument against social reform, since helping the poor was regarded as preserving the unfit. The white, upper-class, nineteenth-century Englishman and his culture were believed to be the ultimate among men, the final and perfected products of selective evolution. Proponents of Social Darwinism chose from history examples that supported their thesis of biological determinism and ignored contradictory evidence. Institutions such as the family were believed to have evolved to monogamy as the highest and most perfect form. The many examples of monogamy within nonliterate, tribal societies, as among the African Bushmen, were ignored. The notion of white supremacy prevailed despite the fact that the founders of Western civilization, the ancient Egyptians, were a mixture of African and Semitic stocks, and the Dark Ages in Europe coexisted with a period of high technological development in China.

Social Darwinism still persists in some quarters to explain or justify differences in the power and privileges of human beings. An example of this kind of thinking is the assertion that American blacks have genetically determined "patterns of ability" that differ from those of whites.[15] Specifically, this refers to an assumed lesser, hereditary capacity for practical problem-solving behavior and abstract reasoning. It is argued further, that while "the full range of human talents is represented in all the major races of man, Negroes brought here as slaves were selected for docility and strength rather than mental ability and that through selective mating the mental qualities never had a chance to flourish."[16] Once again the specter is raised of "dysgenic effects" on the total population, such as lowering the general IQ level, of current welfare practices, which presumably preserve the genetically unfit.[17]

Few would argue that there is a hereditary component in the intelligence of individuals. Despite serious methodological problems, studies of identical twins reared apart and numerous other kinds of studies support this argument. However, there is no evidence to support the claim of genetically determined intellectual abilities specific to particular classes, nations, races, or the sexes.

In the argument about American blacks, a major untested and questionable assumption is that docility and strength, traits that presumably characterized the initial slave population, are negatively associated with hereditary intelligence. Furthermore, despite strong sanctions against racial intermarriage and interbreeding, the initial gene pool of blacks in this country has not been preserved in pristine state. Physical anthropologists estimate that at least 70 percent of American blacks have some degree of white ancestry in their biological makeup at this point in history.

At the present time, Social Darwinism and biological determinism are discredited, generally, by most social scientists. But ideologies that justify political and economic inequality have a tendency to resurface, especially in a time of worldwide social movements to promote greater equality in the opportunities and resources of minority groups.

Sociobiology is a contemporary, interdisciplinary attempt to explain the differences between the cultures and the achievements of various peoples and the two sexes largely on biological grounds.[18] Sociobiologists assume the existence of specific genetic coding for specific, complex behavior traits such as homosexuality, selfishness, or fear and hostility toward strangers.

In a recent monograph, two sociobiologists argue that cultures evolve as a consequence of adaptive genetic change or mutation that are transmitted genetically from generation to generation in the form of discrete "culturgens"—genetically coded behavior patterns.[19] Cultural differences between societies in technological development, therefore, are biologically based and cannot be readily changed by well-meaning reformers or by self-serving profiteers.

The concept of culturgens is a mythical hybrid that cannot be empirically observed or supported by scientific evidence. It ignores the role of accident, discovery, and invention in technological evolution and cultural change. It ignores the fact that cultural diffusion occurs in the absence of interbreeding of human populations. It ignores the common problems of human existence for which common nonbiological solutions have been found. It cannot account for the very rapid increase in technological and cultural change in Europe within the past 250 years, and even faster—100 years—in Japan. Evolution and genetic change in human populations do not occur rapidly enough to explain technological and cultural change.

Social Darwinism and its never ending spin-offs cannot provide a valid explanation of social change, cultural differences, and large-scale inequalities among human populations. Yet the evolutionary model, divorced of biological underpinnings, does have explanatory value when applied to technological change and the accumulation of scientific knowledge in human societies. This particular application of the model, in fact, has become quite popular recently in sociology and anthropology in interpreting world history, family history, and the changing relationships between men and women.[20]

In the realm of technological change, there has been a trend toward the selecting out of more efficient and effective techniques in controlling the material environment. Historically, there has been a progressive harnessing of energy, from animal power, to steam power, to electric power, to atomic power, and a progressive accumulation of scientific knowledge. Some societies have remained stationary, in this respect, for thousands of years, while others have regressed technologically, usually after a defeat in war. Ancient Rome is an example; its defeat ushered in the technologically impoverished Dark Ages in Europe. Still others have skipped stages, sometimes quite dramatically, through cultural diffusion, borrowing techniques, skills, and knowledge from more technologically advanced societies. The rapid industrialization of the Soviet Union and China are examples.

While the claim that differential technological development is related to different genetic endowments of human populations cannot be supported, the theory of a progressive and cumulative trend in technological development as a basic factor in the course of world history does seem to be generally valid, despite some fluctuations and reversals.[21]

We cannot claim, however, that there has been an evolutionary pattern in other, nonmaterial spheres of life—in the realm of attitudes and values and in the psychological quality of human life. It would be very difficult to support the argument that there has been a progressive trend toward greater happiness, justice, morality, and freedom in human societies.

Patterns of killing and maiming have changed: cannibalism, scalping, and human sacrifice have been supplanted by more efficient techniques such as atomic and germ warfare, gas chambers, and napalm. But hatred and cruelty persist. We no longer hang people for stealing a loaf of bread, but justice favors the rich and the powerful. Upper-class people do not get executed for murder. And white-collar crime, which is far more costly to taxpayers and to society, is punished far less severely than street crime. Bribery, corruption, tax fraud, and the manufacture and distribution of unsafe products under unsafe conditions are middle- and upper-class crimes, secret, less immediately obvious than muggings and murders, committed by people with the power and money to resist or even prevent prosecution and punishment.

Of human happiness we have no measure. The sources and reasons for unhappiness have changed, but discontent, hopelessness, and despair persist. The misery that results from actual material deprivation has declined in industrial societies, but the misery that results from rising but unfulfilled expectations has increased. The mass media, particularly television, have whetted appetites in a way that far surpasses the unaided imagination of isolated people in traditional societies.

Freedom has increased in the sense that a greater number of people have more choice in determining their individual or collective destinies, but again this is largely a matter of class. The poor have few choices. And involuntary servitude persists in prisons, in mental hospitals, and in other, less obviously restrictive, groups and organizations.

Technological change, however, up to the point of achieving the possibility of destroying the world by contamination, depletion of natural resources, nuclear warfare, and overpopulation (science and technology keep people alive) has been progressively adaptive—if we use the standards of the sources of energy available and the accumulation of empirical knowledge about the world.

This aspect of the evolutionary model, the progressive development of science and technology, will provide a useful criterion for constructing a typology of human societies in chapter 3. On the basis of this typology, it is possible to understand and explain many of the patterns and the changes in family structure, functioning, and values that have taken place in different societies during the span of human history.

The Marxian Model

A second model of society that has been influential in the social sciences, especially in Europe, is the Marxian model. This model is commonly referred to as "economic determinism" by American social scientists. The Marxian model is one in which the basic conflicts, the distribution of power, and the nature and course of social change in societies are believed to be products of the economic organization of the society: the way in which goods and services are produced and distributed. Conflict, between societies, the classes, and men and women, based on differences in the control of productive property and in economic interests, is seen as the motive force in human history. The means of production in this model refers to technology and economic resources; the relations of production refer to the class system. Social change rests, ultimately, on technological development and the conflicts that derive from differences in property and power.

This explanatory model, relabeled the conflict theory model and modified to give weight to other, nonecomonic factors in determining social order and social change, has grown more popular in the United States, now that economic and political crises are recurring features of the American scene. The emphasis on conflict and the economic sources of conflict (class conflict in the original model, plus race, sex, and generational conflict currently) now seems more appropriate to an explanation of American social reality than it did during earlier decades, such as the period of enforced consensus in the silent 1950s. There are fads in models as well as in concepts that reflect societal needs for explanation at any particular time.

The Marxian model, particularly as it promotes sensitivity to the relationship between economic resources and power, can be very helpful in interpreting changes in family life historically. Authority relations within the family, between husband and wife and parent and child, are and have been strongly influenced by economic factors. The changing status of women during the course of world history has been closely tied to their changing economic roles in various types of societies, as we will see. And, at any particular time in history, including the present, the economic class location of families in a society is a very important factor in understanding typical differences in family values and family relationships in that society.

Structural Functionalism

Structural functionalism, usually referred to simply as functionalism, is a model of society that derives its name from the fact that the existence of any phenomenon in a society or group— the family, social inequality, the incest taboo—is explained in terms of the function it performs for the maintenance or preservation of the society or the group. Societies and groups are viewed as bounded structures or systems, composed of interrelated parts. The primary focus is on the needs of systems, such as the group or the society, rather than on the needs of individuals: "The basic function fulfilled by the family in all societies is the replacement of dying members."[22] The function of social stratification, the system of unequal rewards and privileges in a society, is to "insure that the most important positions are conscientiously filled by the most qualified persons," and the occupations that are most highly rewarded in terms of income, status, and power are those that "(a) have the greatest importance for society, and (b) require the greatest amount of training or talent."[23] The poor have higher rates of illegitimacy because "the society will be less concerned with illegitimacy when it occurs in the lower social ranks, since their position is less significant for the larger social structure."[24] Incest taboos are found in every society ever observed because "they force the young in each generation to leave the nuclear family in order to find mates. Therefore the society is made more cohesive, for many links are forged between families that might otherwise turn inward on themselves."[25] Individual needs are subordinated to social needs as explanatory principles in the functionalist model.

In the functionalist view of society as a system of interrelated parts, change in one part of the system reverberates throughout the system and reacts back on the original source of change. Change may occur independently in any major institutional sector: the family, the economy, religion, or government. Causation, therefore, is multiple and reciprocal. This is a major difference in the model from that of the biological and economic determinisms of Social Darwinism and Marxian economics.

Social integration, according to the functionalist model, is based on agreement and consensus within the society, particularly about values. Economic interdependence as a source of integration is deemphasized,[26] as is the integration forced by political repression. The role of technological and economic factors in social change is minimized. Ideological factors, attitudes, values, beliefs, are given greater weight relatively.[27] The concepts of power and conflict are usually omitted from the model.[28] In this respect functionalism is antithetical to the Marxian model of society. Functionalists, guided by their model, see order and consensus wherever they look; Marxists, surveying the same social terrain, see disorder and conflict.

Some functionalists posit a state of equilibrium as the natural tendency of society, corresponding to the tendency toward homeostasis in the human body. They interpret permanence and change in a society in terms of this standard. They believe that social phenomena that are dysfunctional for the equilibrium of the system are cast out or modified and absorbed into the system, just as antibodies engulf and absorb invading microbes in the human body. Thus, revolution leads to counterrevolution and back again to a new stability in the interrelationships between the major institutions in a society. Attitudes and values tend to catch up with changes in the economy that disrupt social order. The dislocations, disorganization, and suffering caused by the Industrial Revolution are eventually balanced by changes in attitudes and values that lead to a redefinition of the role of government. The government, in socialist or welfare state form, takes over the functions that the lord of the manor or the extended family no longer performs. Equilibrium is thus restored by virtue of society's inherent self-regulating propensity and, in the process, all major interdependent institutions in the society are transformed.

An objection that has been leveled against the equilibrium aspect of the model is that the assumption of an inherent tendency for societies to restore themselves can be used as an argument against deliberate reform and planned social change. Furthermore, when societies are in constant change, how does one determine disequilibrium or restored equilibrium?

Probably most contemporary American sociologists, including those who would not identify themselves as functionalists, would accept the multiple causation aspect of the model. They view the major institutions in society as interdependent and interrelated. They accept the importance of consensus in society but feel that conflict, dissent, and disequilibrium are equally intrinsic to social life. They feel that both aspects of social reality must be accounted for in an adequate general description or model of society.[29]

Many sociologists also feel that both individual and social needs must be taken into account in analyzing social phenomena. The family does function to replace dying members of society, but this is not necessarily a more basic function than that of providing for the needs of newborn members of the society. Both are equally valid reasons for the universal existence of family groups.

The incest taboo controls envy, conflict, and hostility within the family, thus facilitating the fulfillment of family members' needs for a stable source of love and security. These needs are as important as the need of society for links between family groups. Actually, marriage in urban, industrial societies no longer fulfills the function of forging links between families and promoting social chohesiveness. Marriages based on personal preference and relatively free choice and resulting in independent, mobile, increasingly isolated nuclear families are not the alliances between families that they once were when families, particularly in the upper classes, arranged the marriages of their offspring.

The Conflict Theory Model

Sociologists who do not accept the consensus and equilibrium aspects of the functionalist model, but who are not traditional Marxists, are usually identified as conflict theorists. For them conflict and instability are the natural state of society. Many conflict theorists, unlike orthodox Marxists, however, give independent weight to ideological factors in explaining social change and historical trends and, as pointed out earlier, they focus on other sources of societal conflict in addition to economic differences.

Traditional China provides an excellent example of the role of ideology in the history of a particular society. This country possessed many of the technological preconditions of industrialization. China invented paper, printing, gunpowder, and the compass. While learning was valued, however, the memorizing of the Confucian classics and the mastery of over two thousand elaborate ideographs was not the kind of learning that promoted technological development. On the other hand, the ideology of the socialist revolution in China has inspired rapid and far-reaching technological change in that country in recent times.

It is now generally accepted that attitudes, beliefs, and values in a society can have a powerful inhibiting or accelerating effect on technological and economic change. In this country the American Dream has probably been a very important factor in the slow pace of economic reform in America relative to certain other European democracies.

Ideologies affect the rate of technological development and the content of technological innovation. A country that values power very highly is more likely to develop rockets and atomic bombs than a country that values peace at almost any price. Other factors such as cultural diffusion, climate and geography, migration, war and conquest are also significant in determining the direction and pace of technological development.

Ideological factors become more important in affecting social change in industrial societies. The concentration of power at the top levels of government, democratic, oligarchic, or totalitarian, the existence of mass communication and mass transportation, which make it easier to reach and control all citizens in a society, and the fact of far greater economic and technological resources at the command of political leaders, all combine to enhance the role of ideology in social change. It is much easier now for rulers to implement decisions based on ideological principles than it has been in the past.

The conflict model has become more popular in American sociology recently, while functionalism is declining in influence. This reflects the greater prominence of overt conflict in American society in recent times. Either model used alone can distort the observation of social reality, and yet both have a handle on the truth. The distortion in the functionalist model lies in its overemphasis on consensus in societies. This stems, in part, from the fact that the model was originally formulated on the basis of data from nonliterate tribal societies, where overt conflict *is* usually repressed and where consensus regarding values *is* almost universal. Class, ethnic, racial, or religious minorities are rare in these societies; there is little contact with widely differing societies and alternative values, and the rate of social change is slow. In this type of society, one can speak of a social phenomenon as being functional or advantageous for the entire society because interests within different segments of the society are not that dissimilar.

In complex heterogeneous societies, however, one has to ask, functional for whom? The social stratification system of these societies is not equally functional for all segments of the society. There are stumbling blocks to perfectly free social mobility; parents pave the way for their children, if they can. Unequal rewards of power and privilege may be functional for the society in that they motivate people to train for more difficult occupations at the middle levels. Nevertheless, stratification systems are most functional for those at the top and for their children, regardless of their occupations and contributions to society.

Social inequality also has dysfunctional as well as functional consequences for the preservation and the maintenance of the entire society. The anthropological evidence points quite clearly to the fact that there was much less conflict, envy, and hostility within simple hunting and gathering societies, where differences in economic rewards and privileges were minimal. The sharing of the catch and the kill was common; it was essential for survival. Organized group warfare and pronounced intragroup hostility arose with the development of technology and the accumulation of an economic surplus in societies that was not shared equally by all. War was unknown for 99 percent of human history.[30]

Of course there are other factors involved in the close association between warfare and more advanced technological development. When hunting declines and other animals are no longer the object of the kill, human aggressive impulses, everpresent because frustration is everpresent, become directed toward other humans, strangers and friends, especially if the culture does not prohibit this or if social control mechanisms are ineffective.

The conflict theory model may also distort the perception of its users so that the actual or potential conflict in a society is overestimated. Affluence diminishes the intensity of intra- and intergroup conflict. This is the rationale behind reforms from above instituted by the ruling classes in capitalist societies. Cooptation usually works. Conflict between groups also has positive functions in that it promotes solidarity within groups. The civil rights movement in the United States enhanced feelings of a common identity and a common heritage among American blacks, as revealed in the concept of "soul" and in the borrowing of family appellations such as "brother" and "sister" to refer to fellow blacks.

Models and Interpretations

Proponents of any one of the three original models—Social Darwinism, Marxism, and structural functionalism—have interpreted the same social fact differently. An illustration will make clear how models shape scientific investigation and explanation.

Male superiority within the family, in prestige, authority, and privilege, is a fact of life in almost all known societies. No valid instances of true matriarchal societies have been known to exist. Even in martilineal societies where descent is calculated through the female line and where newly married couples live with the wife's relatives (matrilocal residence) authority in the family is usually invested with the wife's male relatives. How can this be explained?

Herbert Spencer, probably the most prominent of the late nineteenth-century Social Darwinists, attributed male superiority to the biological fact that women experience "a somewhat earlier arrest of individual evolution . . . necessitated by the reservation of vital power to meet the cost of reproduction." The "mental manifestations" of the earlier biological maturation of women are a "perceptible falling-short in those two faculties, intellectual and emotional, which are the latest products of human evolution—the power of abstract reasoning and the most abstract of the emotions, the sentiment of justice—the sentiment that regulates conduct irrespective of personal attachments and the likes or dislikes felt for individuals."[31]

Functionalists would interpret male superiority in terms of the more significant roles males play in the fulfillment of certain societal needs: their greater role in war, in government, in the economy, and in ceremonials that promote social solidarity and cohesiveness, particularly in nonliterate tribal societies and in preindustrial societies. "The higher the skill and responsibility of the man in extrafamilial roles, the greater is the effective superiority of the husband in family decision-making."[32] Notice that this explanation rests on the male's level of skill and responsibility within the society and not necessarily on his relationship to the economic means of production.

According to the Marxian model, male superiority arises from, and is related to, the control of private property by males. Frederick Engels traced an evolutionary pattern in husband-wife relationships within the family that corresponded to stages of economic development. The earliest stages, where property was communal, were characterized by the relatively unstable matings of group marriage or temporary "pairings." Women's status was not only high, it was "supreme" because the biological fathers of offspring could not be identified and because in the communistic household "the administration of the household entrusted to women was just as much a public function, a socially necessary industry, as the procuring of food by men."[33] We see here, incidentally, in the relating of the performance of "socially necessary" functions to the status of women, that this model overlaps with the functionalist model. The reverse is also true. Functionalists find it difficult to avoid economic interpretations in their analyses.

Engels claimed that women lost their high status after the domestication of animals took place. This led to the accumulation of wealth and the concept, as well as the fact, of private property. Men, who commanded the herds, took command in the home also. "Women were stripped of their dignity, enslaved, [and became] the tools of men's lust and mere machines for the generation of children.'' Monogamy arose, not as the ''fruit'' of individual ''sex love'' but to guarantee the transmission of the patriarch's property to his legitimate heirs.[34] Monogamy (fidelity), however, applied in fact, only to the female. The double standard, prostitution, and hetaerism coexisted with monogamy as a consequence of the male's superior power and privilege. The class struggle and oppression in the wider society were paralleled by the struggle between man and wife in the home.

Engels' solution was the abolishment of private productive property and the employment of women in public industry. The necessity of women to surrender themselves for money would then disappear, prostitution would be abolished, and effective monogamy for both sexes would become a reality. Economic considerations would become irrelevant to the choice of a marriage partner, since both mates would be economically independent. There would be no motive for marriage except mutual inclination, and women would not tolerate infidelity because they would no longer be dependent upon their husbands for the support of themselves and their children.[35]

Ample support can be mustered for Engels' thesis of a relationship between economic factors and free choice in courtship and marriage. Historically, the higher the class, the more likely that marriages were arranged by the two families involved, with or without the consent of the prospective married pair. On the other hand, in traditional rural China, marriage was decided and arranged by family elders even among the poorest peasants. In this kind of situation, where there was strong emphasis on family lineage and respect and deference for elders and where the young couple lived with the husband's parents, the personality of the prospective bride and likelihood that she would be compatible with her new relatives, especially her mother-in-law, were important reasons for the control of marriage by parents. Economic factors were not absent, however, since likely prospects were also evaluated in terms of qualities such as physical strength, good health, and ability to work hard.

In contemporary American society, while romantic love is the culturally prescribed basis for marriage, economic factors are obviously not irrelevant since the great majority of marriages take place between people of the same class. The effect of economic factors on marital choices may be indirect, however, since class is associated with attitudes, values, education, and other factors that affect feelings of mutual attraction.

While male superiority is a pattern in all societies, the degree of difference between men and women in power and privilege tends to decline considerably in urban, industrial society. How would the three models be used to explain the rising status of women in highly industrialized societies?

Social Darwinism cannot explain this fact since genetic endowment does not change rapidly enough to account for a change that has occurred largely within the past fifty years.

An explanation in terms of economic factors has greater validity. Women have always contributed to the economic resources of the family. In agricultural societies, they produced crafts, did piece work, and tended the smaller animals.[36] They bartered or sold butter, eggs, poultry, and produce from their gardens. They took in laundry and boarders. They worked as domestics. They converted raw materials brought in by males into food, clothing, and household necessities. Not until later stages of industrialization did large numbers of women go out to work in factories, offices, stores, and schools and begin to acquire a significant source of *independent* income. As women became less economically dependent, the patriarch eventually lost his almost exclusive control over family economic resources and a major basis for his arbitrary authority within the home.

Functionalists would explain the rising status of women in industrial societies in terms of their greater participation in nonfamilial activities that are important to the maintenance of society in modern times, particularly in the economy, but also in recreation (entertainment) and, to a much lesser extent, in government and the military. This, in turn, has to be explained and, in fact, it has been explained by functionalists largely in terms of changes in the economy and technology since the Industrial Revolution that have propelled women into gainful employment outside the home to a greater extent in modern times.[37]

In industrial societies, women become essential to the corporate economy. Even if we assume complete interchangeability in work roles, the male unemployment rate does not begin to approach the number of women in the work force. If all women were removed from the economy, the vast, interdependent network of exchange of goods and services that characterizes industrialized economies would collapse. Most men would not take jobs, such as secretary, nurse, or elementary schoolteacher, that are sex-typed as feminine.

The proposition that control over economic resources has an important relationship to authority within the home is supported by accumulating survey research evidence. Married women who work have more authority in decision-making processes within the family; the longer they have worked the greater is their authority; and, the higher the prestige and income of their occupation, relative to their husband's, the greater is their authority in the home.[38]

Studies in less highly industrialized societies, however, such as Greece, Yugoslavia, and France, indicate that where strong patriarchal values persist, they diminish the effects of gainful employment of the wife on family authority patterns. The cultural context has to be taken into account in making this kind of generalization.[39] The trend, nevertheless, is clearly in the direction of even greater female participation in the work force for more years of their lives, and toward the greater legal, political, personal, and marital authority of women in modern societies.

Further evidence on this point is provided by anthropological accounts of horticultural societies. These societies have the technique of plant cultivation, but they do not have the plough and they do not have the knowledge of irrigation, fertilization, and crop rotation techniques. In horticultural societies, women are more likely to do the planting and harvesting, since the gardens and fields are close enough to the hearth so that this kind of work does not interfere with their childbearing and child-rearing obligations.

Matrilineal and matrilocal types of family organization, in

which women have higher status and authority, are most likely to be found in this type of society. In advanced agricultural societies and in industrial societies, where men make the most significant direct contribution to the subsistence needs of the family, these patterns of family organization are rare.

The responsibility of providing for the economic resources of the family is not the only basis for authority in the family, however. Other resources, such as intelligence, education, good health, and physical strength that may be differently distributed between husband and wife also affect authority patterns within the home. In the working class, in all countries for which there is evidence, including the United States, male authority may take the form of dominance based on greater physical strength. Wife beating may maintain the husband's authority even where the wife works and has an independent source of income.

A Sociological Perspective

An analysis of family life through time and across cultures that claims to present an adequate sociological perspective should attempt to integrate the valid aspects of the evolutionary, functionalist, and Marxist or conflict theory models. These models are useful to an understanding of the problems of order and change in total societies—the macrosocial level of analysis. They can help answer questions such as why some societies have developed along certain economic, political, and cultural directions while others have had very different histories.

THE ROLE THEORY MODEL

A sociological perspective should also provide a framework that joins the individual in the family group to the larger society and the culture. The role theory model provides this missing link. This model applies to the microsocial level of analysis— interpretations of face-to-face interactional processes within social groups.

As pointed out earlier, theory is concerned with explanations, with answering questions of *why* certain phenomena exist or occur. At a more concrete and more readily observable level, theory is also concerned with explaining *how* certain events unfold and take place. The focus is on the socialization process, the learning of roles or scripts that establish the guidelines for behavior in various kinds of recurring group situations, including the family.

This model contains fewer untested or untestable assumptions than Social Darwinism, Marxism, or functionalism. It falls within the realm of what Robert Merton called "theories of the middle range."[40] Sociologists and social psychologists who employ role theory in their research do not answer ultimate questions about social life and social change, but they tread on less controversial ground because their propositions are more closely tied to the collection of data.

It is easier to be convincing when one is explaining how and why the process of socialization leads to typical values, such as obedience to authority in the working class, than to support the thesis that there is a tendency toward equilibrium in societies.

The basic assumption of the role theory model is that human beings are not born with hereditary instincts, or genetic codes— the modern euphemism for hereditary instincts—that determine complex, goal-oriented behavior. A second assumption is that humans behave in patterned and more or less predictable ways because they learn roles that define mutual expectations in typical and recurring social relationships.

While few social scientists would quarrel with the first assumption, there are some who would claim that there are very few specific and widely agreed-upon roles or scripts associated with any particular status. They would argue that most individuals improvise behavior from cues in actual interactional settings; and that they establish patterns in succeeding interactions on the basis of trial and error rather than preconceived, culturally defined expectations. The other extreme allows for very little deviation from what are believed to be rather rigid and unmanipulable role prescriptions for most social relationships. Reality, in urban, industrial societies, lies somewhere in between.

STATUS AND ROLE. Role is a central concept in sociology, comparable to the concept of personality in psychology. Humans are social animals. In most of their relationships with other human beings they act from the vantage point of a widely recognized position or status, such as mother, doctor, president, or priest, and they tend to abide by internalized roles, or guides to behavior that are defined as appropriate to these statuses by the groups with whom they identify or who control them. These scripts or roles specify the rights and obligations of individuals occupying a particular status. They consist of prescriptions for behavior, thought, and emotion that are normatively regulated.

College students, entering a classroom for the first time at the beginning of a semester, follow certain general guidelines and fulfill generally agreed-upon expectations in their behavior. They take a seat. They listen and take notes. They raise their hands if they wish to speak. They use formal and polite rather than personal or intimate language. And they leave usually after a prescribed period of time. Variations of ritual are permissible, but usually within explicitly defined limits.

Professors also fulfill mutual expectations in their role performance. If they stood on their heads instead of lecturing, the situation would become unstructured, unpredictable, and even ludicrous. Much humor, incidentally, stems from the unexpected stepping out of a role by participants in a familiar and recurring social situation. Laughter is often the response to inappropriate role behavior that startles, confuses, or embarrasses partners in typical social interactions.

CULTURE AND SUBCULTURE. The culture, the basic heritage of knowledge, skills, attitudes, values, and behavioral norms, that is learned and transmitted to almost all members of a society defines the limits, the extremes of variation in role prescriptions. No infant in American society is weaned at the age of six or swaddled from head to toe at birth, although these patterns have been typical in other societies. Most Americans speak English, learn to read and write, and value achievement.

Within the broad limits set by the culture, subcultures contain typical variations in role definitions and specify somewhat different intellectual, emotional, and behavioral requirements for playing the same roles. The major subcultures in urban, industrial societies are those associated with class, national origin, race, religion, sex, and age. Subcultural variations in role prescriptions reflect differences in life circumstances of various segments of the society. As these life circumstances change, and they change very rapidly in highly industrialized societies, roles change. The lag between traditional role conceptions and changed social conditions accounts for much confusion and suffering in society today, especially in family life.

In addition to subcultural differences in role definitions, the ultimate source of variation in role performance, and a very important one, lies in individual differences in intelligence, constitution, and temperament, and in unique life experiences. For this reason, no two individuals occupying the same status will play the prescribed role exactly the same way, although certain similarities based on cultural and subcultural dictates and common life experiences will be obvious. In any stable group such as a particular family, furthermore, the adaptive process consists of a selective screening of cultural role definitions modified by individual perference which results in a special variant of the cultural or subcultural ideal.[41] Any single family, in other words, has a collective life of its own, typical and yet not quite typical, especially in rapidly changing, complex societies. Here we will be concerned with the typical, as culturally prescribed, but the uniqueness of individuals and families is important to acknowledge and to bear in mind.

SOCIALIZATION. Role conceptions, embodied in the culture and subculture, are transmitted by socializing agents—authority figures and peers—who use positive and negative sanctions to ensure conformity to their norms. Negative sanctions range from teasing, ridicule, and gossip to expression of disapproval, withdrawal of love, physical punishment, imprisonment, expulsion, and death. Positive sanctions are rewards such as friendship, affection, love, promotions, honors, fame, and fortune that reinforce the pursuit of goals by socially prescribed means.

Conformity, which reflects the effectiveness of social control, varies with the strength and nature of group ties. Where group ties are weak, individuals are less bound by group norms, a condition characterized by Emile Durkheim as "anomie."[42] Juvenile delinquency and crime are practically unknown in nonliterate societies because group ties are strong and all-encompassing. Social control in these societies is highly effective, and most people play their roles willingly and with commitment.

The degree of commitment to the role, or conflict about the role, will be affected not only by the unique experiences of socialization that the individual has undergone but by social structural and cultural factors such as rates of social change, ambiguities, contradictions, modifications, and alternatives in prevailing role definitions, the availability of resources for adequate role performance, especially economic resources, and the strength of group integration, solidarity, and social control.

In industrialized societies, these factors associated with role performance become increasingly problematic, adversely affecting the commitment to prescribed roles and to the achievement of identity. Role and feelings of identity are closely related, but not necessarily congruent. At deeper psychological levels, confusion and doubt about identity may coexist with apparent certainty and confidence at the behavioral level. The two tend to concide, however, and the prevailing social context affects the degree to which they do coincide. Widespread problems of identity in society are a modern phenomenon related to inconsistent, confused, and outmoded role definitions.

Not all role learning takes place within groups, although much of it does. Individuals may pick up attitudes, values, and behavior patterns in anticipation of a status that they hope to achieve. An example is the deliberate adoption by members of the working class of ways of dressing, speaking, and acting that are customary in the middle class. This kind of socialization by working-class people who are hoping to rise in the class structure may not occur as a result of group interaction, since group memberships are usually limited to people of the same class. Individuals will use models that are not in their immediate environment, such as those in the mass media, to learn the appropriate norms of the middle-class status that they want to achieve. In traditional societies, the learning of role behavior from individuals outside the primary group is rare, as is mobility, for that matter.

Another point that should be stressed, because it is often overlooked, is that the role theory model is concerned with normatively regulated *thought* and *emotion* as well as behavior.[43] The knowledge and skills appropriate to the role of the professional, for example, are sanctioned by degree and licensing requirements established by authorities in the field of specialization. In addition, however, professional associations sanction attitudes and emotions insofar as these are embodied in conceptions of professional ethics.

At the level of the emotions, psychological traits—the use of particular mechanisms of defense such as repression, projection, displacement—may be characteristic of large numbers of people who are similarly located in the society and who undergo certain common socializing experiences. In the lower working class, especially, subcultural definitions of the masculine role prescribe toughness, stoicism, and denial and avoidance of introspection in the face of anxiety and threat. Confiding and the communication of intimate inner feelings are regarded as effeminate and sissified. It is for this reason that lower-working-class men tend to experience great difficulty in responding successfully to the conventional insight therapy relationship; mutual trust, emotional openness, and empathy are curbed in their relationships with important figures in their lives. They dislike talking about their problems and they prefer medication and direct advice from therapists.

Emotional defenses are psychological traits, but they are sociological facts if they are a result of socialization into subcultural values and norms—in this case, those that define the masculine role and male identity.

In recent years, in the United States, the role theory model, with its focus on actual, day-to-day, ongoing family relationships, has become more popular in sociological research.[44] The emphasis on familial and individual sources of marital happiness or discontent, emotional maturity or disturbance, successful functioning or failure, as defined by the society, and on family change rather than societal change is not new. It reflects the traditional preference for psychological rather than economic and political explanations and solutions to the problems of families and individuals in the United States.

The radical political and economic values of the counterculture of the 1960s did not survive into the 1980s. Other values, the emphasis on the me and the now, on personal fulfillment and growth, on getting in touch with one's feelings, on communication, openness, honesty, and intimacy in human relationships did survive. These interests and values are reflected in recent trends in family research, which, like all social science research, accommodates to the changing clichés of human existence at any particular time.

The election of President Ronald Reagan in 1980, and the cutbacks in public programs and research grants to social scientists promoted an in-depth focus on small numbers of self-contained family groups, because this kind of research can be done by individual researchers.[45] More costly, large-scale research by research teams has shifted gradually to those with the money to do this kind of work—private national polling organizations, and federal agencies. Even here, and also for economic reasons, telephone interviews and mailed questionnaires are replacing more costly face-to-face interviews.

Social Location and Family Roles

A few examples, at this point, of how the status of class, race, and age is associated with varying role definitions, how these definitions affect family life, and how they are related to past, current, or changing economic and political circumstances will be helpful.

CLASS. Class has very significant implications for role conceptions and performance. Class will determine, to a large extent, the amount of independence the individual has in all areas of life, and particularly on the job. Factory workers have much less control over their work conditions than professionals. Professionals do not punch time clocks, they make more independent decisions, and they are not closely supervised by superiors. It is understandable, then, that working-class parents in bringing up their children are more likely to emphasize obedience to authority and conformity to externally imposed rules than middle-class parents.[46] In the middle class, parents stress general principles rather then obedience to discrete rules in their disciplinary efforts. The child is allowed and encouraged to make more independent decisions. This finding holds true cross-nationally, wherever studies on child-rearing practices have been conducted, despite differences in history, culture, or stage of economic development in different societies. Parents encourage independence and self-reliance when their children will need these traits in adulthood.

In this country today, class determines certain typical variations in the way the role of wife and mother is conceived and played out. The traditional role is now played by a minority of married women. Basic variations in the role are found in the subcultures of the very rich and the very poor. And newly emerging variations are becoming widespread, especially among the college-educated, urban upper-middle class.[47]

The traditional obligations of married women in agricultural societies have been to bear and raise children, to perform household chores and farming chores, to subordinate self-interests to the needs of other family members, and to accept the authority of the husband in decision-making, particularly decisions having to do with finances. They have had the right to economic support and security, loyalty and fidelity of the husband, and gratitude from the husband and children for nurturing services performed.

This picture is obviously an idealized one, but it represents the conception of the role that guided the behavior of a majority of wives and mothers in the middle economic levels of American society in the past. Companionship between husband and wife was not a crucial requirement of the role, although it became more important as affluence, leisure, and the life span increased in the twentieth century.

In the United States today, within the old upper class, companionship is the basic value in the relationship between husband and wife. Wives are rarely gainfully employed. Empty-shell marriages may persist for the sake of preserving family alliances, and fortunes—but no longer is this a generally accepted duty in this particular stratum of society. Divorces are becoming more frequent and mistresses are becoming less frequent (as a permanent arrangement).

The wife is not obliged to perform domestic service in the home other than as manager of paid helpers who do the actual cooking, cleaning, marketing, errand running, and child rearing. She has a great deal of freedom, travels widely, and is provided with ample funds for clothes, recreation, and educational activities. She shares recreational and other pleasures with her husband. Her obligations are to maintain her beauty and intellectual alertness and to provide stimulating companionship and erotic gratification for her husband. The rights to fidelity and marital security rest on these obligations rather than on domestic services or child rearing. In the mass media, women in this class who are not employed, are currently referred to as Ladies Who Lunch. In the Soviet Union, able-bodied married women who are not employed and are not rearing young children are referred to more bluntly as parasites.

Among the poor in our society, married women with husbands present have few rights and heavy domestic and economic obligations usually. Security, support, or alimony in the event of divorce are not expected, primarily because they are not economically possible. Illegitimacy and common law marriages are a reflection of this fact. Companionship is almost nonexistent, as this is a luxury of time and economics. Contrary to stereotyped notions of impulsiveness and abandon among the poor, husbands and wives are less active sexually than in the middle and upper classes.[48] Survival is the crucial value in these family relationships.

Among urban professionals, particularly, a new role is emerging in which the wife is employed full time and contributes as a partner, according to her ability, to the economic assets of the family. She may not perform homemaking or child-rearing services, which are sometimes delegated to others. She shares authority more equally with the husband. Companionship is highly valued but is limited by time-consuming career obligations. In the event of divorce, the wife receives partial child support but not alimony. The marital tie rests on mutual compatibility rather than the symbiotic nurturing functions of the wife and economic functions of the husband.

Most employed married women in the United States play a junior partner rather than an equal partner role. The greater the equality of occupational prestige and income between husband and wife, the greater the sharing of child care and homemaking responsibilities, usually.[49] But married professional women are most inhibited by the presence of children. And regardless of family circumstances, occupational prestige of husband and wife, or presence of small children, married women perform almost all household and child care activities with little help from their husbands. They receive more help at night, more help with the children than with household activities, and more help outside the home, with lawn mowing or shopping, than inside the home.[50]

Reality is, of course, more complex than the foregoing descriptions indicate. Many women combine several aspects of the major kinds of roles, shift from one type of role to another in different stages of their life cycle, or experience conflict between their role conceptions and their husbands' expectations.

RACE. Race, particularly when combined with class, is another very significant determinant of role expectations and behavior in family life. Until the 1970s, almost all research on black family roles in the United States was limited to families in the lower working class. The black poor were compared unfavorably to white middle-class families. The lower levels of black educational and occupational achievement were attributed to black subcultural values, family "deterioration,"[51] and family "pathology."[52] This, in turn, was related to prejudice and poverty.

More recently, sociologists have shifted their focus to middle-class black families and have discovered a very strong emphasis, stronger than in the white middle class in some respects, on work and achievement, on education, on religion and church attendance, on equalitarian husband-wife relationships, on marital stability, and on low fertility.[53] Class overrides ethnic differences in family roles when economic and educational opportunities are available and are perceived as available.

Urbanization, unemployment, and inadequate income have been very destructive to black family life, but until recently, the ethnocentrism of white researchers perpetuated certain myths about the black family. The concept of black matriarchy is a white distortion of the greater equalitarianism that has existed within intact black families.[54] This, in turn, reflects a greater equality between husband and wife in economic roles, historically in Africa and in the United States, and at present. Despite the ravages of slave trading, the black family was not destroyed during slavery, if only because intact families were more productive economically. According to information from marriage applications and birth records, a majority of African Americans, of all social classes, lived in two-parent nuclear families on plantations during the slave era, and in a number of cities between 1880 and 1925.[55] In Philadelphia, between 1850 and 1880, blacks were only slightly less likely to live in two-parent nuclear families than were immigrant and native-born whites.[56]

Current changes in urban, black family life—huge increases in female-headed households, divorce, illegitimacy, and in the percentage remaining unmarried—are paralleled by similar trends within the white population. These conditions are far more widespread within the black community because inadequate income, unemployment, and underemployment are far more widespread.

AGE AND GENERATION. Age and generation are also associated with typical role definitions ("Act your age!") which, in turn, are a reflection of changing life circumstances and the biology of the life cycle. The family roles of older people differ, typically, from those who are middle-aged or young. They differ in the 1980s, as compared to the 1950s, or the 1900s.

Major demographic changes have taken place since the turn of the century. Life expectancy has increased considerably, from forty-nine to seventy-four years of age. Widows over age sixty-five outnumber widowers about five to one. Very few women now die in childbirth and women have greater natural resistence to certain diseases. Birth rates are much lower in industrial societies and there are fewer grown children to care for elderly parents, who are living longer than ever before. At the same time, in industrial societies, levels of education and income, from pensions mainly, are higher. Government support services are more available than in agricultural societies, and there is, generally, less conflict between the elderly and their children over economic resources and power as both generations experience greater economic independence.[57]

In the United States today, despite high rates of geographic mobility, eight out of ten people over sixty-five live less than an hour away from at least one grown child. Fewer than 10 percent live in institutions and in retirement communities. There is probably more intergenerational communication, psychological support, agreement, and affection now than in a dear, dead past that never was.[58]

Among the elderly and retired, differences in the economic and household roles of husbands and wives diminish. There may be a significant reversal of the traditional roles, to wife as provider and husband as homemaker, when the husband is retired and the wife, usually younger, continues to be gainfully employed. Again, this is largely a matter of class and culture. Men tend to become more nurturing, passive, and sociable. Grandfathers are usually able to express more affection toward their grandchildren then toward their children. Women tend to become more assertive, ambitious, and less self-sacrificing as their children grow up, leave home, and become independent.[59] Both sexes exhibit a turning inward and a greater preoccupation with physical needs as they age, reflecting the decreased social interaction and the failing bodily functions of old age.

The work ethic is still quite strong in the present generation of people over sixty-five in the United States. In industrial societies, with mechanized technologies and labor surpluses, retirement is "functional" for the society. It permits the younger generation to take over with a minimum amount of disruption in ongoing economic activities. As indicated by compulsory retirement laws, however, retirement is usually not voluntary, except in the case of physical disability. The wealthy and the powerful, who have more choice in these matters, do not willingly withdraw from the arenas of power and action. This has been a prime source of conflict between the generations in societies, at least since the invention of planting and the creation of an economic surplus, some twelve thousand years ago.

The Socialization Process

We are now in a position to understand how role theory provides the bridge between the individual, the culture, and the society. Cultural and subcultural role prescriptions are transmitted to the individual through the process of socialization.

The socialization process begins at birth and continues until death, or as long as the individual takes on new statuses. Newborn infants must learn the role that is defined by their family and their society as appropriate to their status. They learn a series of obligations: to sleep at night and through the night, to prefer certain kinds and quantities of food, to eat this food at specified times and, eventually, to eliminate in places set aside for this purpose. They also learn to express emotions in certain ways, or to repress them, typically, in conformity to the dictates of their culture. The basic right that is granted to them, at least ideally, is to receive help from their families in the task of achieving physical, emotional, and intellectual maturity.

The final status that individuals occupy is that of a dying member of the society. Even this role is normatively regulated, more or less explicitly. Individuals learn the role that is defined as appropriate by their culture and subculture, and they usually play it out that way, whatever their feelings of estrangement or doubt.[60]

The role theory model is applicable to an understanding of

group interaction and individual personality development and change, particularly as this is typical in certain segments of the society. It is not adequate for understanding overall social change in the total society. It is at this level that the evolutionary, functionalist, and conflict theory models, corrected for distortions, can be helpful with the never-ending challenges of explanation in social life. One hundred years from now these models will probably be obsolete in certain respects. One hundred years ago, Social Darwinism was ascendant in the budding social sciences. We work with what we have.

An Integrated Approach

The four current models in contemporary sociology—evolutionary, functionalist, conflict, and role theory—can be integrated hierarchically in terms of the time and space perspectives that they encompass. The technological evolution model is basic and subsumes the other models in that it applies to total societies and change through time in these societies.

The functionalist model is subsumed by the evolutionary model in that it is cross-sectional and provides a view of society at a particular time, the emphasis being on values, consensus, and institutional interrelationships. The conflict model parallels the functionalist model, but the focus is on conflict, dissent, and the economic and political sources of social change within societies.

Like the evolutionary model, the conflict model has a longitudinal dimension, but technological development underlies and limits, if it does not determine forms of economic and other institutions in societies. In societies where science and technology are rudimentary, the accumulation of an economic surplus is impossible, as are large populations, permanent settlements, highly developed occupational specialization, an economic class structure, a leisure class, literacy, a money economy, government, military, religious, and educational bureaucracies, and innumerable other preconditions of the complex and complicated life.

The conflict model is a valuable interpretative tool in that it focuses attention on the effects of heterogeneity, stratification, and differences in interests, values, and economic and political circumstances on family roles and relationships. The interest in poverty and its effects on minority group family life, or on power within families as this varies according to the economic resources of husbands and wives, are examples of important areas of study where this model is frequently employed.

The role theory model has the most limited scope of the four, since it is restricted to the group and group interaction. Changes in the content of roles, particularly in values and attitudes, are usually related to changes in social conditions, primarily in the technological and economic spheres. It is important to remember, however, that processes of change are multidirectional. The individual, furthermore, is the ultimate source of social change, especially in industrial societies, where social constraints are more tenuous and alternatives are more readily available. Individuals are not blank tablets; they react to the group and the society. Acting singly, or with others, they invent, discover, and dissent; they accept or reject the accumulated heritage of their culture and other cultures.

Most sociologists have used one or another of the four explanatory models in attempting to answer the basic questions of order and change within the family and within the wider society. They have added or dropped concepts according to the accumulated state of knowledge in the field and changing explanatory needs. The concept of adolescence, for example, was not to be found in the nineteenth century in most societies. Adolescence was not a problem at that time, and there was no word to refer to this particular social status.

At the present time, American sociologists have become more interested in macrosocial analysis, after decades of being the vanguard in international sociology in the analysis of small-group processes and quantitative survey research. This shift probably reflects the increasing concern among intellectuals for the overall fate of American society. The United States has lost its privileged status of splendid geographic isolation now that atomic bombs and missiles are a part of the arsenal of war. In the past, European sociologists, whose countries have been less protected by the accident of geography, have been more concerned with questions of the fate of total societies through time.

Sociologists, in their study of family structure and functioning, have viewed the family as the prototype of all social groups, its members functioning according to culturally defined roles that have varied with time and place. They have studied the process of internalization of roles, which results in the kind of order and predictability in family relationships that is based on agreed-upon and mutual expectations between family members. They have also studied the societal sources and consequences of conflict and change in family roles that result in new expectations and new definitions of mutual rights and obligations in family life.

In employing the concepts of the role theory model, my emphasis here will be on the content of family roles—on culturally and subculturally defined values, attitudes, beliefs, and norms that have guided and prescribed family relationships—and how and why these have changed. Lack of space and lack of adequate historical data preclude an analysis of the interactional processes of socialization at the microsocial level—the actual learning of roles in family groups, historically and at present.

In the realm of values, the major change in family roles, historically, has been the shift from traditional values such as familism, fatalism, ethnocentrism, religiosity, and authoritarianism to modern, urban values such as individualism, achievement motivation, tolerance, rationalism, and equalitarianism in family roles and relationships. This will become clear as my story of the family unfolds.

The family has usually been viewed by social scientists as an object of social change, or a facilitator or inhibitor of certain kinds of change. It has rarely been viewed as a source of social change. Changes in other areas, in technology and the economy, particularly, usually impinge on the family. The family is the preserver of tradition. In revolutionary situations, the family is attacked by new regimes that attempt to remove the young from its influence as much as possible. Cultural innovators, whether they be criminals, scientific or artistic geniuses, or leaders of social movements, usually have weak family ties.

After approximately one hundred years of social scientific study of the family, certain basic sociological generalizations about family life have been accumulated. A review of some of this information, beginning with the very distant past, concentrating on the complex and constantly changing present, especially in the United States, and venturing into the future, indicates that certain current trends are likely to continue, given the continuation of human societies.

Human biology underlies and sets certain limits to the possible range of variation in family roles. The question, even, of the continued existence of a family group in human societies is tied to the basic bological needs and characteristics of the human animal. We begin, then, with a discussion of these biological traits as they affect family functioning and as they bear on the question of the necessity of the family and the survival of the family, as a human group and as a social institution.

TWO

The Biological Base

All known societies have family groups. Certain patterns in family life are universal, and while certain other patterns appear to be arbitrary, they are rarely unique. Before we can go on to a discussion of the range of variation in culturally defined family roles, it is important to try to determine to what extent these definitions have been arbitrary and to what extent particular patterns in family life are inevitable because of the imperatives of human biology.

A discussion of the biological traits of humans, as distinct from other animals, is a logical preliminary to an understanding of past and present family functioning. We can then have some idea of the possible limits to variation in family roles and the essences and accidents in the role of wife and mother, husband and father, daughter and sister, and son and brother. What is biological, inevitable, and unchangeable? What is circumstantial, arbitrary, and changeable? These questions become very significant in a time of constant crisis and widespread uncertainty about what is right, desirable, possible, or impossible in family life.

The Problem of Definition

We begin by defining the family. To do this is not easy if we include all types of families that have existed in all known societies. If we define the family according to specfic functions it performs—economic functions, for example—we can define away the family in certain societies where the family does not have the responsibility of providing for the economic needs of its offspring, at least not directly. The Israeli kibbutz is an example of this kind of community.

If we define the family as a group that fulfills certain needs of the society, such as replacing dying members, it is possible to argue that other kinds of groups could perform these functions just as well, perhaps even better. One would then be unable to explain why the family, in terms of the definitions of the people involved, is universal. If we focus on the universal biologically based needs of human beings, however, we will have a sounder basis for describing what families do and have done and, incidentally, for predicting whether they will continue to exist, regardless of how they may change.

The family is a group that engages in socially sanctioned, enduring, and exclusive relationships that are based on marriage, descent, adoption, or mutual definition (as in common law marriages). Common law relationships are included in this definition because participants define themselves as families, because the phenomenon is relatively frequent among the poor in certain industrializing and industrialized countries, and because these relationships are socially sanctioned within some subcultures of poverty: they are recognized and defined as acceptable, although not preferable.

The family group has functioned everywhere and at all times, more or less adequately and more or less completely, to fulfill the emotional, physical, and intellectual needs of its members. These responsibilities may be shared with nonfamily members of a society to a varying extent at different times and in different places. The family, however, has the initial responsibility because it is usually there first. Different cultures may emphasize one or another of the universal human needs in prescribing family roles as, for example, in the Israeli kibbutz where the satisfaction of emotional needs is the paramount value underlying family relationships. No society, however, has ever assigned the satisfaction of the fundamental emotional needs of all its members to nonfamily groups.

The basic family group is the nuclear family, which consists of mother, father, and children, regardless of whether or not they reside in the same household. This unit is recognized in all societies, but it has greater or less independence in different societies. It has less independence if it is part of an extended structure, such as a clan or tribe. The extended family, actually, is any form in which several nuclear families, or parts of nuclear families, defer to the same authority, exchange essential services, and either live together in the same household or close enough to be in daily contact.[1] Polygamous forms are extended families in which the husband has several wives at one time (polygyny) or, and this is rare but not unheard of, the wife has several husbands (polyandry).

The Human Animal

Why have all societies recognized family groups and regulated the behavior of family members? The ultimate answers lie in the biological characteristics of the human animal.

Humans have the longest life span of any animal, with the exception of the tortoise. They require more intensive care and a longer period of nurturing than other animals. Full physical growth and sexual maturity may take anywhere from fourteen to twenty years; most other animals achieve maturity in a few weeks or months. The evolution to an upright posture in humans was accompanied by a narrowing of the pelvis to hold in the intestines.[2] At the same time, humans evolved a larger skull to accommodate the bigger brain necessary for language. Human infants must, therefore, be expelled from the womb at a point when their heads are small and they are less mature than non-humans are at birth. This increases the degree of dependency and extends the period of infancy in humans relative to other animals.

Humans also have the most complex physiological and neurological endowment and are far more dependent upon learning than their nearest ancestors. They are born with only a few adaptive reflexes. The behavior of lower animal forms, on the other hand, is guided largely by instinct, although the evidence now indicates that these instincts are not fully developed at birth and depend on learning and environmental experiences for normal development and expression.[3]

Because of their complex neurological structure, humans are capable of language, the use of symbols that have shared meanings within the group or the society. Language enables humans to instruct their young, to transmit the accumulated wisdom and folly of their culture, and to spare their offspring much trial-and-error behavior. Nonhumans cannot be told that fire burns. They learn this fact after they have been burned. They learn by gesture and imitation, but they cannot be warned in advance of threats that are not immediate. They cannot be controlled by promises of future reward or punishment, or prepared for future statuses in life by verbal instruction. While many species are superior to humans in speed, strength, and sensory perception, only humans have the ability to use abstract concepts in adapting to their nonimmediate environment.

One other biological feature that is unique to human beings and a few, but not most, of their close relatives is the fact that the female does not have to be in heat before mating can take place. Humans have no mating season, at least not one that is physiologically determined. Uncontrolled sexual behavior in societies could be an important source of conflict, jealousy, and destructiveness that would undermine the human need for prolonged and stable care from birth to maturity. It might prevent even a minimal degree of the cooperation that is necessary for human survival at any age. The incest taboo and marriage are human inventions that set limits to human sexual behavior.

The incest taboo is a universal means of controlling the continuous sex drive of men and women. It is found in all societies, although it may be extended quite arbitrarily to include non-blood relatives or individuals who share varying degrees of common biological ancestry. In the United States, for example, some states define marriages between uncles and nieces as incestuous; others similarly define marriages between second cousins. This varies for no obvious reason.

The taboo is apparently not based on instinct, since it has often been broken, and sometimes by subcultural prescription. Among the ruling classes in ancient Egypt, Peru, and Hawaii brother-sister marriages were customary and obligatory. We do not know why this custom arose. We can often explain the persistence of social norms: in this case the custom operated to preserve family fortunes. But other means of accomplishing this have been adopted elsewhere. The origins of this practice, as with many other cultural norms, will very likely always be a mystery. Probably the custom originated as an idiosyncratic act by an individual of high status and a strong physiological need that was too powerful for the cultural taboo to contain. It was then adopted by others of similar psychological bent and the prestige and power to get away with it. With time it became a norm in the subculture of these particular ruling groups, shared by others in the group, and transmitted from generation to generation through the process of socialization.

The practice of brother-sister marriage was not sanctioned for the masses in these societies, however. The justification that the ruling groups put forth to legitimize their practice—that it kept the family fortune intact and that it protected aristocratic families from defilement by the blood of commoners—seems unsophisticated from the vantage point of twentieth-century depth psychology. It could explain the persistence but not the origin of the custom. But it is in the nature of ideologies that they are convincing to the people who hold them—a fact that is often not recognized by individuals who have different ideological persuasions.

Another major way of controlling sexual relationships in societies is by assigning some degree of sexual exclusiveness and permanence to the marital relationship. What outsiders have labeled adultery or promiscuity in other societies has often occurred under normatively controlled conditions of time, place, and circumstance. This applies to practices such as wife-lending and the right of the first night, in which the king, lord of the manor, chieftain, or medicine man was given the right of initial sexual access to newlywed virgins. Fidelity has been differently valued and enforced in different societies, but some degree of sexual exclusiveness and permanence is always implied in marital contracts.

The personnel even in the very rare and not fully authenticated cases of group marriage did not vary. Exclusive and enduring sexual relationships were bounded by the family group, even if they did not take place, apparently, on a permanent pairing basis. In communal experimental groups sexual behavior has almost never been completely random or uncontrolled by group norms. Where this control is absent or minimal, sexual rivalry and conflict are major reasons for the breakup of communes.[4]

Permanent mating relationships are rare among other animals. Nonhuman animals are usually promiscuous, mating with parents and siblings and rarely maintaining a durable lifetime relationship with a single mate. The care of the young is guaranteed, however, by the existence of a maternal instinct, which is controlled by female sex hormones. Maternal behavior can be induced in animals by injecting these hormones. In males, a hormonally based paternal instinct does not seem to exist. The male, as a matter of fact, is often a threat to his young or, at best, is uninvolved or indifferent to their needs. Yet there are species among fish, for example, where the male takes over the care of the fertilized ova completely.

Humans, unfortunately, cannot depend on their hormones to provide them with the appropriate sentiments for rearing their children. No one has been able to demonstrate the existence of a hormonally based maternal instinct or drive in human females. If a maternal instinct does exist, it is easily overlaid by life experiences and cultural role dictates. Anthropologists have reported on societies where women experience little maternal warmth, view pregnancy with dread, and strongly reject and unwillingly perform the obligations of childbearing and child rearing.[5] Daily news accounts of brutality toward children are a further indication that learning and life experiences can overshadow any hormonally based propensities to nurture their young that may be present in human females. The cortex of the brain, seat of learning and memory, is much larger in humans than in other animals. It intervenes between biological predisposition and actual behavior to a much greater extent than in nonhuman animals.

Family responsibilities, incidentally, are not necessarily based on blood relationships. In some societies, the contribution of the father to conception was unknown, since pregnancies were believed to occur as the result of the bounty and good will of the gods. In other societies, the identity of the biological father could not be determined because the marital contract did not specify an exclusive pairing relationship between one male and one female. Among the Todas of southern India, for example, where polyandry was practiced, the wife was shared by the brothers in a particular family. In these situations, where the fact of biological paternity was unknown or could not be established, a sociological father was assigned to each newborn child. He fulfilled the role of father, as defined by his culture and as sanctioned by his society.

While not all societies have emphasized the fact of biological paternity, all have attempted to define and regulate male as well as female responsibilities in family relationships. The universal existence of family groups with socially recognized statuses, such as mother and father, and of socially sanctioned roles prescribing sexual behavior and child-rearing responsibilities, serves the need to control sexual conflict in human societies and provide for the prolonged care of the human young.

The intellectual and physical needs of young children could be fulfilled by outside agencies, but the gratification of emotional needs cannot be delegated completely. At the outer limits, culturally defined family roles must contain provision for the gratification of the biologically grounded emotional needs of the human young. Slaves, servants, and professionals have not and do not have the narcissistic investment in the young that parents have. Children are parents' ode to immortality.

Substitute groups who would have complete care of the young in populous modern societies would have to be bureaucratically structured in order to coordinate so vast an undertaking. Bureaucratic structures are, by definition, impersonal. For this reason, also, the task of providing for the emotional needs of infants and children, as well as adults, is not likely to be taken over completely by nonfamily groups. This question will be taken up again when we look into the probable future of family groups.

All that is recognizably human in men and women is a product of social interaction with other human beings. Children who have been reared under conditions of extreme isolation and emotional deprivation are unable to walk, talk, express a wide range of emotions, or use their hands to manipulate their physical environment. The amount of impairment in physical and intellectual functioning, furthermore, is directly related to the amount of emotional deprivation these children have experienced.

Two illegitimate children discovered at the age of six after each had been isolated in attics for years responded quite differently to attempts to teach them to function at a human level. While the kind and quality of teaching varied in each case, it is significant that one child, who had been imprisoned with her deaf-mute mother, responded well and eventually attained what was reported as normal speech and intellectual development. The other child, who had no sustained contact with another human being, responded poorly to attempts to train her and died at the age of ten. Her speech never developed beyond the two-year level. While she learned to dress herself, she was never able to fasten buttons or eat with a knife and fork.[6] The extreme deprivation of human contact that she experienced had consequences that were largely irreparable.

Other Biological Underpinnings

Cultural definitions of family roles are also affected by particular biological needs and changes in the human life cycle of family members—especially during infancy and childhood, adolescence, and middle and old age—and by the biological differences between the sexes. The question here, as in the discussion of basic human biological needs, is to what extent culturally prescribed family roles are bound by biology and to what extent these definitions are, or have been, arbitrary. Here too, while we need much more evidence, we can at least point to possible limits to variations in family roles as determined by the biology of age and gender. We can also point to surviving traditional role conceptions that are incompatible with the typical biological characteristics of particular age groups and of the two sexes. These outmoded, inconsistent, and irrational expectations in family relationships are a source of severe conflict that becomes more pronounced in industrial societies, even as other sources of stress and conflict, such as economic deprivation, disease, and premature death, diminish.

The Human Life Cycle

The major milestones of growth and aging in the individual life cycle are infancy and childhood, adolescence, and middle age and old age. These stages of life are characterized by rather clear-cut physiological, anatomical, and endocrinological changes, although the pace and degree of change will vary for individuals.

Societies and cultures respond to these stages in the life cycle quite differently. In a society in which the average citizen has a life expectancy at birth of less than thirty years, and this has been the case, historically, in the great majority of societies, large and small, a woman of thirty-five may be an old woman, by social definition. Biologically, however, she has not passed through the changes that we associate with advancing or old age. In the United States, today, the higher classes tend to postpone acceptance of the labels middle-aged and old, relative to the working class. Biological and sociological clocks do not necessarily tell the same time.

Societies will also vary in the extent to which they emphasize or deemphasize one or another of these stages and prescribe clearly defined roles for occupants of these statuses. Adolescence, which begins at puberty and ends with the assumption of full adult status in all spheres of life—marital, economic, political, and recreational—is not a clearly delineated status in nonindustrial societies. It is of short duration, if it can be said to exist at all as a recognized social status. In advanced industrialized societies, the percentage of old people who are over eighty-five is rising most rapidly. This stage is also characterized by typical psychological and physical changes,[7] and is becoming more recognized as a distinct stage in the human life cycle.

Philippe Aries, in his account of the history of childhood during the medieval era in Western Europe, argues on the basis of an analysis of paintings, diaries, games, and schools and their curricula that children were regarded as miniature adults in the Middle Ages almost from the time they were weaned, at about the age of seven. They dressed like adults and worked and played with adults, suffering little from segregation and peer pressures.[8] But they lacked the protection of child abuse and child labor laws, which are based on the conception of childhood as a distinct stage in life that requires protection against exploitation by adults.

The aged are another category that is more distinctly recognized in urban, industrial societies. There are more of them, and they are no longer as locked into extended family groups as they once were. They are increasingly separate and segregated from younger people, in rural counties, older urban and suburban neighborhoods, and, recently, in retirement villages. In these retirement communities, a new territorially based subculture is arising, based on common values of leisure, tranquillity, safety, physical comfort, and convenience, which affects family role conceptions in a significant way.

INFANCY AND CHILDHOOD

Infancy and childhood, the first major stages in the human life cycle, have dramatic implications for family functioning. The introduction of a new child into the family group is more crucial for the rearrangement and redefinition of family roles than the gradual changes that occur with puberty and middle and old age.

Culture and social conditions begin to operate on the infant from the moment of conception. The quality, quantity, and type of food that the mother eats, the amount of rest and exercise she gets, the physical labor she performs, and the knowledge she has of prenatal care and the kind and availability of this care will depend to a large extent on cultural and economic factors.

At birth, the infant requires basic emotional and physical care. The family group responds to these needs according to cultural prescriptions of the responsibilities and obligations of family members. Also important are varying life conditions, especially economic and technological, and the individual personality factors of parents, siblings, and other relatives or surrogates who are assigned the responsibility for fulfilling the infant's needs by the society or subculture.

The distinctive personality traits of responsible figures in the infant's life, those that are not directly attributable to effects of culture, stem from differences in intelligence, temperament, and unique life experiences. These idiosyncratic factors become more significant in industrial societies, where the press of culture and subculture is less uniform, due to the greater mobility and greater contact of individuals with differing and rapidly changing values and norms. Probably individual psychological factors will become even more significant in infant and child care in the future as gross differences in child-rearing practices are increasingly eliminated by the homogenizing effects of mass culture and scientific and technological advances.

The gratification of the basic biological need for physical survival and growth involves, also and indirectly, provision for the emotional and intellectual problem-solving needs and capacities of the young. Without a dependable source of warm emotional response, physical growth, intellectual functioning, and survival are impaired in young children. These needs are interrelated and interdependent. Problem-solving capacity is adaptive and is also, ultimately, tied to physical survival, whatever the environmental circumstances. How have families functioned, historically, to fulfill these needs, and what are the possible limits to their role in meeting these responsibilities?

THE PROVISION OF PHYSICAL CARE. The gratification of the

physical needs of the child, so that normal growth processes can take place and biological maturity is reached in good health, is and has been the most difficult responsibility of the family in nonindustrialized societies. Rational control over the physical environment, including disease-producing agents, is minimal in such societies. Childbearing and childrearing are highly inefficient, since the child's chances of survival are low. Women bear far greater numbers of children and often spend their entire lives, and in fact die, giving birth to children. High death rates balance high birth rates in nonliterate and preindustrial societies, and the family requires a constantly renewed supply of hunters, herders, field hands, or gardeners to sustain itself in a labor-intensive economy.

In rural societies, two hands can produce more than one mouth can eat because almost all hands produce food. This includes the young, from the time they can toddle out into the fields and sow seeds or carry small tools. The major problem in these societies is to keep the young alive.

In industrialized societies, providing for the physical needs and survival of children is not a major problem for most families. Science and technology, applied by legions of trained experts, supplement family responsibility. Compulsory health examinations and innoculations for the young, welfare programs, family allowances, and other devices are elaborated to this end. The problem shifts from keeping children alive to keeping the birth rate down because so many stay alive.

While poverty, economic deprivation, and high infant mortality rates persist, they do not characterize a majority of the population in technologically advanced societies. Most individuals who are born reach maturity in more or less good health, the degree of health depending upon constitutional factors and, even more important, upon class factors. The higher the class, the better the nutrition and medical care that are available to children and adults, the fewer the environmental hazards they encounter, and the longer they can expect to live, on an average. Race is also relevant here. Blacks in the United States have a

lower average life expectancy than whites, although the average
tends to be pulled down largely by much higher infant mortality rates.

THE SATISFACTION OF EMOTIONAL NEEDS. As to the task of providing for the emotional needs of children, the historical record
is much less clear with regard to the adequacy of, and limits to,
family responsibilities. The extent of mental illness in a society
is a good index of the adequacy of family functioning in this
area, although other factors must also be taken into account.
What are the standards for making a judgment about the actual
prevalence of mental illness in a society? Definitions vary. In
complex societies the actual prevalence of psychological illness
is almost impossible to determine because investigations are usually limited to data on hospital admission rates, and official statistics are almost always biased in certain systematic ways. Class
factors strongly affect the likelihood of hospitalization. The poor
are more likely than the rich to be hospitalized for mental illness, just as they are more likely to be imprisoned for crime.

Nevertheless, mental illness is universal. In all societies, some
individuals exhibit gross disturbances in their perception of
reality and experience a degree of anxiety and guilt that inter-
feres, to a greater or less extent, with their ability to think, work,
love, and play. Typical forms of mental illness vary in different
cultures and in the same society at different times. In our own
society, psychosomatic disorders, stemming from repression of
sexual and aggressive impulses, apparently are declining. Character disorders, reflecting a failure of identification with parents or other adults, seem to be on the increase. But we do not
know whether actual rates of overall mental illness are more
frequent now than in the past.

A classic study by Herbert Goldhamer and Albert Marshall,
that attempted to shed light on this problem, found no increase
in hospital admission rates for most types of psychosis in the
state of Massachusetts in the mid-twentieth century as compared with the mid-nineteenth century.[9] Rates for age categories of fifty and under remained approximately the same, de-

spite a trend toward hospitalization of patients with less extreme forms of mental illness in this century up to 1955, when tranquilizers and antipsychotic drugs became widely available.

Thus, the amount of severe mental illness does not seem to be higher in modern civilizations than in newly industrializing societies. If this is so, it probably has to do with the extreme brutality of the material environment for the masses of the population in earlier stages of urbanization and industrialization. Whatever the potential for the outbreak of mental illness in a population, precipitating factors, especially stressful economic conditions, appear to have been more potent during the period of early industrialization and unregulated capitalism in the West.

The importance of the economic factor to psychological well-being is also indicated by the fact that rates of severe mental illness are highly correlated with social class in contemporary industrial societies. Class is a major determinant of differential environmental stress that families encounter. A massive study, carried out originally in midtown Manhattan in the mid-1950s and brought up to date in the 1970s, is unique in that an attempt was made to obtain information about the actual prevalence of psychological illness on the basis of door-to-door interviews in an economically heterogeneous, white metropolitan community.[10] Previous studies had been limited to information about the relationship between social class and rates of hospitalized mental illness.[11] The midtown studies revealed quite dramatically that in successively lower class levels there is a progressively greater likelihood that children will reach maturity with some degree of psychological damage.

The adequacy of family functioning in rearing the young to a healthy emotional maturity is, and apparently has been, closely tied to economic factors. It is not possible to answer, unequivocally, the question whether the family functioned better in this respect in the past. Historians, anthropologists, and social critics have tended to idealize the past, with the contemporary family often coming out badly by comparison. The answer depends ultimately on the values of the observer. Judgments of relative weaknesses or strengths of family functioning depend on the standards one is using and the adequacy of historical and anthropological data.

To take just one example, if family structure, culture, and social conditions promote stable, secure, and enduring affectionate relationships for infants and young children, we can assume that the emotional needs of children will be gratified. Using this standard, families in nonliterate and nonurban areas of preindustrial societies would have an advantage. Family structure is more likely to be extended in agricultural societies where the family group is tied to the land. Even when the extended family does not occupy a common household, there are usually more available family members in the immediate community to provide stable emotional support and the socializing experiences that the child needs to mature and reach adulthood as a competent, functioning member of society.

The experience of losing a parent is not so traumatic when it occurs in an extended family setting. Ready substitutes, familiar and stable, are usually available to take over the role of mother or father. In urban, industrial societies, orphanages, foster homes, or legally appointed guardians are hardly the equivalent in providing continuity in emotional gratification for the orphaned child.

On the other hand, parents were more likely to die at an early age in rural societies. At the present time, marriages in the United States are more likely to break up as a result of divorce rather than death. Children of divorce may experience separation from a divorced parent as less traumatic than the death of a parent. But they are far more likely than in the past to have to contend with hostility and competition between a stepmother or stepfather and a biological mother or father who is still alive.

Furthermore, recent evidence compiled by social and psychohistorians indicates that family conflict, rivalry, and envy in human societies are as old as the existence of extreme differences in power and in the control over economic resources between generations of the same family. The physical, psychological, and sexual abuse of children was widespread in agricultural societies.[12] In industrial societies, children are a luxury rather than an economic necessity, to be enjoyed rather than exploited, expensive to rear, and certainly not profitable in terms of economic returns on the child-rearing investment. Children are treated more gently when their respect and friendship must be earned and cannot be taken for granted as a culturally prescribed given.

Social conditions such as rapid social change and large-scale movement up and down the class structure promote family conflict in industrial societies. Rapid social change destroys mutual expectations about rights and obligations in family relationships. The social mobility of children, relative to their parents, increases the possibility of parental guilt or envy—guilt if the children move down in the class structure, envy, or fear of losing them, if they move up. This adds a sociological dimension to other possible reasons for parental envy of their maturing offspring, such as their greater virility, energy, freedom, and youth. And there are fewer grandparents, aunts, uncles, and other relatives around to act as buffers and to mediate family conflicts in industrial societies.

Still, it is at least easier now to escape these conflicts, if not to resolve them. The young can leave the battle arena and take up residence in another city or town. In agricultural societies, with few urban centers, there is usually no place to go. The individual is bound to the land and to the family group since it is almost impossible to survive outside it. There are no laundromats, supermarkets, or fast food chains to provide for the needs of unattached individuals.

We see, then, that in making historical and cross-cultural comparisons it is very difficult to make absolute judgments of the relative adequacy of family functioning in providing for basic emotional needs. It is necessary to be specific about what one is comparing and what one thinks is more or less desirable. In the above illustration the two conflicting values are emotional security, which in some respects was more prevalent in agricultural societies, and individualism and freedom, which unquestionably are more widespread in industrial societies. Security and freedom can go together, but often they do not. Which is preferable? Again, it depends on the observer's values.

The related question of the possible limits to family responsibility in providing for the basic emotional needs of children also cannot be answered definitively, given our present state of knowledge. For lack of a better substitute, this function, unlike many others, is not likely to be diminished greatly as societies continue to develop technologically.

What, then, is the best amount and kind of emotional support that is necessary for optimum physical, emotional, and intellectual growth and development? The answer to this question is the goal and has been the goal of a vast amount of research in the social sciences over the past hundred years.

The current belief is that the quality of parent-child contact rather than the quantity, in terms of the amount of time spent together and the actual number, type, and extent of services performed for the child, is the significant factor in the emotional health of the child. This is the implication of more refined and more carefully controlled studies of the effects of maternal employment on children. Significant differences in the number and kind of neurotic symptoms between the children of working and nonworking mothers have not been found, as mentioned earlier. Other factors such as class and the availability of continuous warm and accepting care by a mother substitute have been found to be more important than maternal employment per se. The mother who stays at home out of a sense of duty and obligation, furthermore, is likely to be too angry or depressed to provide this kind of care.

THE DEVELOPMENT OF INTELLECTUAL POTENTIAL. The other major responsibility of the family is to develop intellectual competence in its young members. This requires the development of skills and the imparting of knowledge that will enable the child to function adequately in adult roles, particularly in the occupational sphere.

The question of the genetic limits to intellectual functioning in human beings is a matter of definition and the problem lies in establishing standards. Then there is the problem of measuring this potential accurately, a problem that has not yet been solved.

A related question is: how successfully have various types of societal institutions, the family in particular, since this is our concern here, functioned to tap the maximum limits of this potential? Here again the problem lies in the lack of absolute standards.

The question can be discussed only in terms of how adequately mature human beings in a society are able to function in the roles that require intellectual competence of some kind. If there are shortages in some adult occupations for lack of skilled people and if large numbers of individuals are ill prepared to function at the necessary level of skill and training required by the technology of the society, we can then make at least a relative kind of judgment about the adequacy of family functioning in this respect. This approach also has its problems since it must isolate the responsibility of the family from that of other socializing agencies concerned with the intellectual development of young children—the schools, primarily, and, indirectly, the government in modern societies.

One component of intelligence is the capacity to solve practical problems. In societies with highly developed technologies, skill levels are far more complex and problem-solving challenges are constant. In this type of society the family is much less able to carry out the responsibility of developing the intellectual potential of the young. This is yet another function the family once monopolized but now shares with trained experts. The degree of encroachment on the family's role has paralleled the development of technology in societies and the proliferation of specialized occupations.

In nonliterate hunting and gathering and tribal societies, the family had the sole responsibility for educating the young. Not until puberty, and not even then in all nonliterate societies, were children separated from the family and instructed by specialized, nonfamily personnel. These individuals were not usually full-time instructors, however, and after initiation rites were over, they returned to their daily chores.[13] The curriculum, furthermore, was not vocational. Arts and crafts were sometimes taught to the initiates, but not gardening, hunting, or fishing skills. The emphasis was on myth, lore, religion, and magical knowledge rather than on necessary economic skills, which were easily transmitted and taught by family members.

Social mobility was unknown since children usually performed the same occupational roles as their parents. The rate of social change was slow and skills rarely became outdated. The development of intellectual skills necessary for adult functioning was handled quite effectively by the extended family. Teaching was oral, based on the principles of apprenticeship and learning by doing and example. Because there was no economic class structure in the less developed nonliterate societies, almost all children of the same sex were educated equally, with few disparities in the amount and kind of training available to the young.

In preindustrial societies, the extended family continued in its role as prime educator for the masses of the population. Mobility was rare, and social change continued to be relatively slow. Only the elite were literate; the common people did not need to know how to read or write in order to till the fields and harvest the crops. The instruction of the elite, usually by religious functionaries, was nonvocational, emphasizing character training, service, and development of the poised, well-rounded, cultivated man and woman.

In urban centers, which contained only a small proportion of the population, children were often apprenticed outside the family for instruction in trades and crafts. In rural areas, priests occasionally took on the instruction of a few promising peasant children, but teaching was limited to imparting simple literacy and the virtues of piety and docility. For the majority of the population in these societies, however, the family functioned relatively adequately and unaided in preparing its young to anticipate and cope with the intellectual challenges of adult life—as adequately as the general level of knowledge and technology permitted.

In industrialized societies, the family loses its monopoly over the development of intellectual skills in the young. The scope of this loss, in terms of the number of families who experience it and the lowering of the age when children are removed from its exclusive province in this respect, is greatly expanded. Not only literacy, but far more than that is required for intellectual functioning in technologically advanced societies.

The family's responsibility and adequacy in developing the intellectual potential of its children becomes, at the same time, contracted but crucial. It is crucial because the family, at least at present, still has the initial contact with its children and the earliest responsibility in preparing them for the formal educational experiences they will have in school and elsewhere.

The family loads the dice not only by its child-rearing practices but by the fact that it places the child initially, and by the event of birth, within a particular location in the class structure. Both factors, and they are closely related, are very significant influences that will affect the nature and the amount of formal education children will have and their receptivity to this experience.

Class overrides ethnic origin and race as a factor affecting the preschool preparation of children. The great divide, in this respect, is between the child-rearing practices of the working class, particularly at the lowest levels, among the poor, and the middle and upper classes. Lower-working-class mothers, overwhelmed by more numerous, closely spaced children to care for and by unremitting problems of physical survival, spend less time talking, smiling, and playing with their infants.[14] Later, they spend less time reading to their children. They are more likely to issue orders without explanations. Their spoken language is less like written language, grammatically, than that used by the middle class. They use concrete language. Their sentences are short, with little use of qualifying phrases. They discourage curiosity and question asking in their children because they are often too distracted to respond to questions. They tend to ignore the crying of their infants—which some psychologists feel is the origin of feelings of impotence and helplessness that the children of the poor often display in later life. In testing situations, for example, these children tend to give up and are less persistent at difficult tasks than are middle-class children.

Actually, the feelings of fatalism and helplessness that impoverished children often display are characteristic of adults as well as children in the subculture of the very poor. Daily experiences reinforce these feelings in almost all areas of life. Mothers have no reason to encourage optimism in their children, and their children have no reason to feel it in test situations, real or artificial.

The list of the ways in which the material circumstances and child-rearing patterns of poor families do not prepare children for optimum intellectual functioning in school and thereafter is extensive. Differences between poor and middle-class children in this respect show up very early. The value of constructive use of leisure time is applied by middle-class mothers in their expectations from their children practically at birth, with educational objects and toys that teach perceptual discrimination, grasping, and motor skills. Idle hands and minds are disapproved in this class.

How important are these early class-based environmental differences for the intellectual future of the child? A large body of evidence has been accumulating that points to the existence of "critical periods" in infant and early childhood histological (tissue), neurological, and biochemical development that are of the greatest significance for learning and behavior.[15] In toilet training, for example, there is an optimum time for teaching this behavior in terms of the child's neurological development.

In the development of intelligence, the research evidence seems to indicate that children's future intellectual competence is strongly and critically affected by the experiences they encounter in the first three or four years of life, the period when the central nervous system develops most rapidly. The human brain at birth is only about one quarter of the size it will reach at maturity—at about twenty years of age. It grows very rapidly during the first few years of life and reaches 90 percent of its final weight by the age of six.

This does not mean that change and catching up cannot occur

in the child's intellectual functioning after this period; it means, simply, that environmental influences, attention and teaching by the mother and other figures who are significant in the child's life have a maximum impact on developing intelligence at this time. After this critical period, more effort is usually required to produce a change in the level of intellectual functioning.

This emphasis on the first three years of life, incidentally, parallels Sigmund Freud's belief that the first five years of life are crucial for personality development. The difference lies in the fact that Freud's interest was in the effect of experience on the emotions and drives. The new group of investigators is more interested in the relationship between early environmental experiences and intellectual growth.

Given this new emphasis on the importance of the first few years of life and the accumulating evidence that points to the need for additional help within poor families in providing for the intellectual as well as the physical needs of their children, we can predict that eventually the role of the family in this respect, at least for those who are at the bottom of the class structure, will be curtailed further. Probably this will not come about on a widespread scale for some time yet, in the United States. A really serious concern with developing human resources in this country is not an overriding consideration in allocating the national income at present. Countries that are poorer in natural resources, such as the Scandinavian nations, invest in human resources instead. The United States has not had this kind of pressure and, currently, is moving in the opposite direction.

It is very important, however, to be aware of the economic factor, not only in determining class differences in teaching and contact between mother and children, but in determining the academic and vocational success of most children, *regardless* of ability and the specific child-rearing techniques of their parents.[16] Statistically, middle-class children as more likely to be placed in college preparatory tracks than working-class children of equal ability, as measured by grades and test scores.[17] Middle-and upper-class children with average ability are more likely to enter and graduate from college than working-class children with higher measured ability. And middle-class children with poor grades and low test scores are sent to private school, when possible, to avoid downward mobility.[18] This occurs not only in the United States, but in England, France, and in other countries as well.

Most families do what they can to develop the intellectual potential of their children. But social class location intervenes, crucially and effectively.

ADOLESCENCE

BIOLOGICAL CHANGES. Adolescence is the next major stage in the human life cycle that affects family roles, rather dramatically, in modern societies. It is a status that has a physiological onset—puberty—and a sociological ending—full adult status, as defined by the society.[19] The biological changes that occur in adolescence are triggered by hormonal secretions which depend, in turn, on developmental changes in the central nervous system. The adolescent experiences a spurt in growth and in the development of primary sexual characteristics. The penis and scrotum become enlarged and ejaculatory capacity develops in males. Females begin to menstruate, and their analogous sexual organs, the clitoris and labia majora, grow in size.

Secondary sexual characteristics also appear at this time: the enlargement of the breasts and pelvis and the growth of pubic and axillary hair in females; voice and skeletal changes and the growth of pubic, axillary, and facial hair in males. Both sexes experience an enlargement of the sweat glands without a proportionate growth of the secretory ducts of these glands. This often results in skin disorders, a common and normal affliction of adolescence.

These are the basic biological changes of adolescence. The sex drive becomes pronounced after a period of relative latency, depending on the society, and sexual and growth changes are accompanied by an increase in energy and emotional tumult—again, depending on the society. It is these latter phenomena that have the most direct effect on the family and are most directly affected by cultural role definitions and family behavior.

THE SOCIAL STATUS OF ADOLESCENTS. Societies vary in the requirements they lay down for the achievement of adulthood—requirements that may or may not coincide with the physiological end of puberty. The steps to adulthood can be many or few, clear-cut or vague, achieved by some adolescents under certain culturally prescribed conditions and never achieved by others—slaves, for example.

Most nonliterate societies provided for a dramatic, ritualized ordeal or initiation ceremony, a *rite de passage*, to symbolize the attainment of adult status. While this usually involved damage to the skin, teeth, or genitals, individuals had the assurance of achieving a socially recognized maturity after a definite and circumscribed period of time. Their scars were visible symbols of an adulthood that was achieved early, rapidly, and unqualifiedly. And adulthood coincided with puberty.

In nonliterate and in preindustrial societies individuals usually began their adult occupational activities during childhood. Marriage represented the final achievement of full adult status. This, too, tended to coincide with puberty, since physiological maturity occurred much later in nonindustrialized societies. Developments in technology, medicine, and public health practices improve the food supply and the general health of the population in industrialized societies. Growth is speeded up, and sexual maturity occurs much earlier.

In industrial societies, adolescence as a status with a different biological and social termination becomes recognized, protracted, and defined as a social problem. Developments in science and technology make necessary an increasingly lengthened period of formal training for the young. The increased energy characteristic of this biological stage of the life cycle is, furthermore, not usually channeled into productive work until after, and usually long after, the beginning of puberty. Socially recognized adulthood does not occur until the young person enters a full-time and more or less permanent occupation.

The marginal status that adolescence represents is extended at both ends. It not only ends later, it begins earlier. Long-term records on the onset of menstruation in female populations indicate a decline in the average age of menstruation during the past hundred years, from seventeen to thirteen years. The theory that this is related to the adequacy of diet and medical care is supported by the fact that puberty occurs somewhat later among the poor and is also delayed during periods of war and depression, when food supplies are less adequate.

The period between childhood and socially recognized adulthood is not a time of unrestrained freedom. Behavior is regulated, often very stringently, by peer groups. Collective behavior—proneness for fads, fashions, and social movements—is characteristic of individuals who occupy an insecure or marginal status. Since they are not locked into marital and full-time occupational obligations, adolescents are more available to what is new. They are particularly susceptible to this type of behavior.

Adolescence is not a paradise of fun and games, panty raids, capers and pranks, as often portrayed in the mass media. In mobile, class societies especially in the middle class, it is a time of preparation and competition for eventual jobs and marital partners. The family can guarantee neither in industrial societies, although it plays an important role in limiting possible choices. In traditional societies, the family not only limited but often determined both the occupation and the mate. The child did not have to ask "Who am I?" or "What will I be when I grow up?" The family, rather than the vocation or profession, established the individual's adult identity in these societies.

In industrial societies the achievement of full adult status is piecemeal, arbitrary, and inconsistent. In the United States, the adolescent pays adult fare at age twelve, may drive an automobile and is no longer subject to child labor laws at sixteen, serves in the military and achieves legal maturity at eighteen, and may achieve adult marital status without having achieved adult economic status. Student marriages, relying on parental support, or the earnings of the wife, are an example of a pattern that was fairly widespread in the American middle class before the current women's movement.

Adolescents, like the aged in technologically developed society, are outside the productive process. They are, at the same time, a source of enormous profit to business and a costly burden to the nuclear family, especially in countries where higher education is not free to all students and where students do not receive government stipends. If they attempt to find work, they are usually restricted to marginal, low-paying jobs. Work-study programs and volunteer programs such as the Peace Corps, while also low-paying, represent attempts at partial rescue of at least a handful of adolescents from their preparatory status and their state of economic suspended animation and dependency.

THE GRATIFICATION OF SEXUAL DRIVES. A major source of frustration among adolescents in agricultural and industrial societies stems from the difficulty they may experience in gratifying their heightened sexual drives. Societies that are economically and politically stratified usually prohibit premarital sexual relationships for their young, at least ideally. Courtship and marriage are more easily regulated by the family when premarital sexual activity is controlled. Historically and cross-culturally, the higher classes have always been more concerned with controlling the marriages of their children in order to protect or increase family power and wealth. No society, however, has succeeded completely in preventing sexual relationships that are prohibited, and some have been notoriously unsuccessful. The mother-son incest taboo is the only sexual taboo that seems rarely to have been broken in human societies.

While extramarital relationships have been prohibited except under normatively regulated conditions in almost all, if not all, societies, premarital sexual relationships have been permitted in a majority of nonliterate societies. This was particularly true in hunting and gathering societies where differences in wealth and power between families were minimal. In more technologically developed nonliterate societies, where these differences became more prominent, a mixed pattern sometimes existed. In Samoa, for example, commoners were permitted premarital sexual freedom, but princesses were carefully guarded and were expected to be virgins until they were married.[20]

Illegitimacy was not a problem in the nonliterate societies that permitted premarital sexual activity since marriage occurred shortly after puberty—and sometimes before. Not only did young people reach puberty at a later age than in industrial societies, but protection was also provided by the biological fact that very young girls are less fertile for a period of one to three years after the onset of menstruation than they are later on.

In agricultural societies, premarital sex is generally prohibited by the culture and reinforced by religious sanctions. Discrepancies in wealth between various segments of the society become much more pronounced since improved technology permits the accumulation of a greater economic surplus. Political and religious elites, often with interchangeable personnel in the early stages of agricultural development, extract a disproportionate amount of this surplus in exchange for protective and spiritual services.

Theologies that explain the unknown and promise retribution for sufferings and wrongs encountered in this world become codified and are promulgated by a hierarchy of specialized religious officials. The traditional organized religions of East and West have not only legitimated the unequal distribution of material goods in stratified societies in the past, they have also stressed sexual abstinence as an ideal.

Sexual gratification is a pleasure that all humans can experience, and forgo, regardless of their station in life. This is a possible reason for the position of the traditional organized religions on human sexuality. Faith is stronger when based on self-denial. The requirement of sexual abstinence or that sexual gratification be only for the purpose of procreation applied to all members of society, rich and poor alike, at least officially.

The evidence seems to indicate, however, that in practice enforcement of restrictive premarital sexual norms was less than perfect, particularly at the lower levels of preindustrial societies. Unfortunately, since only the elite were literate, and they wrote mostly about themselves or each other, the historical record of the sexual practices of the masses is not very adequate. Love and feelings of intense physical attraction and emotional attachment have occurred in all societies, but societies have varied not only in the extent to which they have permitted sexual gratification for young unmarried members, but also in their definitions of the appropriateness of love as a basis for marriage.

In American society today, individuals who marry without a feeling of love feel deprived or guilty. In traditional societies, particularly in the East, love was often regarded as a "laughable or tragic aberration" by the extended family.[21] In societies where the family unit rather than the individual is paramount in importance, a love relationship between husband and wife is discouraged since it detracts from family loyalty and may be disruptive of authority and deference patterns in the extended family. Love is also discouraged as a basis for marriage because of the possibility that it might cross class or caste lines.

In traditional India, love was culturally prescribed as appropriate to the husband-wife relationship, but only after betrothal or marriage. In traditional China and Japan, respect rather than love was the culturally prescribed value governing husband-and-wife relationships. The significant emotional tie was between parent and child. Families in traditional societies used a variety of devices such as child betrothal and marriage, sexual segregation, and the isolation and chaperonage of women to prevent love and premarital sexual liaisons from occurring.

Romantic love as a positively sanctioned and culturally prescribed norm regulating the relationship between men and women arose in the West among the feudal aristocracy during the age of chivalry, in the twelfth century. Initially, the pattern was consistent with Christian attitudes toward sex in that norms of courtly love applied outside the marital relationship and were grounded on the principle of chastity. The lady and her knightly love, who was not her husband, did not consummate their relationship. They suffered and fetishized instead. The European nobility of the seventeenth and eighteenth centuries finally joined sex and love—but still outside the marital relationship.

As societies industrialized in the West, the middle classes rose to prominence, and it is they who joined love, sex, and marriage. But premarital sexual restraint remained the norm. The language of love became part of the courtship procedure—but only after bethrothal, which was still arranged by the family with an eye to the economic status of the prospective bride or groom. Chaperoning was used to prevent premarital sexual consummation of the relationship.

In industrial societies, the norm of premarital chastity declines and becomes more difficult to enforce. Science and technology provide safe and effective contraception and control of venereal disease. At the same time, the family is less able to control the economic and marital future of its children. Family farms and businesses are replaced by impersonal corporations that recruit personnel on the basis of rational rather than traditional standards such as ancestry, noblesse oblige, or paternalism, at least ideally. Social status becomes somewhat less a matter of birthright and somewhat more a matter of personal achievement.

The decline in the restriction of the mating and premarital sexual behavior of the young in contemporary industrial societies is a logical accompaniment of the decreased significance of the extended family as an economic and social unit. Individuals are freer from family control to work out their own destinies in all spheres of life. The choice of a marital partner has less importance for the fate of the entire family. And, for the individual, the personal qualities of a potential marital partner become more significant than ancestry and inherited social status. Despite these trends, sexual frustration and sexual problems in adolescence and beyond, that were unknown and not even conceivable throughout 99 percent of human history, in nonliterate societies, persist for both sexes, in the United States and elsewhere.

In coping with the biologically based changes of adolescence and the needs and energies that become more pronounced at this time, the family in industrial societies has lost its previous effectiveness. It can no longer provide satisfactory outlets in productive work and arranged marriage for its young. Here again the problem can be formulated as a cultural lag in which other agencies—the government, especially, but also the church, the economy, education, and recreational institutions—have failed to recognize and channel the adolescent's drives and energies adequately. This failure is very costly in terms of human life.

In the United States, the death rate is declining for all ages except among adolescents.[22] The sharp jump in deaths among young people aged fifteen to twenty-four is due primarily to auto accidents among whites and murders among blacks, which, in turn, are related to drug and alcohol abuse and emotional problems. Suicide rates are also rising sharply. Fortunately, the adolescent's reflexes are fast. If not for this, the rate of deaths by accidents would be even higher.

CONFLICTS WITH PARENTS. Psychoanalysts view adolescence as a time of storm, stress, and "frenzied conflict."[23] With the development of adult genital sexual capacity, the adolescent, if permitted, will express hostility and contempt toward parents, as a defense against unconscious feelings of sexual attraction toward the parent of the opposite sex. While the majority of adolescents do not rock either the societal or the familial boat, the sexual maturity of offspring can have profoundly disruptive effects on family life. This, too, varies according to class. Among the poor, for example, father-daughter incest is not infrequent. In the middle class, especially the upper-middle class, parents may seek sexual gratification outside marriage. The heightened sexuality of the adolescent can be contagious, and a sexually mature son or daughter can be a serious threat to an impaired husband-wife relationship.

Same sex parent-child rivalry and envy may also increase during this period for other reasons. Adolescents are at the height of their powers. Middle-aged parents are experiencing unmistakable signs of physical decline. The menopausal mother is confronted with a daughter whose reproductive capacities are budding; the father may no longer be able to defeat his son in athletic tests of speed and strength.

Depression is a common response to loss, and guilt is a frequent component of depression. Adolescents may experience depression in response to the loss of their parents as primary love objects in their life and guilt in response to the unconscious erotic feelings toward the parent of the opposite sex that become reactivated at this time. Parents may feel guilt about their envious feelings and may respond with depression to the anticipated loss of their maturing child. These feelings are intensified in competitive, mobile industrialized societies. Depression over the potential loss of a child is not unrealistic, particularly in the middle class, since children are increasingly unlikely to settle next door or in the family compound when they grow up.

It should be emphasized at this point that negative feelings between parents and their children are a matter of degree. Parent-child conflicts occur in most extreme form in families where serious and obvious psychological problems are present. But the difference is relative rather than absolute. Another point to remember is that these feelings coexist with positive feelings that are usually stronger. Ambivalence in familial as well as in other social relationships is a price humans pay for their evolutionary development. Other animals are more fortunate in this respect.

Feelings of envy and aggressive and hostile impulses are not likely to be captured in research questionnaires, however. Deeper, less acceptable feelings between parents and their children tend to be repressed, particularly in authoritarian homes, where the conventional morality is strongly supported and where hostility and aggression on the part of children are not readily tolerated. For this reason, survey research studies that attempt to measure the existence of a generation gap, or conflict between the generations, usually obtain negative results.[24] What these studies uncover is a basic agreement in attitudes, values, and role conceptions between most parents and their adolescent children. In study after study, a clear majority of students have reported good communication and understanding and a close relationship with their parents. Even in the realm of sexual behavior, young people often feel that their standards are not so different from those of their parents. Parents become more conservative about sex as they age. But their children apparently recognize the discrepancy between what parents say and what they do or have done. The present adolescent generation is more open about their sexual behavior and more likely to set up premarital housekeeping arrangements. Otherwise, their behavior is not so different from that of their parents.

At a psychological level, however, conflict between the generations is not likely to be tapped by attitude questionnaires. One way to gauge the actual prevalence of conflict at deeper, less consciously accessible and less readily admissible levels would be to use projective tests of the Rorschach and Thematic Apperception variety on a widespread scale. At the moment, these tests are too costly and time-consuming to administer to large, statistically representative samples of the population. As research techniques continue to be refined and improved, however, survey instruments that tap deeper feeling levels and penetrate psychological defenses may yet be devised. Only then will it be possible to answer accurately the question of the extent of intergenerational conflict in contemporary societies.

Sociologists can, however, point to cultural and social structural conditions that reduce or promote feelings of psychological conflict between the generations and, particularly, between parents and their adolescent children. As mentioned earlier, the fact of nuclear family structure removes potential mediators and buffers such as grandparents and aunts and uncles from the daily interacting family unit, thus probably intensifying both negative and positive feelings. Rapid social change and ambiguous, contradictory, or changing role definitions disrupt family functioning and intensify psychological sources of conflict, particularly in the area of authority patterns within the family.

The increasingly prolonged economic dependence of adolescents on their parents also promotes conflict and mutual resentment, especially in a society that values independence and self-reliance. While some adolescents have the opportunity to change the economic circumstances of their lives in modern societies, in the process they become impaled on a series of contradictory cultural values and experience severe role conflict. In the middle class—notably in the United States—creativity, independence, work, and achievement are highly valued and are incorporated more and more into the role prescriptions for adolescents of both sexes. Adolescents are exposed to these values and, at

the same time, to the necessity to conform in bureaucratic settings, and to a prolonged dependency in an economy that cannot
use them. They have been taught that all humans are equal, but
they must compete to show their superiority. They must compete
and at the same time love their fellow human beings.

As economic opportunities decrease, competition, frustration,
and hostility increase and love becomes a luxury that few adolescents can afford. Parents, teachers, and other authority figures who work with adolescents are more frequently bedeviled,
battered, and burned out. According to public opinion polls, discipline is believed to be the most serious problem in American
schools today.

Male adolescents probably suffer more severely from the economic dependence of adolescence since the culture continues to
prescribe greater independence to males than to females. On the
other hand, males generally are less sexually repressed than females and are less likely to experience conflict with the requirements of impulse gratification in an era of greater sexual freedom. Females are freer in their sexual behavior than formerly,
but they are still affected by survivals of the traditional double
standard. Females who have numerous sexual partners usually
experience greater disapproval than males experience. Faithful-
ness and exclusiveness in sexual relationships continue to be more
expected of females.

Female adolescents have their own unique culturally based
conflicts that become more pronounced during adolescence. They
are taught to be aggressive and competitive with males in school.
At the same time, however, feminine role prescriptions require
that they be dependent, nurturing, and receptive in their relationships with other human beings, especially with males. The
requirements of female passivity, dependence, empathy, and
conformity, furthermore, are poor preparation for the resourcefulness, impersonality, toughness, and independence that are
often required in rapidly changing, bureaucratic, and anomic
industrial societies.

These sources of conflict stem from outmoded role conceptions
and are additional to or may reinforce psychological conflict

The nature and intensity of role conflict vary, however, by class. In competing for marital partners and jobs, adolescents who are rich are more protected by family power, wealth, and contacts from the worst ravages of competition and insecurity. Adolescents who are poor are often not even in the economic race, and marriage is frequently the result of a drifting together and a fatalistic acceptance of the inevitable, particularly if the girl next door becomes pregnant.

Adolescents have reacted to their unique stresses and frustrations by withdrawing, by fighting, or by persevering and enduring, which is the most common adaptive response. Each path has its own particular subcultural trappings and peer group supports. Time, if not the major social institutions in industrialized societies, is on the adolescent's side, fortunately. Biologically, at least, adulthood is inevitable, for those who survive.

MIDDLE AGE AND OLD AGE

BIOLOGICAL CHANGES. During childhood and adolescence, biological changes in human beings are pronounced and easily observable. During the years of young adulthood, physical change is slower : youth tends to ebb unremarked and almost unnoticed.

In middle age, beginning somewhere around age forty-five, and varying by class as well as by genetic predisposition, physical changes once more become marked. Family roles in industrialized societies, however, are affected more by social definitions and expectations and changing economic conditions than by the actual biological changes that occur as family members age.

Aging individuals experience cumulative, irreversible, and progessive losses of energy and muscular strength, a decline in sex hormone production, a slowing in speed and reaction time, impairment of the functioning of the five senses—vision, hearing, taste, smell, and touch—and some changes in intellectual functioning.[25] The question of just how much, if any, intellectual deterioration occurs in healthy older people is a matter of controversy. Measurement devices are imperfect, and psychological factors, such as motivation and drive and the level of initial intelligence, affect the fate of the intellectual capacities of particular individuals differently in old age. Investigators tend to favor and report studies that support their own beliefs and attitudes about the topic. Detachment about the aged is difficult to achieve, particularly in a society such as the United States where a high value is placed on youth.

Intelligence is a complex trait. Certain aspects of practical problem-solving ability may decline with age, while others increase and still others remain unchanged. Generally, individuals over seventy, who are healthy, tend to perform better than young adults on tests of vocabulary, verbal comprehension, and simple arithmetic. They perform less well on tests involving speed in decoding information.

Much of the evidence that has been cited to show a decline in overall intelligence with age reflects, rather, the decline in reaction time, which affects IQ scores negatively. The basic ability to learn new material, furthermore, does not seem to decrease with age. The ability to perform finely coordinated voluntary movements is impaired but is counterbalanced by the longer experience (where this is not made obsolete by technological development) and better work habits of older individuals. For this reason, studies of worker performance in industry show little change in productivity up to age sixty or sixty-five. Older workers are removed from the economy less for reasons of biological decline than for reasons of pressure from below—to make room for younger people who need employment and who are less expensive to employ since they start at lower salaries.

AGING AND FAMILY LIFE. The effect of biological aging on family functioning varies according to the stage of technological development in different societies and largely according to class within a particular society.

In nonliterate societies, very few individuals and only those with exceptional health, strength, and luck were able to survive to old age.[26] Physical strength and quick reflexes were highly prized attributes in these societies. Older people, who could no longer perform tasks that required speed or strength, such as hunting, were given less physically demanding work. They dressed the kill, processed hides, repaired equipment, or helped with young children. The aged often worked until their death. Labor-intensive economies, which have few sources of energy available other than muscle power, utilize the old in less physically taxing but socially necessary tasks.

The burden of caring for the aged who were incapacitated was distributed among the many members of the extended family. Euthanasia was usually practiced in societies where life conditions were extremely harsh and brutal. The majority of nonliterate societies, however, did not detach, disengage, or disaffiliate their aged members from the world of the living and the productive.

Since the aged were so extraordinary in having survived in these societies, their survival was frequently attributed to the benevolence of supernatural forces. Gentle treatment by younger family members was often sanctioned by the fear of ghostly revenge. The aged were also a socially valuable repository of oral tradition, knowledge, magic, and skills in societies that had no written language. This was another factor that enhanced their prestige and encouraged good treatment by the younger generation.

As societies have developed technologically and become more stratified economically, the treatment of the aged has been less benevolent and has varied largely according to their power and economic status. A close reading of the historical records of the ancient Hebrews, Greeks, and Romans, and of medieval Europe and colonial America, reveals that the ideals of respect, deference, and kindness toward the aged were little more than the official rhetoric of these societies. In fact, only a few old people, and largely those who were within the upper classes, were able to command good treatment. The majority suffered neglect at best, and cruelty at times. The wife shared the fate of her husband, and lost her privileged status, if she had it, upon his death.

In industrialized societies, physical strength and speed become less socially necessary attributes in the population, but social conditions—increased population, the possibility of operating the economy with far fewer people—disqualify the more numerous aged from economically productive work. They lose status dramatically upon compulsory retirement, and those who suffer most are those who have been most highly achievement-oriented during their working years.

It is an irony of modern times that men and women who have been most successfully socialized into the traditional masculine and feminine sex roles during earlier stages of their life experience the greatest stress in old age. Very dependent, nurturing women are less able to redirect their energies into nonfamily activities when their children leave or if their husbands die. Very aggressive and highly competitive men have more difficulty shifting to the recreational activities that are more appropriate to the status of retirement.

Definitions of the obligation of the family and the state toward the aged in modern Western societies have varied largely in relation to the course and nature of technological development, the degree of urbanization, and the value placed on economic productivity and success in the society.

As the mobile, nuclear family becomes the typical form in modern societies, and as the aged are increasingly removed from the work situation in economies that cannot or will not use them, the burden of supporting the aged becomes more and more difficult for the family. Three-generation households in which the aged live with their grown children are not desired by a majority of old people or by their middle-aged children. In the United States, the pattern exists more frequently in the working class, which has less choice in this respect. A widowed mother may live with her grown daugher. Even here, however, it is far from typical. Yet it is becoming more frequent as purchasing power declines, social programs are cut, and the life span and the number of physically dependent people over eighty continue to expand. The middle class is more likely to provide cash income supplements for their needy aged parents, but this, too, may change, and for the same reasons as in the working class.

The role of the state in sharing the responsibility for the aged with the family varies in Western industrialized societies. The United States, in this respect, compares unfavorably with other

Western democracies. In England, for example, government-supported home nursing care is provided for those who cannot take care of themselves. In the United States, the incapacitated old person must move in with an adult offspring or be disengaged from the household and community and placed in an institution, after turning over all property and savings. A society that values youth and success to the extent that the United States does is not tolerant of those who are left behind. Breaking ties is less painful than daily confrontation with human frailty and vulnerability. Nevertheless, in both societies, only a small percentage of the aged live in institutions. More than three quarters of the old people in the United States, furthermore, live near at least one grown son or daughter whom they visit regularly.

In Sweden public housing for the aged is extensive, and old age pensions are tied to the cost of living and provide completely for the material needs of old people. These pensions are granted to all, regardless of private means or the amount of previous tax contributions.

England and Sweden industrialized earlier than the United States and are still more highly urbanized. This explains part of the difference in government policies, but ideological factors have also been operative. The American belief in rugged individualism and individual responsibility for one's fate, and the dislike of "charity" and paternalistic government, also accounts for the relative reluctance to assume full responsibility for the needs of the aged that the small nuclear family can no longer cope with, in the United States—or anywhere else, for that matter.

Biological Sex Differences

Differences in hair color are not regarded as having a necessary relationship to behavior and are not accorded great significance in human societies. Differences in skin color, however, are a very important basis for evaluation and behavioral expectations. Biological sex differences have also been a major source of cultural definitions of expected behavior, particularly within family groups. The biological fact of maleness or femaleness has been elaborated into conceptions of masculinity and femininity that have varied greatly in different societies.

Almost any personality trait or human activity, even the care of young children (which was assigned to secondary husbands in polyandrous Marquesan society) has, at one time or another, been defined as either masculine or feminine or both in various societies. Since women give birth to and nurse children, one would expect child care to be the most important aspect of the female role in human societies. A careful examination of the anthropological and historical evidence, however, indicates that in no known nonliterate or preindustrial society was the mother the sole caretaker of young children, nor was she even "principally involved" in this care in three quarters of these nonindustrial societies.[27] The separate, single-parent household, almost always headed by a woman, and now, more often, by a middle-class woman, is a phenomenon of urban, industrial society. In many hunting and gathering societies, furthermore, women, who did the gathering of wild vegetation, were the major food providers, although the meat brought in by male hunters was more highly valued. The relationship between biology and destiny is a subject to be investigated, not assumed. And the question to be investigated is not biology *versus* environment, but the relative *weight* of each set of factors in determining typical differences in male and female roles and personality traits.[28]

More specifically, to what extent are persisting sex differences in family roles and in personality, especially in such areas as temperament, sexual behavior, and family functioning, biologically determined and unchangeable? To what extent are these differences a variable product of socialization—of time, place, society, and culture? Evidence on this highly controversial question can be found in comparative studies of different types of societies, studies of the behavior of nonhuman male and female primates, studies of pathological hormonal or chromosomal conditions in humans, and studies of male and female newborn babies who have not yet experienced the effects of postnatal socialization and cultural conditioning.

HORMONAL DIFFERENCES

Hormones are chemical substances, produced in the endocrine glands—the pituitary gland, the thyroid gland, the pancreatic inlets, and the ovaries and testes. Hormones regulate various bodily processes—metabolism and growth rates, for example—and the development of primary and secondary sex characteristics. In the male, the most important hormone for developing and maintaining biological sex characteristics is testosterone, one of a group of hormones known as androgens. In adulthood, normal males produce about six times as much testosterone as females. In females, the estrogens and progesterone are most important in the development and regulation of biological sex characteristics. Actually, to label the androgens and estrogens "male" or "female" hormones is misleading, since both types of hormones are produced by both sexes, but in differing amounts.

ANATOMY. The most obvious, hormonally based, typical differences between males and females, in size, strength (ratio of muscle to fat), and speed, and in reproductive organs, have been regarded as all-important in determining typical differences in sex roles in contemporary societies. A look back through the entire span of human history, however, indicates far greater variety than hormonal differences alone could account for. The degree of male dominance, for example, as pointed out in chapter 1, has varied greatly in human societies. Moreover, this dominance has had far more to do with differences in the production and control over economic resources by women and men in different societies at different times than with typical differences in hormone levels. This will become quite apparent in chapter 3, where the changing economic roles of women and men in major types of societies are described in greater detail.

TEMPERAMENT. The hormones have also been regarded as all-important factors underlying typical temperamental differences between the sexes in childhood and in adulthood. Temperament is a genetic predisposition to react to the environment in certain specific ways.[29] It refers to energy or activity level and to emotional sensitivity and intensity. The latter refers, specifically, to mood and to behavioral expressions of love or hate—to nurturing or aggressive behavior.

In nonhumans, the relationship between the sex hormones and behavior is clear and direct. Injection of female sex hormones intensifies nurturing behavior; injection of male sex hormones increases aggressive behavior. Nonhuman females do not have territorial defense patterns, nor do they engage in competitive and dominating behavior, typically.

The relationship between the sex hormones and human behavior, however, is much more difficult to establish. Culture intervenes, and biological factors are not easily isolated. In humans, the more highly developed cortex can override hormonally based predispositions. Studies of newborn infants who have experienced minimal cultural influences have not demonstrated consistent, reliable, or extreme sex differences in such areas as emotional response (irritability, crying) or sensitivity to various stimuli. Individual infants differ significantly; male and female infants, as a category, do not.

Adult males do have a somewhat higher metabolic rate on the average than females, but again, numerous studies have not found typical and consistent differences in the activity levels of female and male infants. These studies have limited value in relating behavior to sex hormones, however. Differences in male and female sex hormone production do not become pronounced until puberty and are a consequence of the development of the central nervous system. By that time, typical differences in the socialization experiences that males and females undergo from the moment of birth obscure the role of the hormones in determining sex role behavior.

Studies of infants who, in the past and as a consequence of prenatal hormonal disorders, were born with genitalia that could not readily be identified as male or female (hermaphrodites), provide important evidence on the question of the relative importance of genetics and early socialization experiences in determining sexual identity and sex-typed behavior. John Money and his associates at Johns Hopkins Medical School, who spent years studying children who were assigned to the wrong sex at birth, concluded that early socialization experiences are so important that by the time the child reaches the age of eighteen months it is too late to correct the mistake without causing severe psychological damage.[30] With newer techniques for determining genetic sex chromosome structure, where the sex of newborns is in doubt, these infants can now be assigned to the correct sex on the basis of chromosome tests and are treated hormonally. Nevertheless, results from older studies provide indisputable evidence of the importance of early learning experiences in determining sex-typed behavior and sexual identity.

While there is evidence that high levels of the female sex hormone estrogen are associated with positive mood states and low levels with negative emotions in many women, this does not have crucial implications for sex role definitions. The fact that a large number of women seem to be somewhat more irritable, depressed, and anxious just before menstruating, after delivering a child, and during menopause does not mean that women should be excluded from certain occupations and activities. Men, as well as women, are irritable, depressed, and anxious, at times, whatever the state of their hormone levels. Men also experience mood swings that correspond to changes in their hormone levels, although they are less likely to admit to their anxieties because of traditional male sex role prescriptions that stress bravery and stoicism.

The relationship between sex hormones and the emotions in men and women needs much more study. Much of the research on women has failed to distinguish between the effect of changes in hormone levels and preexisting personality traits of the women who have been studied. It has failed to allow for the power of suggestion since the subjects of these studies have usually been aware of the investigators' interest in their menstrual cycles. And it has failed to emphasize how male and female emotional reactions vary, typically, in different cultures and subcultures, during different periods of history, regardless of hormonal levels and changes.

The most obvious biological differences between males and females, in physical size and strength and in reproductive functions, have been most clearly tied to sex role definitions, especially in the past. Hunting, for example, required not only great physical strength but greater mobility and freedom to roam, often great distances, and for weeks and sometimes months at a time. Women, who gestate and nurse the young, have been less available for these activities. On the other hand, in many societies women have been assigned more physically demanding chores than men. They have dug ditches and carried heavier physical burdens on their heads and backs.

With technological development, the tie between biological sex characteristics and behavior becomes more tenuous and the possibility of modifying sex role norms in even more radical ways arises. Push-button technologies and weaponry in highly industrialized societies do not require physical strength. Women are less likely to nurse their young, and biological scientists may yet devise a substitute for the womb to gestate the young. The dead hands of culture and biological and economic necessity weigh less heavily in modern societies, and individual choice and inclination have freer play.

In the past, the differences between males and females in reproduction have had highly significant implications for the restriction of the sexual behavior of the female, especially in societies with an economic surplus that is not shared equally by all families. The reasons are obvious: paternity cannot be established if the sexual outlets of the female are unlimited, and it is the female who is directly burdened with an illegitimate child. Advances in the technology of birth control in industrialized societies have been a very important facilitating factor in the decline of the double standard.

SEXUAL BEHAVIOR. In the past, the double standard was also justified on the grounds of a presumed stronger male sex drive, which in turn, was related to higher levels of testosterone in males. More recently, however, it has also been argued that females, in fact, have a stronger sex drive than males. Mary Jane Sherfey, for example, claims that females have an insatiable sex drive comparable to that of nonhuman female primates when they are in heat.[31] She argues that stronger cultural restrictions on female sexuality have been essential to preserve the family group from destruction by the biological sexual voraciousness of the human female. Which view is correct?

Anthropological studies of nonliterate societies, where there were few or no differences in cultural restrictions on male and female sexual behavior, provide important evidence on this question.[32] In these societies, and again for 99 percent of human history, there were no typical or significant differences in the sexual behavior of males and females. Both sexes engaged in sexual intercourse once a day, usually, and women were as likely, and not more or less likely, than men to initiate the sexual act. Nonhuman female primates who are in heat are more aggressive sexually because they do not achieve orgasm, apparently, nor are they able to sublimate their sexual impulses into other types of physical or intellectual activities. A minimum level of testosterone is essential to adequate sexual functioning. Both sexes have this minimum. Typical differences in sexual behavior are far more a matter of culture and expectation than biological imperative.

The recent explosion of a number of myths regarding female sexuality will change sexual practices and attitudes and values even more than they have changed recently, once they become widely publicized. It has been established, for example, that the clitoris and the lower third of the vagina are the primary erotic zones in female orgasmic response. The female-superior coital position has, however, been unpopular in this country and has been defined as unfeminine. When it becomes more widely known that this position allows for more direct clitoral stimulation and is thus more likely to be gratifying to the female, notions of the relationship between masculinity and who is on top are likely to be discarded.

In the sexual folklore of the West and the East, the size of the penis has long been equated with masculinity and the capacity to gratify women. Recent empirical investigations have revealed, however, that there is little anatomical difference in this respect between males, when the penis is erect. The publication of this kind of information and the knowledge that female sexual response derives largely from external stimulation and does not depend on the depth of penetration are likely to promote more rational sexual techniques, devoid of anxious and irrelevant male concerns about their comparative anatomical adequacy.

AGGRESSION. Aggression is another personality trait that has been linked to higher levels of testosterone in males. Aggression is a trait that has been culturally defined as desirable for males in most societies that have advanced beyond hunting and gathering in technological development. Since the invention of plant cultivation, approximately twelve thousand years ago, men have usually been required to suppress emotions related to love to a greater extent than women and have been allowed greater freedom to express emotions related to hate.

The question is, then, and this is a very important question, bearing on the fate of human societies and the inevitability of war: to what extent is male aggression genetically determined? The relationship between male sex hormones and aggressive behavior in nonhumans has been clearly demonstrated, as has been pointed out. Females are more likely to engage in nurturing, withdrawing, pacifying, and grooming behavior than males. When male sex hormones are injected into pregnant monkeys, the female offspring are more active and aggressive than the female young in control groups. Injection of male hormones upsets the dominance order in adult animal groups.

The fact of hormonally based aggressive behavior stemming from the sex drive is of a different order of significance, however, than the claims that have been made for an independent, spontaneous, genetically based aggressive or ''killer'' instinct in men. The work of Konrad Lorenz and Robert Ardrey, assuming the existence of an indigenous, nonreactive urge to kill in human beings, which they believe is phylogenetically programmed, convinced many who sought explanations, and perhaps absolvement, for the persistence of war.[33] Many contemporary sociobiologists make the same assumption.

These authors and their compatriots in the currently fashionable pursuit of futility and despair ignore the evidence of zoology, anthropology, psychology, and physiology in their arguments.[34] Animals kill for survival—to satisfy hunger needs; they do not kill for the sake of jealousy, rivalry, or pleasure. Humans elaborate the notion of killing for survival, often irrationally, but this is not proof of genetic predisposition.

Territorial defense patterns in nonhumans, which are a means for establishing differential food and sexual privileges in animal groups, involve threatening display rather than killing. Furthermore, humans' closest relatives, other primates, do not have the pattern of territoriality and are not usually belligerent except when provoked. Even prehistoric humans, according to the anthropological evidence, did not hunt to satisfy a predatory instinct but to satisfy their hunger needs and those of their dependents.

Physiologists have not been able to demonstrate the existence of chemical and physical changes in humans and other animals, comparable to the drop in blood-sugar levels as hunger builds up, that indicate a continuous internal accumulation of aggressive energy without reference to an external stimulus.

From the field of psychology we have a vast body of data demonstrating that much of the aggression manifested by human beings is a *reactive* response to attack or to frustration— the blocking of needs or goal-directed behavior.[35] If aggression is universal in human societies, it is because frustration is universal. Social conditions affect the amount of frustration in the population, and the culture encourages or inhibits the expression of aggression. It also identifies the objects of aggression: strangers, minority groups, noncomformists, and other outsiders. The list of individuals and groups who have served as objects of displaced aggression in human history is long.

War, if it is inevitable, is programmed not in the genes but in frustration-inducing social conditions, abetted by cultural values that make extreme distinctions in definitions of femininity and masculinity, equating masculinity with killing and stoicism and repudiating love-related sentiments as effeminate. Societies pay a price not only for their requirement of extreme aggressive behavior in the male, but also when they ascribe extreme passivity to the female. They lose the potential contributions to the culture of many of their citizens, who are encouraged to contribute to the growth of population rather than culture. We now need knowledge, ideas, and direction far more than we need people. Masochism, the correlate of passivity in the human female, can also have tragic effects on the family. It promotes resentment and subtle retaliation by those who suffer and encourages the aggression of those who benefit.

Long-haired youths in the 1960s exalted love and repudiated killing in their slogan ''Make love, not war.'' They also deemphasized differences in male-female sex role definitions. The sex act is not only a nondestructive alternative to militarism, it also contains an element of aggression and allows for a partial release of these impulses. To make love and not war is grounded in profound psychological truth. Societies that have valued power rather than love have been more likely to start wars than to institute internal economic reforms.[36]

Nonliterate societies that have made little distinction between the ideal personalities of males and females have emphasized physical and love-related pleasures such as eating, drinking, and sex. This type of society, however, did not survive after technological advance created economic surpluses that became the objects of destructive conflicts.

If we are to redefine the cultural ideal of masculine aggressiveness it will have to be a worldwide phenomenon. The balance of love will have to replace the balance of terror; otherwise, the pioneers in this undertaking will perish. Greater economic abundance has encouraged impulse gratification, freer emotional expression, and a greater honesty and openness among younger people in industrial societies. We can anticipate continued changes in this direction. But the have-not nations will have to be carried along in the sweep of future automated splendors; otherwise, the envy and frustration of the other four fifths of the world will undo us all.

CHROMOSOMAL DIFFERENCES

Males and females also differ in chromosomal makeup. Females have an XX chromosomal structure; males have XY chromosomes. In the past, attempts were made to relate violently aggressive male behavior to abnormal XYY chromosome patterns and to trace male passivity and low virility to XXY patterns, but with little success. Research has indicated no consistent and direct relationship between chromosome structure and behavior. A slightly higher proportion of violently aggressive males have had an extra Y chromosome than in the general population, but the great majority of XYY males are not criminally violent.[37]

Sex differences in chromosome structure do have indirect implications for family life and for the relationship between the sexes, however, especially as these differences affect the sex ratio, susceptibility to disease, and the death rate.

The composition of the Y chromosome is unknown, but the X chromosome appears to provide protection against certain genetic and nongenetic diseases. Some researchers have speculated that the second identical X chromosome in females provides a stand-in replacement for defective chromosomes. In any case, while more males than females are conceived, more male fetuses are spontaneously aborted. The female infant mortality rate is lower, and women have a longer average life expectancy that men. This is true throughout the animal kingdom, incidentally.

In societies where males outnumber females by a considerable number, as in India, Guatemala, and Ceylon, we can assume that the practice of female infanticide continues, informally and illegally.

Females have fewer genetic disorders such as color blindness and hemophilia and they are more resistant to the damaging effects of malnutrition and other types of physical trauma. As Ashley Montagu pointed out some years ago, women are not the weaker sex, except perhaps in muscular strength.[38]

What consequences does this have for family life and sex-typed behavior? In the United States, there is a surplus of approximately six million women in young adult and in older age categories. This can have indirect implications for the persistence of traditional differences in the personality traits of men and women. If men, and higher-level jobs, are in short supply, women may be less likely to express strong assertiveness, independence, and achievement motivation. These traits continue to be discouraged for females, especially in the white working class, despite approximately twenty years of a women's movement in the United States.

Elderly women whose husbands have survived are very likely to be nursing husbands with chronic diseases. This pattern is reinforced by the persisting tendency for men to marry younger women, especially in second marriages. Widows over age sixty-five are very unlikely to find an eligible male to remarry. Two thirds of all widows, in fact, never remarry.

The future of the sex ratio, however, is likely to depend more on medical and scientific developments than on genetic sex differences. Techniques for preselecting the sex of offspring may soon become a reality. Most parents in the United States prefer two children: one male and one female. While preference for male children is less strong in the United States than in other countries that have been surveyed, those who plan to have one child usually prefer a male.[39] This preference should operate to diminish the present imbalance in the sex ratio, when parents are able to choose the sex of their children.

At the same time, continued developments in the cure or control of all types of diseases, especially heart disease and cancer, the two major causes of death in the United States, should help equalize the life expectancies of men and women. Men have been more susceptible to heart disease in middle and old age. Biologists do not predict a great extension of the human life span in the near future, but with anticipated medical advances, especially in chemical therapy and organ replacement techniques, more males will survive to the present limits of the human life cycle.

Another important factor that will close the gap in life expectancy between men and women is the increased tendency for women to be gainfully employed in highly competitive, psychologically stressful occupations. In larger cities, where more women are gainfully employed, especially in higher-level jobs that are sex-typed for males, average differences in male and female life expectancy are declining.

It should now be clear that the basic biological needs and traits of human beings throughout the life cycle establish certain broad limits to the content of family roles. It should also be clear that role conceptions and definitions can vary greatly within these limits, especially as societies industrialize. If biology is destiny, it becomes much less so in modern times, with the aid of science and technology.

Biological maturity and all that this implies, including the intensification of the sex drive, coincide less with provisions for economic independence and sexual gratification and marriage in modern societies. Biological changes during other phases of the life cycle also tend to become less consistent with cultural dictates, as retirement, for example, becomes compulsory, largely for technological and economic rather than biological reasons.

Sex typing declines, in certain respects, as basic differences between males and females, particularly in size and strength, become less significant for economic functioning in industrial societies. Sex differences in reproductive functions continue to define parental roles, but less so than in agricultural societies. The continued existence of the family group is based on the biologically grounded emotional needs of the human young, especially the need for a stable source of love, which underlies and strongly affects physical and intellectual development and growth. The content of the role of mother or father changes as societies develop technologically, but the status of parent is unlikely to be eliminated because of these basic biological needs.

A look into the past with an eye to changing economic conditions, as science and technology develop, will further illuminate this point. We will also see, then, why certain values—particularly the values of individualism, equalitarianism, rationalism, achievement motivation, and tolerance—become more widespread, and are incorporated into family roles as societies move toward increasing control over their material environments. Our heritage offers an ever-expanding possibility for deliberate and rational change in family life and in social life, generally, given the values that guide us. Scientific knowledge accumulates, however it is used, misused, or ignored by those whom it would benefit.

THREE

Types of Human
Societies

Human societies, and the major institutions within them—the family, religion, government, economy, education, and recreation—can be seen to have varied in rather typical ways, when these societies are classified on the basis of the level of technological development and the state of scientific knowledge that have characterized and distinguished them.

In science, typologies are constructed for the purpose of classifying observed facts according to some explanatory or interpretive principle. Scientific typologies, ideally, meet the standards of all inclusiveness and mutual exclusiveness: all relevant facts can be classified, and the location of any particular fact or item, once the classifying principle is established, is logical and irrefutable.

The Problem of Typologies

When human beings, their activities, or their societies are being classified these standards are difficult to meet. Individual variability and cultural complexity may defeat the most enthusiastic typologists in the social sciences. In the United States, it is currently fashionable to attack typologies as sterile or oversimplified. This is a symptom of the antiintellectualism that has always characterized American society and that has been enhanced recently by severe political and economic strains and a growing ethic of despair. Scientific typologies have, in fact, played an important role in the history of science and in the progressive accumulation of information and understanding about human beings and their material and nonmaterial worlds.

When viewing human societies as falling into several major categories on the basis of the level of scientific information available to them and the primary means by which resources are produced and energy is obtained, it is important to bear in mind that the model and the concepts are abstractions. Reality is almost infinitely complex: societies usually present a mixed picture and boundaries are often blurred and hard to establish.

Many societies, furthermore, have not changed in a pattern of step-by-step progression and advance in the ability to harness energy, manipulate the environment rationally, and accumulate verifiable knowledge about the world.[1] Some societies have regressed, usually after a defeat in war—Western Europe and the Mediterranean nations after the fall of Rome are examples. Other societies, such as hunting and gathering societies that have survived into the present have stood relatively still. Still other societies, like the industrializing societies of sub-Sahara Africa, have skipped stages, sometimes quite dramatically.

Social conditions and social trends that have been associated with gradual technological development in the West—increased urbanization, rationalism, secularism, bureaucracy, and mass literacy—have occurred and proceeded at varying rates in currently industrializing societies. The very rapid introduction of advanced industrial techniques and scientific methods for controlling disease and curbing death has produced transitional conditions, such as the population explosion, that have little precedent in Western history. These nations may or may not emulate the West in the economic, ideological, political, or familial patterns that will ultimately characterize them. Their experiences will provide additional answers to the question of the relationship between ideology, technology, and institutional forms, as they undergo rapid social change.

Whatever the problems of typologizing—of definition, placement, and judgment—the thousands of separate and discrete societies that exist and have existed, from small bands or tribal enclaves of 50 to 200 souls to behemoths of almost a billion toilers and dreamers, can be classified. When they are, on the basis of tools and weaponry, the state of scientific knowledge, the amount and kind of property and economic surplus, and the nature and degree of mobility within and between their borders, all of which are interrelated, we find certain associated patterns and regularities in family life.

A Typology of Societies

The major types of societies, viewed in broad perspective, have been nonliterate hunting and gathering and horticultural societies, agricultural societies, and urban, industrial societies. Agricultural societies that industrialized in the eighteenth and nineteenth centuries are sometimes referred to as preindustrial societies, to distinguish them from agricultural societies that are currently industrializing. It is possible to construct a highly generalized portrait of family life as it has varied typically within these various settings, focusing on courtship and love, and husband-and-wife and parent-and-child relationships.

PRELIMINARY CONSIDERATIONS

Two technological innovations that have occurred in human history have had such enormous consequences for social life that they can be called revolutions.[2] The two revolutions are the Agricultural Revolution and the Industrial Revolution. The concept of revolution, in this case, refers to degree rather than speed of change.

The changes associated with the Agricultural Revolution—the increase in the size and permanence of settlements, in the number of specialized occupations in trade and commerce, and in the degree of economic inequality, the development of class structures, and the elaboration of political, economic, religious, and educational activities into more formal structures—took thousands of years to unfold.

The effects of the second technological revolution have been progessively speedier, largely because cultural borrowing and diffusion occur more quickly as mobility and communication increase and isolation and provincialism decline. By and large, and sooner or later, however, more efficient techniques for adapting to the environment have tended to replace less efficient techniques, although values have played an enormously inhibiting or facilitating role in this process.

The Agricultural Revolution, in which the technique of cultivating plants was discovered, is believed to have occurred first in the Middle East about twelve thousand years ago. Horticulture, the first stage in this revolution, involved the knowledge and use of the hoe and digging stick, but not the plow, in plant cultivation. Animals were domesticated in horticultural societies and used as a source of additional food production, but the use of animal power to replace human muscle power, the harnessing of oxen to the plow, for example, was not known.

Archeologists do not agree about whether the techniques of horticulture developed independently in the New World or whether they diffused throughout the world from their origin in the Middle East to Britain in the West and to Asia in the East, and then across the Bering Strait to the New World. Whatever the path and the vicissitudes of this particular technological innovation, however, the consequences for the quality of human life and for human values were tremendous.

With the advent of the Industrial Revolution in England in the eighteenth century, machine power gradually replaced muscle power, and standardized goods came to be produced by standardized machines using interchangeable parts. Mass production and mass consumption are paramount consequences of this additional source of power. Industrialized technology enhances the material comfort of all segments of the society—although disproportionately—in a way that the Agricultural Revolution did not. Inhabitants of modern urban slums often wear fashionable factory-made clothing that is in sharp contrast to the shabbiness of their shacks and tenements.

NONLITERATE HUNTING AND GATHERING SOCIETIES

Any discussion of nonliterate societies must rely mainly on studies and observations of isolated surviving nonliterate communities made before these communities began to change dramatically through contact with industrial societies. Since the rate of social change in these isolated societies has been very slow, we assume that family life and social life have not varied greatly through the ages.

The human animal has inhabited the earth for at least two million years and possibly much longer. Modern humans (Homo sapiens) appeared sometime between 70,000 and 35,000 years ago. Until the discovery of horticulture, humans survived as hunters and gatherers, moving constantly, sometimes every week, as local food supplies were exhausted, living in small, isolated, homogenous bands, with little or no specialization of occupations other than on the basis of age and sex, and no surplus food. Life was short, but not necessarily brutish and nasty. While there was no leisure class and all who were physically able participated in the quest for food, the three day average work week of hunters and gatherers has yet to be achieved by a majority of humans in modern societies.

The realm of the sacred, that part of the world that is set aside, treated with reverence and awe, and regarded as unpredictable and uncontrollable, was all-powerful. Animism, the endowment of the physical environment with supernatural properties and forces, was common. Humans in nonliterate societies often did not distinguish between themselves and the material environment with respect to such qualities as life, motivation, and power.

Superstition, chance, including games of chance rather than games of skill and strategy, and fatalism were widespread; knowledge of rational techniques for adapting to the environment was very limited.

The rate of social change was so slow as to be almost imperceptible. The number of elements of technology and knowledge in the culture that could be combined or recombined into new forms was small, and the rate of invention was negligible. The number of people comprising the intellectual and motivational pool from which could arise innovation and new solutions to the problems of existence was limited. Contacts with other societies, and the possibility of borrowing more efficient or effective techniques, were sporadic or nonexistent.

Most hunting and gathering societies had leaders who emerged temporarily at times of decision-making to mediate discussions of when and where to migrate or how to plan food-foraging expeditions. These individuals were usually not full-time leaders, however. Typically, there was no permanent, widely recognized status of leader to which was attached automatic rights of deference and authority regardless of the personal qualities of the occupant. Leaders returned to the mundane survival activities of daily life when their stewardship talents were no longer required. And this was often true of the only other specialized occupation in these societies—the shaman or medicine man, specialist in magical salvation or destruction.

Magic occupied the life space that organized religion and science occupy in more technologically developed societies. Shamans coerced the spirits and demons into intervening in the concerns of their clients, bringing them health, long life, love, the defeat of enemies. Shamans were self-employed; they were not functionaries in a permanent religious organization. Priests have represented a moral community; shamans worked alone and without the backing of a systematic, all-embracing theology.[3] They neither competed with nor supported family values, beliefs, or behavior.

While monotheistic religions existed in a small number of nonliterate societies, rarely was there a conception of an all-powerful, everpresent supreme being who was actively concerned with sanctioning and implementing a system of ethics.[4] This development is associated with more complex technology, more populous and more heterogenous societies, and the decline in the effectiveness of the family and the community in exercising social control.[5]

Private property as we conceive of it was unknown in hunting and gathering societies: the ownership of land that was soon to be abandoned was pointless, and the accumulation of liquid capital, or its equivalent in shells or other media of exchange, was impossible in the absence of an economic surplus and trade. The notion of personal property, however, did exist and was vested in such items as ritual rights to songs, dances, and names, and the small amount of tools, weapons, or clothes that individuals were able to transport on their backs. It was easy to discard and duplicate new equipment that was simply and quickly constructed out of materials that were readily available at the new site. The impetus for both possession and accumulation was lacking in hunting and gathering societies.

Men hunted, and fashioned their spears, axes, and bows and arrows out of wood, stone, and bone. Women collected edible vegetation, hunted small animals, bore and nursed children, often throughout the entire span of their short lives, succored the ill, the wounded, and the dying. Communal sharing of the kill was common. Luck and chance were powerful forces; families and individuals could ill afford the independence that stems from economic security. They might be next in the capricious battle with the forces of accident and destiny.

Villages rarely contained more than fifty people and were often even smaller. Sometimes villages sharing a common culture and language were united into a tribal structure, reinforced by out-marriage, but these were usually not under the effective rule of a centralized authority. It was difficult for one family to accumulate the equipment and the power to subdue the rest.

Population remained fairly constant, automatically regulated by balanced and very high birth and death rates. Where this balance was upset, infanticide was often practiced. Inefficiency was the rule in reproduction and in survival—in all areas of life, in fact, except art, music, and religious ritual, where the standard of efficiency did not apply.

Except where protected by natural, geographic barriers, most hunting and gathering societies that did not discover the use of metals in fashioning tools and weapons and the technique of deliberately cultivating plants were doomed to extinction by the expansion of societies that did make these self-preserving discoveries.

NONLITERATE HORTICULTURAL SOCIETIES

With the introduction of horticultural technology in human societies, the press of the search for food lightened. Population increased, since population in nonindustrialized societies tends to expand in proportion to the available food supply. Settlements become more permanent; the exhaustion of the land took longer to accomplish than the exhaustion of the local supply of wild animals and vegetation by hunting and gathering societies.

Tribal federations became more unified and effective political units, under the control of families that had forged ahead in power and wealth. The families who achieved this initial advantage probably did so because they happened to have produced more children, and children who were more aggressive than their compatriots. Expelled misfits of extended families or survivors of decimated, weaker families sought the protection and swelled the ranks of the more powerful families, bringing still more workers and fighting power to these families.

More efficient food-procuring techniques made an economic surplus possible, and a new source of distinction between families and individuals appeared. Humans evaluate people, places, and things. They arrange objects in their environment in a hierarchical order and judge them as more or less good, worthwhile, desirable, or important, according to their values.

In hunting and gathering societies, prestige was differently allocated to members of the society on the basis of age, sex, and personal qualities such as physical strength, bravery, intelligence, or resourcefulness. With the development of an economic surplus, the differential possession of the land and its fruits became an additional criterion for evaluating families and individuals.

Religious ideologies provided the motivation for families to produce more than they could consume and the justification for turning over this surplus to the priests and to the heads of more powerful families, who traded protection for tribute. Hereditary, family-based advantage in property, power, and prestige became established, and class structures came into existence. More efficient techniques for supplying food released some members for full-time specialized occupations in the arts and crafts, religion, and politics. Pottery and weaving appeared, and the use of metals, other than iron, was discovered. Specialized occupations meant the production of more goods of a particular type than individuals, their families, or their village could use. These new and often luxurious products were either transferred to the dominant class or were traded by barter. Trade and commerce encouraged cultural diffusion and mobility; the rate of social change increased somewhat.

Women usually did the planting and harvesting in horticultural societies. Men often did the heavier work of clearing fields. They continued to hunt to supplement the subsistence needs of the society, their contribution in this respect varying from society to society. In societies where hunting was more important than plant cultivation in providing for subsistence needs, the status of males relative to females was usually higher.

Human sacrifice, organized group warfare, cannibalism, head-hunting, and the taking of slaves are practices associated with horticultural technology and the accumulation of an economic surplus. In the absence of written records, scalp collecting became popular in many societies—a prototypical form of conspicuous consumption in which the number of accumulated scalps served to validate the status of the brave and the strong.

Not all societies developed a more advanced technology—some for reasons of geographic isolation or climatic idiosyncrasy, others for lack of an ideology that encouraged accumulation, aggression, and innovation. On the ruins of the less isolated of these societies arose the great agricultural societies of historic times.

AGRICULTURAL SOCIETIES

Agricultural societies appeared in Egypt and Mesopotamia approximately five thousand years ago. These societies not only had the plow, they arnessed oxen to the plow, thus taking a giant step in the direction of conserving human energy and supplementing the sources of power available to the society. With rare exceptions, these societies were distinguished from hunting and gathering and horticultural societies by three features: the development of a written language, which was limited to the elite, the existence of urban centers, and the yen and capacity for empire building.[6] Horticultural societies such as the Maya of Yucatan, who possessed an ideographic system of writing, a calendar, and a numeral system that included the concept of zero, the Incas of Peru, who were empire builders, and the Chinese during the Shang and Chou dynasties, who had a written language, urban centers, and a feudalistic system of government, were unique exceptions.

Other differences that distinguished horticultural from hunting and gathering societies became even more pronounced in agricultural societies. The size and permanence of settlements, the variety of occupational specialization, the extent of trade, the degree of social inequality, the level of productivity, the size of the economic surplus, and the size of the noneconomically productive class all expanded.

Warfare in horticultural societies was usually sporadic, limited to raiding, plundering, capturing slaves, driving off interlopers. In agricultural societies, wars of conquest and occupation became the preferred form. Conquest and subjugation were faster and more efficient ways to increase wealth than patiently to await the rewards of continuing technological development. Technological innovation in agricultural societies, furthermore, was discouraged by the fact that the fruits of new discoveries were likely to be preempted, promptly and mercilessly, by the religious and politically dominant class.

Occupation, governing, and tax collecting from huge, heterogeneous territories require organization and personnel. Agricultural societies developed vast political and military bureaucracies to handle these tasks as well as religious bureaucracies to cope with the problem of social control.

Bureaucracies develop when it is necessary to coordinate the activities of large numbers of people in carrying out large-scale tasks. If one person is collecting taxes from ten people, that person can keep track of who is paid up and who isn't. If a thousand collectors are collecting taxes from a million people, somebody back at the home office has to keep records, coordinate functions, and provide supplies to avoid waste, loss, duplication, and chaos. And so the administrator is born.

As the tasks of protecting, controlling, building, and expropriating economic resources grew in scope in agricultural societies, bureaucracy proliferated in the political and religious spheres. No single extended royal family could provide the talent or numbers to coordinate the activities of governing and worshiping. And so they recruited administrators, tax collectors, and professional armies from other wealthy but less powerful families.

Literacy is also a usual precondition for governing large territories, and, incidentally, a precondition of bureaucracy. Records must be kept of tribute exacted and rewards dispensed to loyal functionaries. Since the written language was very complex in less technologically developed agricultural societies, a specialized occupational group of scribes came into existence. Here, again, recruitment was largely from wealthy and powerful families, since only they could afford to release their sons from productive work and could pay the costs of long years of education.

Formal legal systems developed in response to the need to control large populations with local and varying cultures and conceptions of justice. Codified law represents an attempt to substitute impersonal, universal principles for the blood-revenge tactics of family-dispensed justice. Where formal law and agencies of law enforcement are lacking or ineffective, injured parties and their families usually engage in the spiraling and interminable cycle of retributive acts characteristic of blood revenge. This can be disruptive of the civic order and predictability required for the effective operation of centralized governments.

Technological development proceeded unevenly and slowly in agricultural societies, but most of them eventually learned how to harness wind and water power and developed increasingly more efficient tools and weapons, particularly with the discovery of iron.

Centralized governments were usually monarchical and autocratic. Oligarchic republican forms of government appeared in maritime societies, where land was less significant as a source of wealth. The degree of centralized control by a king or emperor was related to the size of the territories governed, the existence of natural barriers, and the consequent ease of transportation and communication within the society. Feudalism, a system in which power is dispersed among lesser elite families within a loose federation headed by a king or emperor, existed where highly centralized control was difficult to maintain.

Conflict was a constant feature of agricultural societies, stemming from economic, religious, and ethnic differences in interests and values and from the barely endurable life conditions of the peasants. Spontaneous peasant revolts, particularly in more advanced agricultural societies, were standard occurrences.

While the royal family and the governing class together comprised probably less than 2 percent of the population in these societies, they owned from one half to two thirds of the national wealth.[7] Religious faith and political coercion, where faith was inadequate, kept the supply of tribute, rents, and taxes flowing from the masses to the dominant class. Privilege was divinely sanctioned; excellence, for those who were chosen, was measured by success in extracting the surplus to the fullest extent possible. Good works served God, not the masses. The haves and the have-nots worshiped, usually, with equal conviction. The privileged were as convinced of their right to worldly goods as the masses were resigned to their suffering.

Land was the most important source of wealth in agricultural societies, and wealth and power truly walked hand in hand. Political power was not viewed as a public trust, even ideally, but as a God-given right to be exercised to the fullest for family and personal gain.

Urban settlements developed as seats of government and religion and as centers of industry and trade. In the towns and cities, peasants could exchange what little was left of their surplus for tools, spices, and other products they could not produce. It was in the urban centers that the middle class became prominent, consisting of merchants, self-employed artisans, and minor clergy and officials who served the governing classes. The emergence of a middle class had great significance eventually for the redistribution of power and for changes in family life. The urban middle classes have been the innovators and the leaders not only in political and religious revolutions but in many of the significant changes in values that have characterized family roles and functioning in modern times.

Despite the fame of urban centers in agricultural societies, they contained only a small proportion (5 to 10 percent) of the population. The masses continued to exist close to the land, illiterate and short-lived, subject to unremitting hardship and the unrelenting coercion of economic necessity and authoritarian political power.

Magic, superstition, and fatalism were preeminent features of peasant society as they had been in less technologically developed, nonliterate societies. For the masses, knowledge of rational techniques for coping with the environment had increased somewhat, but control over one's fate and the availability of opportunities and alternatives had changed very little from prehistoric times.

INDUSTRIAL SOCIETIES

With the Industrial Revolution, humans took a mammoth stride in the direction of increasing control over their environment and edged that much closer to destroying it. Probably the most important precipitating factor was the invention of the steam engine. The shift to manufacturing as an important source of national wealth, and the establishment of the factory system, transformed Western economies and societies and led eventually to the dominance of the West in world politics, prerogatives, and privileges.

The effects of the Industrial Revolution have reverberated throughout the world over approximately two hundred years as humans shifted their energies from extracting activities such as farming, mining, lumbering, and fishing, to manufacturing, from stoking and operating machines to watching and adjusting machines, from flying shuttles and spinning jennys to automated plants and computerized services, from producing to selling and distributing, and from accepting and obeying to innovating and experimenting in all spheres of life. Creative energies have been released that lay dormant for thousands of years in agricultural societies, curbed by repressive economic conditions, fatalistic ideologies, and highly effective social controls.

To explain a complex social phenomenon such as the Industrial Revolution, it is necessary to select from a multitude of historical events those that seem most relevant. History is objective fact; interpretations of history vary with time, place, and the world views, predispositions, biases, and interests of societies and their citizen-writers of history. Causal explanations in science, furthermore, are subject to the process of infinite regress.

Where should one begin?

Contemporary Western historians and social scientists usually trace the sequence of events that culminated in the Industrial Revolution to the voyages of exploration and discovery that began in the fifteenth century in Europe. Natural science, mostly concerned at that time with understanding and explaining the mysteries of the solar system, was given a tremendous boost by the knowledge that became available about the shape of the earth. Physicists, academists, and biologists were also stimulated to seek a more empirical, experimental basis for their propositions and predictions, to venerate past authority less, and to trust in observation more. Technology, the practical application of scientific knowledge, benefited accordingly.

Myths about the material universe and, much later, the social order began to be struck down, gradually but inexorably. Rationalism came to be valued; its fruits were apparent in profit and power and, less immediately and less obviously, even now, in benefit to human life.

The age of exploration and the colonization of the New World resulted in a flood of previously scarce metals into the mother countries and a great acceleration in world trade and commerce.

One important consequence of the influx of gold and silver into European countries was the spread of the money economy and the decline of the barter system.

In the less technologically developed agricultural societies of antiquity, grain served as a medium of exchange when simple barter was inadequate. Since grain is cumbersome and perishable, scarce metals of various kinds came into use as substitutes for payment in kind or in grain. At first the size and weight of metals used in commerce were standardized for local areas. Then, as empires were consolidated by ruling families, centralized governments assumed the responsibility for minting standardized metal currencies.

The spread of the money economy in the fifteenth and sixteenth centuries had tremendous implications for social life. It facilitated trade. With a less cumbersome medium of exchange, it was easier to calculate profit and loss rationally, to invest and reinvest in business ventures, and to accumulate the kind of wealth that could later be easily diverted into industrial enterprises. Liquid capital gradually replaced land as the major source of the wealth of nations, families, and individuals.

As trade and commerce increased, merchants and artisans multiplied. Merchants stimulated new needs and acquisitive impulses among the populace. Their mobility in agricultural societies provided an important channel for cultural contact and diffusion. Their pursuit of gain and their calculation of profit in monetary terms were prototypical manifestations of the values of individualism, rationalism, competitiveness, and active mastery over the environment which are basic to achievement and innovation-oriented industrializing and industrialized societies. These new values eventually undermined the cooperative, conservative, fatalistic, nonventuresome, and nonrisk-taking values of the landlocked peasant in traditional societies of the West and had enormous implications for family life.

In addition to the material benefits that derived from the era of exploration and colonization, the Protestant Reformation, in the sphere of ideology, is also credited by some scholars with having had a major facilitating effect, if not an independent causal effect, on the social trends that eventually resulted in the Industrial Revolution in the West.[8] No comparable innovation in religious beliefs and values occured in the East; Eastern religions continued to value other-worldly spiritual goals and future-worldly rewards. For life on earth their advocacy of patience and resignation remained unchanged.

The Protestant Reformation was itself a response to social conditions that had been changing at least since the time of the Crusades. The Crusades opened up new culture contacts and new trade routes, stimulated new material wants, and enhanced the importance of urban centers. The doctrines of Protestantism, as enunciated by Martin Luther and John Calvin in the sixteenth century, provided a set of values and beliefs that eventually filled the spiritual needs of urban merchants and craftsmen, supporting and reinforcing their interests and economic activities.

Luther exalted honest work in one's calling as a way of serving God, thus removing the association of work with punishment and sin, which was the view of the medieval Catholic Church. The Church had frowned upon accumulation beyond that which was necessary for existence, and had stigmatized the merchant and the moneylender as thieves and parasites.

Calvin regarded profit-making as a respectable source of income, as respectable as wages and rents. His doctrine of predestination, which held that individuals were destined at birth for salvation or damnation and could do nothing to change their fate, had the unintended consequence of promoting rationalism in business life. This-worldly success came to be interpreted as a sign that the individual was favored by God in the lottery of fate and was, therefore, among those who were destined to dwell in His house forever. Continuous work, thrift, self-discipline, and self-denial brought not only worldly success, but relief from the constant anxiety that Protestants felt (difficult for modern humans to imagine) about whether or not they were in fact among the chosen.

The Puritan sects, prominent in England, Scotland, Holland, and New England, declared that individuals were alone before

God. Their closest friends might be among the damned. They must seek success at the expense of their competitors and must rely ultimately only on themselves. Individualism was given powerful ideological legitimation, and loneliness, the corollary of individualism, eventually became the existential condition of the most independent, the most self-directing, and the most steadfast of the practitioners of the success ethic.

Certainly the founders of Protestantism had no idea of the far-reaching consequences of their movement, particularly in promoting, at least indirectly, profit-making enterprise and industrialization. That there was this association initially is indicated by the fact that the first nations to become highly industrialized were Protestant. But the wealth shipped in by the colonies to many of these nations was an antecedent, if not a sufficient factor. In the East, the most highly industrialized nation, Japan, experienced no great change in the religious sphere prior to industrialization. It was, however, a colonizing power.

POSTINDUSTRIAL SOCIETIES

In agricultural societies animal power replaces human muscle power to some extent; in industrial societies, machines become a major source of power. In postindustrial societies, computers increasingly replace human brain power.[9]

Most employed people in postindustrial societies shift their energies, from extracting resources from land and sea or producing goods by machines, to selling their services. They work as salespeople, secretaries, bookkeepers managers, teachers, healers, advisers, protectors, and promotors.

The new middle class of salaried employees becomes the numerical majority in the labor force. Communication skills become more important than manual skills. Many trends in human social life that emerged in industrializing societies—the employment of women in the market economy, for example—have become widespread. In the United States today, most newly created jobs are in the service sector, and most of these new jobs are filled by women.

Modern Social Trends

The social conditions accelerated or sent into motion by the Industrial Revolution and the values that became widespread have profoundly changed the quality of life in contemporary industrial societies. Some of these changes, discussed here, seem most clearly associated with recent trends in family life.

In highly industrialized societies, developments in medical science and public health diminish the death rate and lengthen life, almost doubling the average life span in the past 100 years. Reproduction becomes more efficient since fewer babies die, and birth rates decline. Even with the decline in birth rates, however, world population has increased nearly sixfold in the 200 or more years since the Industrial Revolution.

The high level of technological development results in a greater emphasis on mental skills and selling and distributing in the economic sphere. The middle class eventually becomes the majority; the class pyramid moves toward a diamond shape, with the rich at the apex and the poor at the bottom and most people located in the middle. Movement up the class structure becomes common; movement down becomes feared. In traditional societies, movement either way was rare and irrelevant to the dreams and hopes of the majority of people.

Psychological mobility, the subjective counterpart in expectation, identification, and aspiration of actual, objective change in group membership, also becomes common. The mass media, to which all gradually become exposed, encourage this process by serving as sources of information about life styles, world views, roles, etiquette, speech, dress, consumer goods, distant places, and distant people. Models multiply, as do socializing agents. Superficial differences, urban-rural, regional, and, to a lesser extent, class differences are increasingly leveled by the standardized images publicized in the mass media. The leveling process is underwritten by the efficiencies of mass production and the reality of mass consumption.

Geographic mobility is also common: mobility in search of jobs, education, better housing, greater political freedom or social acceptance, new experiences, adventure, or escape from family and community controls. The more highly industrialized the country is, the higher the mobility rates. The United States has the most mobile population in the entire world.

Factories and offices require concentrated populations; urban centers contain a majority of the population in industrialized societies. In the United States, over 70 percent of the population lives on one percent of the land. Less than 4 percent of the work force can produce more than enough food on the farms to feed the inhabitants of this country and many others.

The degree of urbanization in a society is not determined by the growth of cities but by the proportion of the total population that lives in cities. In India, cities are growing, but the high birth rates in rural areas maintain the urban-rural population ratio at a fairly constant level. The movement from farm to city is a finite process. Eventually, the United States will be a nation of cities. Farms will be factories to which workers will travel from their urban homes to perform their daily shift of work.

Technological development proceeds at such a rapid rate in industrialized societies that economic growth can increase national wealth faster than wars of conquest, at least ideally. Invention and creativity underlie this technological development. Governments with an eye on the future curb the irrational greed of the dominant class effectively and become highly involved and concerned about the quality of education, the level of achievement motivation, and the satisfaction of the economic needs of their citizens.

The specialization of occupations grows constantly. The *Dictionary of Occupational Titles in the United States* (published by the Department of Labor) constantly expands the list of thousands of separate and distinct kinds of jobs in this country. Ever narrower specialization in training and knowledge becomes the only way to keep the pace of technological change and the accumulation of information from becoming an intolerable strain on human intelligence.

The clock and the traffic light replace sunrise and sunset as regulators of human activity. Time becomes an obsession, particularly for those who have much to accomplish. The frontiers of space contract as the population expands. But the frontiers of time expand, as artificial sources of light (oil, gas, electricity) lengthen the waking day.[10]

Human contacts become more and more segmented, impersonal, superficial, ephemeral, utilitarian, and, ostensibly, rational.[11] The cash nexus replaces emotion and sentiment as the foundation of social relationships. Loyalties to place and group decline; sophistication—flexibility and a capacity to adapt to constantly changing social situations—becomes a useful quality of character and often an absolute imperative.

Democracy—nominal, formal, fictional, or actual—becomes the preferred governmental form and the wistfully desired organizational principle in other spheres of life. Educated, skilled, better fed, and more economically secure people are not submissive or compliant; they want a greater role in determining their fate, whether they are workers, women, ethnic and religious minorities, young or old people.

Democracy and bureaucracy become the competing and antithetical ways of organizing authority and decision-making. They are antithetical because authority in bureaucracies flows from the top down. Ideally, in democracies the process is reversed. The preservation of individualism, where this is valued, becomes a new challenge: not only do political coercion and authoritarianism suppress inventiveness and creativity, but so does bureaucracy. It is an organizational form that is intrinsically inimical to unpredictability and change and, therefore, to initiative and to the restless, achieving spirit. But authority in bureaucracies, based as it is on skill and training, is usually not as arbitrarily oppressive as traditional forms of authority.

Intellectuals in highly industrialized societies, whatever the form of government, as long as it allows intellectuals to express themselves, decry the increase in anomie and alienation, the fragmentation of identity, and the endless quest for meaning and purpose. They deplore the breakdown of community and extended family, the decline in solidarity and belongingness, and the increase in self-absorption and narcissism. They point to the destructive possibilities of high rates of unbalanced and uncontrolled technological and social change. They bemoan the glorification of bureaucracy, the functionary, and the expert. They fear the concentration of power and the availability of vastly more efficient and effective means for obtaining and maintaining power and wealth. They mourn the loss of innocence and the decline of utopia, idealism, optimism, and hope.

From Traditional to Urban Values

As societies have changed from traditional (nonliterate and agricultural) to modern (urban, industrial) the family has also changed, especially with respect to the values that become incorporated into family roles.[12] The spread of urban values in industrialized societies—values such as individualism, equalitarianism, secularism, and rationalism, tolerance and sophistication, and active mastery and achievement—is increasingly reflected in all aspects of family life—in courtship patterns, in marital relationships, and in parent-child relationships. It is also reflected in the greater number of alternatives to traditional family groups and relationships.

The value of familism, in which the needs and wishes of the family are more important than the needs and wishes of its individual members, declines as levels of formal education and employment in the nonfamily economy continue upward. The family loses its absolute control over its men, women, and children. As the standard of living rises, as opportunities expand, as mobility increases, individuals begin to value their family obligations and responsibilities less.

Adults will follow job opportunities even if this means breaking ties with relatives. Married women will go out to work even against opposition from their husbands. They will leave unhappy marriages, sometimes without their children, especially in the middle or upper classes. Husbands will leave their economically dependent wives of many years, again, mainly in the middle or upper classes. The presence of children no longer preserves marriages, although women with male children are less likely to be divorced. The oldest child will no longer give up educational or other personal goals to support needy brothers and sisters or aged parents and grandparents. Young people will choose marital partners or live together in heterosexual or homosexual relationships with or without the approval of parents. The emphasis for the fulfilled life shifts from the family to the self. Individualism becomes the preferred standard.

Developments in science and technology promote rationalism and secularism and weaken religious beliefs as a controlling factor in family relationships and behavior. When miracle drugs can save mothers' lives and safe and effective techniques exist for contraception and abortion, death in childbirth and unwanted pregnancies are less likely to be viewed as God's will. Despite the position of the Vatican on birth control, Catholics in the United States are as likely as Protestants to use artificial birth control techniques.

As economic and educational resources and opportunities become somewhat more equally distributed in industrialized societies, authoritarianism—the standard of absolute obedience to fixed and unchanging rules—declines. This occurs in all spheres of life, including the family. The power of rulers over citizens, employers over employees, teachers over students, priests over parishioners, husbands over wives, and parents over children diminishes and becomes more negotiable.

More and more, women are independently employed in the corporate economy or in the public sector for more years of their lives. They achieve more equal levels of education, and, in many families, are more educated than their husbands, Currently, in the United States, working-class males are more likely to drop out of high school. More women than men are entering college. And, in recent years, the number of Ph.D.'s granted to women has been rising while male Ph.D.'s have been declining in number.[13]

Adult children in industrial societies may have more education and a higher income than their middle-aged parents. Young children, potentially, may have more or fewer of those resources than their parents. Families, especially in the middle levels of industrial societies, can no longer seal or guarantee the economic fate of their offspring, nor can they exercise as much control over their less dependent individual members.

Ethnocentrism—the tendency to view the values and customs of one's group or society as superior to all others—also declines. Fear and hostility toward strangers and the inability to tolerate or understand out-group differences become less widespread as societies industrialize. The idea of cultural relativism takes hold, as more people come to view their own customs as possibly arbitrary and certainly not the only good or required way to live.

People brought up more permissively in more economically secure environments tend to be less ethnocentric. They feel less aggressive if they are less frustrated economically. They are less likely to displace their aggressive impulses onto weaker, less powerful outsiders if they are permitted freer expression of aggression within their families—especially toward their parents.

Ethnocentrism also declines as higher rates of geographic mobility and higher levels of education in industrialized societies promote increased contact—direct and indirect—between different kinds of people. Familiarity diminishes fear and suspicion of strangers usually. More educated people are likely to be more open to new and different ways of thinking, feeling, and acting.

Fatalism declines as educational and economic opportunities, real or imagined, increase. Passive acceptance of one's fate becomes unpopular, especially as more people experience some of the benefits of technological advance Achievement and activism become the mode; rising expectations become the motivator.[14]

Women who interrupted their schooling or careers to rear children return to compete and achieve. Men who closed off less practical interests in the arts and crafts as young adults change careers in middle age. Children of migrant workers aspire to become doctors and dentists when they grow up. Impossible dreams become possible, in fantasy if not in reality.

Economic recessions in capitalist societies promote pessimism, but they do not reinstate fatalism. Repeated nationwide surveys in the United States, especially since 1980, have revealed widespread concern and pessimism about the future of the economy and the society, but not about the self.

We now have a basis for understanding why certain values become more widespread as societies develop technologically. Let us go back, now, and trace in greater detail typical variations in family life and family values in nonliterate, agricultural, and industrialized societies so that we can better understand survivals and trends in contemporary family life in the United States and in other countries.

FOUR

Varieties of Family Life

How have technological advances affected the family? How has the family changed from the time when human societies consisted of bands of roving hunters and gatherers, to the time when land became an anchor and a source of wealth? How has the family changed now that mobility is once again an everyday condition of human existence, and wealth is far more abundant, somewhat less equally distributed, and more movable and liquid in form? How have the values that I have called urban values affected family roles and relationships and family problems and conflicts?

The trail is not easy to follow. The historical record favors the literate and the privileged and those who achieved greatness or eternal notoriety. The prehistorical record, as reconstructed by archeological studies of weapons, tools, and art forms, says little about family roles, child-rearing practices, or intergenerational relations in nonliterate societies that are extinct. Again, we must depend on data from isolated surviving traditional societies that have been studied in modern times. We assume that family roles and values in these societies are not so different from those of their extinct predecessors, at least in major respects, given the very slow rate of social change in these societies.

THE FAMILY IN PREHISTORY AND HISTORY

Prehistory and history are time perspectives. Prehistory refers to the era in human societies before the invention of writing and written records. Culture and subculture are associated with place—with territory and society—and with groups. A single culture may be viewed historically, through time. Since rates of social change vary, the two perspectives do not always coincide when we compare societies, using the level of technological development as a basis for classification. In the very long run, however—that is, in terms of thousands of years—certain typical trends in family life have emerged that are associated with major breakthroughs in technology, specifically the Agricultural Revolution and the Industrial Revolution.

In the late nineteenth and early twentieth centuries, scholars of the Social Darwinist persuasion attempted to reconstruct step-by-step stages in family structure and functioning that they believed were associated with each step-by-step advance in technological development. Underlying these exercises was the assumption of progress toward human perfection. It was assumed that the populations and societies that experienced technological advance were intellectually superior. And it was assumed that the family forms associated with technological advance were morally superior.

Usually the family was depicted by Social Darwinists as having advanced from a state of primitive sexual promiscuity to group marriage, to matriarchy, to patriarchy, and, finally, to the most perfect union—Victorian monogamy. Among the more famous scholars who applied this model to family life were Herbert Spencer in his *Synthetic Philosophy* (1860), Johann Jacob Bachofen in *Das Mutterrecht* (1861), Lewis Morgan in *Ancient Society* (1877), and Edward Westermarck in *The History of Human Marriage* (1891).

Frederick Engels in *The Origin of the Family, Private Property and the State* (1902) also rested his analysis on technological development and assumed unilineal and universal stages in family structure and functioning. His analysis, however, fo

cused on technological development as this affects the accumulation and distribution of economic resources within societies and
within families. He did not view historical changes in family
life as progressive. Quite the contrary, Engels felt that family
life had deteriorated morally from a presumed original state of
equality between men and women in societies where property
was communally owned.

We now know as a result of accumulated anthropological research and more complete and accurate historical information
that there has been no universal, step-by-step, one-way pattern
of family development and change in human history. Matrilineal societies, for example, have been common in Asia, Africa,
Oceania, and aboriginal America. These societies, in which descent is traced through the female line and where newlyweds
usually live with the wife's relatives, have typically preceded
patrilineal forms. This occurs because horticulture usually pre-
cedes agriculture and matrilineal family organization tends to
occur where women make primary contributions to subsistence
needs by doing the planting in the society. But this is not an
inevitable consequence in horticultural societies; in fact, the
majority of these societies have been patrilineal.

The economic role of women in a particular society may be a
necessary but it is certainly not a sufficient determinant of patterns of calculating descent in that society. Given similar technological conditions, such as the discovery of horticulture,
preexisting traditions, values, and myths, the origins of which
are forever lost to the scholarly and the curious, have played an
obviously important role in affecting the direction of change in
family roles in particular societies.

We cannot argue, on the other hand, that family values and
ideologies have been an independent or a semiindependent force
in social change, as one sociologist has claimed. William Goode
has pointed to the communal experiments in China, Russia, and
Israel, and the retreat to more traditional forms in the latter
two countries, as evidence of the "independent" effect of family patterns on technology and economy.[1] The decision to institute communes in China, Russia, and Israel was made by polit-

ical leaders, not by families; preexisting family values have promoted the commune movement in China and undermined its success in Russia and Israel. The family, however, did not initiate the communal experiments in these countries.

Basic human needs and basic human emotions are universal; similar material conditions are associated with similar family characteristics. While there is no necessary and inevitable connection between the two in particular societies, we have ample evidence of certain major directions of change in family roles and values as societies have developed technologically and as they have achieved greater scientific knowledge about the world and its inhabitants.

To present an overview of family life throughout human history is an enormously complex task. We can simplify this task somewhat if we select certain major aspects of family life, such as family structure and functions, sexual behavior, love, marital choice, marital relationships, and parent-child relationships. We can describe typical variations that have appeared in nonliterate, agricultural, and industrial societies. We can then attempt to relate these changes to major changes in economics and values historically.

The long-range view yields a very interesting and rather startling generalization: despite vast differences in almost all spheres of life, certain patterns in family life are very similar in the simplest societies (hunting and gathering) and in the most complex societies (postindustrial). In both types of societies, the nuclear family is the predominant family structure; sexual intercourse before marriage is freely permitted; the choice of marital partners is based on personal preference rather than family arrangement; husbands and wives have more equal prestige and authority and share economic, child-rearing, and homemaking activities more; divorce is easy to obtain; and parent-child relationships are permissive—emphasizing independence and self-reliance rather than strict obedience to external rules.

In the realm of family functioning, however, in economic, protective, religious, educational, and emotional functions, families lose their monopoly as societies develop technologically. The function of providing emotional or psychological support increases in importance relative to other family functions in industrial societies, but even this function is shared more and more by friends and paid experts.

How can we explain these similarities and differences in family structure and functioning historically?

The concept of structure, remember, refers to a number of units—molecules, individuals, social classes—that are related to each other in certain interdependent and recurring ways within some sort of whole: a cell, a family, a society. In the family, structure refers to the total number of socially recognized statuses of positions occupied by individuals who are engaged in regular, recurring, and socially sanctioned interactions and relationships. With death, divorce, separation, marriage, remarriage, and childbirth, family structure changes. Statuses are lost or added; roles are redefined or redistributed.

Family structure, historically, has been either nuclear or extended. Anthropologists have preferred the designations "conjugal" or "consanguine." The conjugal or nuclear family structure is one in which the marital tie is paramount. In extended or consanguinal family structures, biological descent is the primary fact of family life, and the marital tie is deemphasized.

The pattern that predominates in a particular society will depend in large measure on the mobility of its members as they pursue economic goals. Hunting movable game and the existence of a job market are associated with nuclear family structure.[2] The extended family is associated with planting as a major economic activity. The extended family is a cumbersome unit, poorly suited to situations where individual members or nuclear families are frequently on the move.

The type of food supply, the size of the economic surplus, the kind and amount of property and wealth, and whether it is family owned or individually obtained, are related factors. All, in turn, are tied to the level of technological development. Because of the importance of the mobility factor, the nuclear family, relatively independent from the larger familial unit with respect to authority and economic functioning, predominates in hunting and gathering societies and in postindustrial societies. In horticultural and agricultural societies, the family is less mobile, or is immobile. It is bound to the land as a major source of sustenance and it strives to maintain the extended structure as the cultural ideal.

Ideals and reality, however, have rarely coincided for the masses of human beings. While the extended family has been the cultural ideal in a majority of societies, it is very likely that the common people have lived throughout history predominantly in semiextended units. Certainly this has been true in the West. In semiextended family units, the nuclear family occupies a separate household, but it is in *daily* contact with other relatives who live nearby—above, below, next door, down the road or street, or in the same neighborhood or community.

Peter Laslett and other social historians have argued that nuclear family households were prevalent in preindustrial societies and were not a consequence of industrialization and increased geographic mobility in pursuit of jobs.[3] Laslett claims that, in fact, the households of the poor in urban areas in England after the Industrial Revolution were more likely to contain extended families.

A narrow focus on actual household composition is misleading, however. It ignores the prevalence of relatives in the neighborhood and in the community who influenced and provided very real support for nuclear families in preindustrial societies, despite separate living quarters.[4] The larger, more crowded households in cities during the period of early industrialization in England were a consequence of poverty and the inability of many nuclear families, or parts of nuclear families, to maintain separate houses or apartments.

During the depression of the 1930s, in the United States, many families were required to double up for the same reason, in the middle class as well as among the poor. Currently, with the decrease in purchasing power, the young and the old in the United States are staying on or returning home, in large numbers, although most would much prefer to live in their own separate households.

Historically, it was mainly the rich and the powerful who maintained extended family households by choice. Harsh living conditions, inadequate food supplies, and little empirical knowledge about the control of disease and the environment operated against extended families. High death rates and the short life span frequently removed key figures in the various generations. In industrialized societies, people live longer, but social and geographic mobility and the increased tendency toward class and ethnic intermarriage are factors that may disrupt extended family relationships, despite lower death rates and longer life expectancies.

Polygyny (the taking of multiple wives) is a form of extended family that has been most prevalent in horticultural and in herding societies. Although it was the cultural ideal in many of these societies, it was practiced mainly by the wealthiest families. Monogamy becomes the ideal as well as the actuality in agricultural and industrial societies. Why does this happen?

We cannot relate the practice of polygyny to the *specific* economic roles of women in various societies.[5] The argument, here, has been that where women do the planting, one man can afford to support several wives and their children. Polygyny does occur in horticultural societies, where women often make the largest direct contribution to economic resources by producing raw materials. But it also occurs frequently in herding societies, where women make a smaller direct contribution to economic production. Women do not usually tend herds.

The economic factor, however, is very relevant to the practice of polygyny. Polygyny was used by ruling families to strengthen alliances between them and to consolidate their wealth and power.[6] It occurred primarily in patrilineal and patrilocal societies, where male dominance was stronger.

The practice of polygyny promoted and reinforced social inequality in economically stratified societies. Strong, wealthy extended family groups were in a position to obtain more wives who, in turn, produced more children, thus adding to the family pool of warriors and workers and improving its claims to protective powers and its right to rule over weaker families.

Polygyny declines in agricultural and industrial societies as extreme differences in wealth decline. But it survives in different form in modern times for very wealthy males who can afford to maintain two households, one inhabited by a mistress or a former wife, and one inhabited by a wife. The near-wealthy, upper-middle-class males, may attempt to imitate this pattern, but with difficulty, unless at least one of the women involved is self-supporting, in a high-paying occupation.

Among areas of the world where polygyny survived in agricultural societies are the Arab countries. Women in Arab societies performed the lion's share of subsistence activities. Men sowed and helped harvest, but women were largely responsible for the daily activities that kept families alive. Work was defined as demeaning and more suitable for the female sex. Cultural definitions of masculinity emphasized bravery, sexual virility, and idleness. Males valued talk and gossip with other males and adornment. They marketed because marketing was not defined as a chore, as it is in Western societies, but as an occasion for social interaction and pleasurable talk. Marketing also enabled males to control the fruits of their wives' labor.

In industrialized societies, extended family patterns are most pronounced among the very rich and the very poor. Wealth is the source of the authority of the matriarch or patriarch among the rich—wealth and the power and social contacts that facilitate careers and guarantee security to younger generations of the family. Among the poor, in capitalist societies, economic need and custom bind the extended family together. Grandparents, aunts, uncles, cousins, comadres and compadres (godparents) provide food and other essential goods and services within segments of the society characterized by extremes of insecurity, illness, deprivation, and distrust and suspicion of government, helping professionals, and other outsiders.

The extended family structure is more functional in traditional societies where land is the basis for subsistence and wealth. The family provides services that cannot be obtained elsewhere. It works as a productive economic unit, pooling and sharing economic resources. Children are essential to economic survival and well-being. A widow with a large number of children is a desirable mate because she brings needed field hands and household helpers into the new marriage.

In industrialized societies, children do not earn their keep and are not necessarily a source of support in old age. Family members are employed on an individual basis. The husband and father does not control the employment of his wife and children. Recruitment into jobs is based, at least ideally, on talent and skill rather than on membership in a particular family group. Economic resources are in the form of money paid to individual members of the family.

In early stages of industrialization, however, the traditional patterns survive to the extent that families tend to work in the same factory under the supervision of the male head of the household.[7] Wages earned by wives and children are turned over to him. Women can rarely sustain themselves on their earnings in a labor-intensive economy. The income that married women earn is used to provide essentials for the family that the labor of husband and children is unable to provide.[8] Only in highly industrialized societies do some married women work for psychological reasons and only in this kind of society can a large number of women earn enough by their own labors to sustain themselves (but not their children) adequately.

Family businesses, headed usually by the oldest living member of the family, also promote the continuation of extended family patterns in early stages of industrialization. With increasing industrialization, however, family firms are bought up and absorbed by nationwide corporations. The son and heir becomes a bureaucrat or an employee in the national office rather than the one-man boss of the local textile mill, glass factory, or shoe factory in Middletown, Yankee City, Plainville, or Springdale, U.S.A.

But nepotism persists. In working-class districts of London, fathers "speak up" for jobs for their sons when they finish school.[9] Unions in the United States show preference to sons of members. The children of movie stars have an edge over equally talented children of nontheatrical family origins. But even the children of celebrities cannot succeed without at least some talent, as fate and family origin become somewhat less intertwined in modern societies.

The extended family fights a losing battle with the necessities of geographic mobility and the attractions of social and psychological mobility in industrialized societies. The young leave the old behind, on the farms and in the older areas of the city, as they seek better jobs, better living conditions, and new experiences. The closing down or relocation of factories and offices out of the city, urban renewal, public housing projects, and corporate transfers of personnel, in the middle classes, provide additional reasons for the separation of extended family members.

Social mobility usually leads to geographic mobility. Extended family ties are further weakened by differences in interests, values, and life styles that characterize members who achieve a higher status or descend to a lower social status than their families of origin. Where geographic mobility is forced, as in urban renewal areas, the severing of extended family ties can be a major reason for severe conflict with public agencies who enforce this mobility. This is particularly true of certain ethnic groups such as Italian Americans, who have very strong extended family bonds. The second and third generations tend to stay together in older, urban, working-class neighborhoods where the immigrant grandparents originally settled, even though the younger generations, at least, have the choice of moving to middle-class neighborhoods.[10]

Extended family contacts survive in urban industrial society, but in much-modified and attenuated forms. The completely isolated nuclear family with no relatives within easy visiting distance is relatively rare. It is most likely to be found where there has been extreme intergenerational mobility, as when a daughter or a son has risen from the working class into the upper-middle or the upper class, or when children have married across racial or religious barriers. Most extended families maintain contact by visiting, corresponding, and telephoning. Help is exchanged in the form of gifts, loans, baby-sitting, and advice, especially during emergencies and even in the upper-middle class, where extended family ties are usually weaker.

These patterns are very different, however, from the daily contact and interdependence based on economic necessity that characterized extended families in traditional societies. At least some of the stresses that families experience in modern societies can be attributed to a lack of adequate substitutes for the services that the extended family performed in the past. Members of the extended family provided care and support for the aged and incapacitated, daily child care and housekeeping help, and a built-in supply of wider social contacts, confidants, and companions in recreational activities.

Loneliness was rare where the extended family provided a network of stable social relationships. In the not-too-distant past, working-class wives in the United States who moved away from their mothers and sisters were the loneliest of women, especially if they did not work. They were not as likely as their middle-class counterparts to be involved in church, club, volunteer community activities, or friendship relationships. This is changing somewhat, for younger more educated, employed working-class women.[11]

The decline of the extended family and familistic values and the rise of individualism in modern times are reflected in language. Many traditional languages contained no word meaning "self" or "individual." These concepts did not reflect a meaningful or significant aspect of social and psychological reality. The question "Who are you?" was answered in terms of familial rather than occupational status: "I am Jacob, son of Isaac and grandson of Abraham." The question in modern societies is not "Who are you?" but "What do you do?" or in its less direct form, in the United States, where status distinctions are more subtle, "Where do you work?"

The type of family structure that is associated with industrialization can and does appear in agricultural societies. In the

United States, for example, the nuclear family, sometimes enlarged by unmarried individuals who were forced to attach themselves to a family unit in order to survive, was typical even before industrialization, which occurred largely after 1850.[12] Preexisting conditions promoted the nuclear family structure and the values associated with this type of family, values such as independence. achievement, and equalitarianism. Probably the most important of these unique conditions was the shortage of women (which promoted equalitarianism within the family), the existence of a frontier (which provided escape from family and community controls and encouraged self-reliance and individualism), the absence of a medieval past (with its cultural rigidities and authoritarian values), and the selective, continuous, voluntary settlement of this country by restless, independent people who were escaping economic, political, and religious oppression.

While the trend in family structure has been in the direction of the nuclear form, as societies have industrialized and as people have become more mobile, technological development is neither a necessary nor a sufficient cause of this development. In present-day mainland China, for example, collectivism is valued over individualism. This has resulted in a continued deemphasis of the nuclear family unit, even as the country is industrializing. This is certainly true in the rural communes. It is also true in urban areas, however, where the aged are encouraged to move in with an adult son or daughter.

In mainland China, the preexisting pattern of familism, with its strong emphasis on the needs of the family rather than the individual, has been utilized in the fulfillment of planned social goals. The individual continues to be submerged within the larger unit: extended family, commune, and state. In Japan, the stem type of extended family structure, consisting of three generations—grandparents, parents, and grandchildren—is still the typical pattern, despite the fact that Japan is now among the top three countries of the world in level of technological development. Housing shortages and preexisting values in Japan, particularly a very strong tradition of familism, have preserved the extended family, at least with respect to residence patterns. Other aspects of extended family life, however, are declining: three-generational, hierarchical authority, the deemphasis on the marital tie relative to the parent-child tie, and the economic dependence of the younger adult generation on the elders. This is true certainly in urban areas.[13]

One other type of family structure that was rare in preindustrial societies, as a separate household unit isolated from other relatives, is the one-parent family.[14] This type of family unit is almost always headed by a female in industrial societies, where children are not an economic resource, and is a result of illegitimacy, desertion, divorce, or death. In the United States today, divorce is the most frequent reason for the absence of the father in a female-headed household. Illegitimate births, one third of which are planned and intended, are also a major reason for this type of family structure. At present, in the United States, most unmarried mothers are keeping their babies rather than giving them up for adoption.

In the past, the prevalence of female-headed households, in the Caribbean and among black Americans, for example, was attributed to subcultural values. Careful examination of historical and contemporary evidence in the United States and elsewhere indicates, however, that female-headed households are more a matter of class than of race or subcultural values.

The increase in female-headed households is a consequence of poverty and unemployment in capitalist, market economy, industrializing and industrialized societies.[15] Impoverished males in these societies are increasingly unemployable because of labor surpluses or the mechanization out of existence of unskilled or low-skilled jobs.

In the United States, illegitimacy among American blacks declined in the 1960s, but rose again in the 1970s, as unemployment rates rose. Not only illegitimacy rates, but mental hospital admission rates and rates of violent crime tend to increase as unemployment rates increase.

The future of illegitimacy rates cannot be predicted simply on the basis of anticipated changes in the overall standard of living in industrialized societies. Right now, for example, in slum areas in New York, legalized abortion is not having the immediate predicted effect on illegitimacy rates among Puerto Ricans. Machismo, the standard of masculinity in which manhood is defined in terms of virility (demonstrated by fertility), is still strong in these areas and impedes family-planning efforts, at least for the time being.

Illegitimacy rates in the United States have increased by more than one third in recent years. The rate is proportionately higher for blacks, who are at least three times more likely than whites to be living in poverty. More children are now being born to unmarried black women than to married black women (who have very low fertility rates). This cannot be explained in terms of values. Illegitimacy is disapproved among the black poor, and unmarried black women who bear children experience lowered self-esteem. Nor can this high rate be explained by the persistence of subcultural supports in the form of the ready availability of grandmothers or other relatives to care for illegitimate children. Young unmarried black women who bear children are now more likely to live in their own household, on welfare, than in an extended family household, although relatives are usually nearby.[16]

Poverty, high rates of unemployment among young black males, and a very imbalanced sex ratio (black males are much less likely to survive to adulthood) are more important factors in explaining black-white differences in the percentage of female-headed households. Impoverished young, black women have fewer options.

The historical relationship between poverty and illegitimacy rates in industrializing societies is supported by recently accumulated evidence.[17] Nonmarital fertility rates in certain areas of Germany in 1880 were two to three times higher than the rate in the United States in 1978. The rates were higher among German women aged thirty and over in 1880 than for black women in the United States in 1978. These rates declined in Germany, France, England, Japan, Jamaica, and other countries that have been studied as educational and job opportunities increased, with industrialization and urbanization.

On the other hand, technological development and the rising economic and psychological independence of women have resulted in a slight increase in voluntary illegitimacy among middle and upper-class white women in the United States and Western Europe. A small number of older, wealthy, unmarried career women are opting to bear children by choice. In the past, they would have adopted children.

The reasons for this choice have little to do with economic deprivation or subcultural role definition. These are idiosyncratic actions rooted in the unique psychological life histories of the women involved. Cultural pressures on high-achieving women in the United States and in most Western European countries, who have been postponing childbearing until they are over thirty and are established in their careers, have grown in the 1980s. This is very likely related to recurring worldwide recessions, and the decline in high-level jobs. Women are being encouraged to value motherhood, as they were encouraged to return to the home during the economic depression of the 1930s. A recent study conducted in France that erroneously reported a sharp decline in fertility among women after the age of thirty, was widely publicized by the mass media in the United States. In fact, the fertility of women does not decline appreciably until they are in their late thirties.[18]

Despite stronger cultural pressures and the apparent easing of the stigma attached to single parenthood, however, it is unlikely that voluntary illegitimacy and female-headed households will become a widespread pattern among middle- and upper-class economically secure women. Quite the contrary, successful women with higher professional degrees (in law, medicine, the academic disciplines) are more likely to marry now than in the past. High earning power is the modern equivalent of a dowery.

Despite the spread of various alternatives in industrialized societies, the two-parent family and child household is still the widely preferred form. Nine out of ten people in the United

States marry at least once (but later). More than nine out of ten married couples have children (but fewer). And three quarters of the people who obtain divorces remarry approximately three years after their divorces (men more quickly than women).[19]

We can predict that the heterosexual pairing relationship, whatever its problems, will survive and endure for most adults who have a choice, economically and psychologically, in all societies. Alternatives continue to be defined as settling for less by most people, everywhere.

Family Functions

Societies have a need to survive. So do individuals in family groups. The two levels of need not only may not coincide, they may be in direct opposition to each other. The need to protect the total society by means of war results in the death of individual family members. Tax policies, and the allocation of societal resources for defense or for the benefit of one particular class in a total society, may deprive many families of the possibility of providing adequate physical care, intellectual growth, and emotional security for their members.

It is for this reason that the universality of the family has been explained in terms of its role in fulfilling human rather than societal needs. People do not ordinarily live their lives to fulfill abstract societal goals. If families do fulfill these goals, they do so coincidentally and incidentally. The process of fulfilling the needs of family members, in fact, can be potentially destructive to the total society.

High birth rates may endanger the survival of the society by overpopulation and related problems of famine and contamination. High birth rates also slow industrialization because increased food production that is used to feed more people cannot be used to buy more machines. Families in countries that are now industrializing will continue to value large numbers of children as long as the governments in these countries do not take more responsibility for the care of dependent and disabled citizens.

All societies must fulfill certain human needs in order to survive. Ideally, the major institutions in modern societies—the family, economy, government, religion, education, and recreation—are organized around the fulfillment of these basic needs.

The maintenance of society requires institutionalized (widely accepted and deeply internalized) norms for regulating sex, reproduction, and the care and socialization of the young. These norms operate mainly within the province of the family and the educational system.

Every society must also have a system for producing and distributing essential goods and services to its members. This is the area where economic institutions operate, and also government, insofar as it is involved in taxation and redistribution of the national wealth through public services.

The total society and individuals within it must have protection against human destructiveness. This includes protection against the destructive behavior of others and self-destructive behavior. The government performs this function also.

Societies must also provide adequate recreational outlets for their citizens. Recreational activities provide an important channel for fantasy and for the catharsis of aggressive and sexual impulses that must be controlled to some extent if individuals, groups, and societies are to survive. All work and no play, furthermore, is physically and psychologically destructive to humans.

Another function, the fulfillment of which is considered by some to be necessary for survival, is the provision of cultural beliefs that give meaning and purpose to life and furnishes motivation for its continued existence. In traditional societies this is the monopoly of religion. In industrializing societies, various secular equivalents of religion appear in the form of political, economic, and psychological movements. Unlike religion in traditional societies, the goals of secular movements are this-worldly and the means are empirical. The supernatural is regarded as irrelevant to the daily affairs of humans.

A controversy over this function centers on whether the motivation for group or individual survival can or must be derived from group goals and ideologies. In postindustrial capitalist societies, where individualism is a dominant value, who is to impose shared beliefs and on what basis shall most, many, or some people accept these beliefs?

It appears that in complex, heterogeneous, rapidly changing societies, threatened by the possibility of atomic destruction, individuals must work out their own unique life plans on the basis of personality, opportunity, and constantly shifting social conditions. Certainly the direction of more recent political and economic movements in more individualistic societies is away from all-embracing ideologies, long-range and comprehensive goals, and widely agreed-upon means.[20] Families, in their socializing efforts, are also much less certain about what is, what must be, what should be, and indeed, what will be. They are more likely now to concentrate on one day at a time.

In nonliterate societies, particularly of the hunting and gathering variety, all functions that sustain the society and the people are fulfilled by the family, as an automatic consequence of its daily operations. The distinction and possible discrepancy between societal needs and individual and familial needs are minimal in societies that are not economically stratified. In these societies, the family regulates sexual behavior, reproduces, socializes, protects, works, distributes and shares available resources and performs religious rituals and recreational activities—largely without the aid of experts, specialists, and outsiders. Family members are police, preachers, workers, teachers, and entertainers. Societies consist of interrelated families, not interrelated formally organized governments, corporations, churches, schools and recreational facilities.

As societies develop technologically and become more differentiated, the family also becomes more specialized in its functions. Its province in the protective, economic, religious, educational, and recreational spheres is diminished and its functions delegated, in part, to outsiders. The economic functioning of the family becomes curtailed as other agencies take over the production of items formerly manufactured in the home: prepared foods, clothing, soap, candles, and numerous other items.

Married women, regardless of whether or not they work outside the home, perform services that have not been entirely farmed out to factories, bakeries, laundries, and other agencies. The economic value of these services, while considerable, is not readily measurable and evaluated. An important determinant of self-esteem in a business civilization—how much one is worth economically—becomes a problem for women. Employed wives tend to have higher self-esteem than full-time homemakers.[21]

But women with high incomes and major responsibility for child care and housework experience what has been called work overload. They are less depressed but more anxious than married women who are not employed, or whose jobs are less demanding. The husbands of women with high incomes, incidentally, are significantly less likely to be depressed or to have low self-esteem. Since these men are also likely to have high incomes, we see once again the importance of class in affecting mood and self-concept.

Married men, because of more efficient technologies and higher levels of wealth, may be able to earn enough to purchase all necessary goods and services that are no longer produced or provided in the home in industrial societies. Nevertheless, married women are increasingly likely to be gainfully employed, and mothers with preschool children are the fastest growing category of employed women in the United States today.

In the 1900s, in the United States, the typical woman employee was unmarried and in her twenties; in the 1980s, the typical woman worker is married and in her forties. Economic reasons may be more important than psychological reasons (a strong need for achievement and recognition, boredom, loneliness, isolation) in determining the decision to work. But most working wives claim they would continue to work even if their husbands earned what they would consider an adequate salary or wage.

The trend in highly industrialized societies is away from regarding children as an economic resource, as a source of security in old age, or as proof of sexual virility. While the birth rate declines, children continue to be desired but for psychological rather than economic reasons. Teen-age unmarried mothers who deliberately become pregnant most often do so, according to the surveys, because they want someone to love.

Protective functions in industrial societies are increasingly shared with specialized agents and agencies—police, lawyers, judges, and all others involved in law enforcement and defense. The courts and law-enforcement agencies are used, in fact, by one family member against another when family authority is disrupted or when definitions of family obligation or tolerable behavior are not shared. Parents more often invoke the law against children, as when aged parents sue for nonsupport.

It is a sign of the times that laws making this type of legal action possible have been repealed in the United States. On the other hand, there have been several instances recently where children have brought suit against parents on the grounds that failure to conform to family norms is insufficient reason for withdrawal of economic support. This type of suit would have been unimaginable in colonial America. Several colonies had laws that specified the death penalty for sons over sixteen years of age who repeatedly disobeyed their parents.[22] The decline in patriarchal authority is probably the single most dramatic change that has occurred in family life in the transition from agricultural to industrial societies.

Families no longer provide all possible role models that the child may want to identify with, nor do parents have the necessary skills and knowledge to train their children to fulfill adult roles available in the society. Blacksmiths cannot teach their children to be sales clerks. Schools constantly expand their jurisdiction, claiming expert knowledge to legitimate their authority when there is conflict with parents over the content, goals, and techniques of teaching.

Passive recreation, commercialized and provided by skilled professionals, replaces the taffy pull, the barn raising, folk dancing, and other activities that usually involved the family as a unit in traditional societies. Active participant recreation—

golf, tennis, jogging, running, swimming—is now more often an individual than a family project. Health clubs are booming. And, incidentally, they are more socially acceptable than singles bars or dances for individuals who are looking for marital partners.

For a while, during the 1950s, it looked as though television might bring the family together again, in the recreational sphere, in front of the television set in the living room. Two-, three-, and four-television-set families have dispelled these earlier visions of a recreational renaissance within the family.

Families are less likely to pray together in industrial societies. The family altar is all but gone. The saying of grace at mealtime is disappearing. The discrepancy between religious ethics and daily conduct grows wider. Nevertheless, strong religious beliefs continue to be the single most important factor associated with traditional norms of premarital virginity, marital sexual fidelity, and marital stability.

One function of the family—the provision of emotional support and gratification—becomes more, rather than less, important in modern societies. The expectation of happiness as a by-product of family interaction was absent or minimal in traditional societies. Happiness is a concept that is closely linked to the value of individualism. The remorseless struggle for life in preindustrial societies did not foster sentiment, kindness, and the luxury of concern about personal happiness and personal growth in family relationships.

Family Histories

New families are founded when people marry. In societies, and in classes within societies, where personal preference rather than family dictate is the standard for choosing a marital partner, sexual behavior is less controlled by restrictive norms and values. Sexual exploration is an aspect of the process of selecting a desirable marital partner. Love as a basis for marriage is also a matter of cultural definition and varies with time, place, and economics.

PREMARITAL SEXUAL BEHAVIOR

Historically, premarital sexual freedom was first curtailed for young females in wealthier families as societies developed an economic surplus. These restrictions became even more severe in preindustrial societies, as differences in the wealth of families became more extreme.

The sexual behavior of the lower classes in these societies appears to have been freer, as indicated by data on illegitimacy rates among the poor. In Europe, furthermore, starting in the sixteenth century, and even earlier in some countries, half or more of the adult female population remained unmarried.[23] This was due not only to poverty, but to the loss of young males, who emigrated to the colonies or who were killed in wars. Despite strong religious sanctions, the ideal of virginity at marriage was irrelevant when marriage was not possible for many or most women who were poor. Marriage was a privilege in preindustrial societies.

While practices such as child betrothal, segregation and seclusion, and family chaperonage appear to have been fairly successful in guarding the virginity of young daughters in wealthier families, some societies in Africa and the Middle East took more drastic measures. Clitoridectomy (the surgical removal of the clitoris) was practiced as a technique to reduce the capacity for sexual pleasure and, it was hoped, the desire to engage in premarital sexual intercourse. The operation was usually performed on girls between the ages of four and eight. At the present time, this practice continues in at least twenty-six Arab and African countries.[24]

In industrial societies, a variety of factors promote freer premarital sexual intercourse, especially among females, and especially within the middle class. The much talked about sexual revolution, in which there was a very widespread increase in the frequency of premarital and extramarital intercourse in this country, occurred, actually, in the 1920s. A parallel phenomenon, but on a less widespread scale, took place at the same time in European countries such as France and England.

The studies by Alfred Kinsey and his associates, in the late 1940s and early 1950s, and a small number of more limited and less publicized studies that had been conducted in this country since the 1920s, exposed the fact that premarital sexual intercourse was far more prevalent in the United States than the official norms would indicate. The most startling finding of the Kinsey studies was that approximately 90 percent of the married males and 50 percent of the married females interviewed had experienced intercourse before marriage. Kinsey and his co-workers also found, incidentally, that about one half of the married men and one fourth of the married women respondents had engaged in extramarital affairs by the time they reached the age of forty.

The gap between ideal sexual norms and values and actual behavior in the United States that was revealed by these studies precipitated a reaction of agitated indignation and attack by representatives of the traditional morality in the United States, who feared a bandwagon effect. It is probably for this reason that the Kinsey studies have not been repeated, although the data by now are quite old. Funds have not been forthcoming from foundations or the government for a new nationwide, detailed study of contemporary sexual practices and attitudes in the United States.

Nationwide public opinion polls avoid questions about sexual behavior. Surveys conducted by popular magazines and freelance writers are biased because people volunteer their replies. The results are biased in the direction of the young, urban, more educated segments of the population, who are likely to be more open about their sexual behavior. This was also a problem in interpreting the results of the Kinsey studies, incidentally.

What precipitated the sexual revolution in the 1920s? A large number of factors, acting in combination, played a role. Beginning around the turn of the century, science and technology provided safer, more convenient birth control devices and some control over venereal disease. Increased industrialization, spurred by World War I, uprooted people, encouraged the movement from country to city, and thereby weakened family, church, and

community controls. The shorter work week provided more leisure time for sexual activities. The automobile, hotels, the spread
of commercial, nonfamilial forms of recreation, and the invention of dating diminished the effectiveness of family chaperoning.

The growing equality of women in education and employment, which was also accelerated by World War I, was another
very important factor. Educated and economically independent
women are less likely to accept the double standard. Women who
are least educated and most dependent economically on their
husbands are most likely to express tolerance of their husbands'
infidelity. They are also, incidentally, more likely to tolerate
physical abuse from their husbands.[25] And they are more likely
to accept arranged marriages in currently industrializing societies.

Increasing secularism and knowledge about the facts of human sexuality also played an important role in the sexual revolution. The late nineteenth-century work of Richard von Krafft-
Ebbing and Havelock Ellis and the publications of Sigmund
Freud, at the turn of the century, became enormously popular
among intellectuals in the United States and, in watered-down
versions, affected the attitudes of the educated middle classes.[26]

Since the 1920s, in the United States, the pattern of sexual
freedom has spread gradually, continuously, and in an evolutionary, not revolutionary, way. Individuals who are most liberal in their sexual practices are those whose ties to traditional
organized religion and to the conventional morality are weak-
est: the highly educated, men in general, blacks, political radi-
cals, and nonchurchgoers. This is true of all age groups, including adolescents.

The fact of recent continued increases in premarital sexual
intercourse in our society is indicated by constantly rising rates
of illegitimacy and of pregnancy at the time of marriage, in
spite of advances in birth control technology. Another bit of
evidence is the decline in organized prostitution which is due in
part to the rising status of women (more women have other al-

ternatives), but also, in part, to the fact that legitimate sources of sexual gratification are more readily available to males.

Research in the 1970s and early 1980s indicates that the major change in recent years has been a merging of the differences in premarital sexual activity between males and females, blacks and whites, and working-class and middle-class people.[27] Genital sexual activity is starting earlier. The overall prevalence of sexual intercourse, before, within, and outside marriage, is increasing. More liberal attitudes toward sex before marriage have also increased, as has the number of partners of sexually active people. This last trend may be reversed, however, if the presently incurable venereal disease known as genital herpes continues to spread at epidemic rates. The United States Government recently approved a treatment (but not a cure) for this disease. It will be interesting to see if government research funds will be forthcoming to find a cure for a disease that may become a powerful inhibitor of casual sexual contact in contemporary societies.

LOVE AND MARRIAGE

Love is an elusive concept. It was regarded as irrelevant, at best, to courtship and to marriage in preindustrial societies. But in all societies, since human beings possess the same basic needs and desires whatever the cultural and economic context, the emotion of love in the man-woman relationship occurs. It consists of two distinguishable, but not always separable, aspects.

What we call romantic love is a feeling of intense physical attraction and a desire for sexual contact with a person of the opposite sex. The personal qualities of the loved one are usually idealized (love is blind). These feelings are often most intense at the beginning of a relationship, and they remain very intense if sexual gratification is frustrated.

Sigmund Freud attributed the depth of feelings of love to the strength of sexual impulses, first experienced in relation to parents, which are frustrated or, in his words, ''inhibited in their aim.''[28] He regarded romantic love as a neurotic compulsion which derives its intensely compulsive nature from the fact of frustration.

Historically, in the West, romantic love as a subcultural norm regulating the man-woman relationship first appeared during the Age of Chivalry in twelfth-century France. The intense pinings and yearnings of noble ladies and their knights were a direct consequence of the fact that these feelings of sexual attraction occurred outside marriage and usually were not indulged, at least not ideally.

A similar situation in modern societies is found in the infatuations that adolescents develop toward unavailable individuals, who are often authority figures or who represent the adolescent's ego ideals (pop singers, movie stars, sports heroes). The intensity of longing and desire is in direct proportion to the remoteness of the loved one.

Romantic love is narcissistic. Individuals are preoccupied with their selfish needs and frustrations. In its pure form, it is distinguished from mature love, which differs in certain respects. There is a more realistic appraisal of the personality of the loved one and a mutual identification and concern about the needs of the other person as well as the self.

LOVE AS A BASIS FOR MARRIAGE. Whether or not romantic love has been prescribed as appropriate to courtship and marital choice in various societies has depended, in large measure, on their level of technological development and, within each society, on the social status of marriageable men and women. Arranged marriages have been prevalent where there have been extreme inequalities in wealth between families, and where the choice of a mate has great significance for prestige, power, and wealth and the inheritance of these attributes by biological descendants of the extended family.

Romantic love as a basis for marriage, on the other hand, implies free choice and a disregard of family needs and wishes in making this choice. Expedient considerations—money, power, actual or anticipated social status—are unimportant or irrelevant. This pattern is prevalent in the simplest and in the most complex societies because the fate of the family is less affected by the marital choice of offspring in these kinds of societies. All are poor in hunting and gathering societies and, ideally, all have the possibility of social mobility in industrialized societies.

If parents are not likely to live with or very near their daughers- and sons-in-law, and are not likely to depend on their children for economic aid or support, and if education, skill, and talent can be more important than inherited social status in determining economic fates, parents will be less concerned, but certainly not unconcerned, about the social origins and personal qualities of their children's marital choices.

The fact that families often arranged marriages in rigidly stratified traditional societies because to do so was vitally important to their fate, explains the motivation of parents. But what of the young people who complied with the family's matchmaking decisions? Why was it so easy for families to prevent and control disapproved romantic attachments between the young in traditional societies?

The obvious explanation is that the economic dependence of the young, reinforced by rigid cultural norms and highly effective social controls, succeeded in repressing spontaneous or disapproved love impulses. It has also been argued that widespread premarital sexual freedom in nonliterate societies reduced the intensity of an emotion that thrives on frustration. Another possible explanation that is sometimes given is that love relationships in traditional societies were less intense and thus easier to control because the parent-child relationship was less intense in societies where the extended family existed.

Intensity of feeling is extremely difficult to assess, especially when the individuals involved are long dead. Despite the presence of other relatives to help with child rearing, mother-child relationships appear to have been quite strong in traditional societies. Certainly this was true in polygynous societies. In matrilineal societies, fathers, who had little authority over their children, seem to have had very warm, affectionate relationships with their offspring. And the mythology, folklore, art, and written products of many traditional societies attest to the presence of individual cases of passionate romantic love (with tragic consequences, usually, especially for the woman) regardless of cultural norms and social pressures.

Whatever the answer to this historical puzzle, the situation changes dramatically in modern societies. In industrialized societies, as the standard of living rises for all classes, and as the discrepancy in income within the middle levels of society narrows somewhat, love as a basis for marriage is more likely to operate not only ideally but actually. The greater economic independence of women in modern societies also fosters this trend. In the past in the United States, surveys of reasons for marital choices have indicated that women have been more strongly influenced than men by expedient factors such as the intelligence, education, earning potential, and ambition of their prospective marital partners. This is changing and should continue to change in the direction of freer, less oportunistic mating as the two-income family becomes the norm.

Neverthless, and despite the ideal of romantic love, marital choices in modern societies are usually restricted to individuals who are of similar class, race, religion, ethnic origin, and educational level. Sociologically, like marries like. This principle also applies, incidentally, to the age, intelligence, physical appearance, physical attractiveness, height, and previous marital status of individuals who decide to marry. Widows tend to marry widowers; divorced people tend to marry divorced people. They have similar unhappy memories in common. People tend to sort themselves out spontaneously on the basis of similar interests and life experiences, and in a way that usually does not offend family standards.

Where like does not marry like, males have usually married down, trading superior social status for the personal attractiveness of lower status women and, incidentally, reinforcing traditional cultural values of male authority and female deference. In interracial marriages, in the United States, the tendency has been for an economically successful minority group male to marry a woman of the dominant race but of a lower class. Economically, women with the highest earning power and men with the lowest earning power are least likely to marry. Yet, although the average age at first marriage is rising, the great majority of people do marry, at least once.

Until recently, area of residence has been a very important factor in determining marital choices. Most marriages have taken place between people who live in the same neighborhood or community—"the girl next door" phenomenon, which sociologists have conceptualized as the principle of propinquity, or nearness, in determining marital choices.

In-group marriage and propinquity as standards in marital choices decline in highly mobile societies for obvious reasons. Geographic mobility and greater exposure to individuals of different social origins diminishes the fear, dislike, or intolerance of strange people and strange ways, and the decline in territorially based group ties and group loyalties promote out-group marriage.

College campuses in the United States, particularly the fastest-growing public colleges and universities, are giant mixing bowls that recuit from an increasingly wide spectrum of the population. Over half of our high-school graduates enter college. It is on college campuses that the seeking and sorting out of potential marital partners is most free of traditional trappings and family intervention. Traditional dating practices appear to be declining. Females are more likely to call males for a date, pairing relationships frequently split off but remain affiliated with groups, and the sharing of expenses on dates is common. This, too, reflects the increasing psychological and economic independence of younger, more educated women.

THE PSYCHOLOGICAL FACTOR. In analyzing the basis of attraction between potential marital partners, the adage that opposites attract is part of the folklore of American society. How is this reconciled with the tendency for like to marry like, for which we also have an adage: Birds of a feather flock together?

Here, the answer lies in the distinction between sociological and psychological factors in determining marital choices. Sociological factors, locating characteristics such as class, race, and religion, affect conscious, deliberate choices—those based on obvious similarities in interests, values, and beliefs. Psychological factors, deeper and often unconscious needs and motivations, may not be consistent with the more obvious bases for mutual attraction. It is at this level, largely, that the principle that "opposites attract" operates.

In the sociological literature, much confusion has resulted from a failure to appreciate the distinction between conscious and unconscious motivations in the trial-and-error explorations of the mating game. Psychological needs are often repressed by human beings, particularly those needs that do not conform to traditional cultural ideals. These motives will not show up on survey questionnaires because they are not recognized, or, if recognized, they may not be admitted. Very few men are likely to admit that they sought out an aggressive and dominant woman because of strong dependency needs, even if they are aware of this fact—and usually they are not.

The evidence that on a psychological level opposites attract is not, therefore, overwhelming. Sigmund Freud formulated an early version of the notion that individuals with complementary needs and personality traits tend to seek each other out in love relationships. He distinguished between narcissistic love, which he attributed to males, and anaclitic love, which he attributed to females. The former is characterized by a strong need to be admired and revered; the latter, by a strong need to be dependent, deferent, and vicarious in the realm of achievement.[29]

In the field of sociology, Robert F. Winch and his associates have elaborated on the notion of complementarity of needs in marital choices.[30] The theory of complementarity suggests that individuals are attracted to each other at the level of psychological need to the extent that they have opposite needs, or different levels of intensity of the same need. The theory has been tested with respect to such traits as dominance-submissiveness, nurturance-receptiveness, achievement-vicariousness, and hostility-abasement.

The evidence for complementarity in personality traits of marital partners is contradictory and not conclusive.

One researcher, Benjamin Murstein, has suggested that the theory may be accurate, but mainly for people with psychological problems.[31] This could explain Freud's observations, which were based on a clinical population. Projective tests and depth interviews are more likely to get at this kind and level of information but, as indicated earlier, these techniques are costly and time-consuming to administer. For this reason, they cannot be used on large, statistically representative populations. Qualitative data, furthermore, are even more subject to investigator bias in interpretation than are survey data which, while superficial, are at least more concrete and less subject to misinterpretation.

Irrefutable support for the theory will have to await further refinements and sophistication in social science methods. The use of projective rather than direct questions on survey questionnaires is one such refinement. Rather than ask directly "would you like to have an extramarital affair?" most experienced investigators would now ask instead "Do you feel that most married men (women) would like to have an extramarital affair?" With the second type of question, respondents can project impulses that they cannot or will not admit, and the social scientist may come closer to the truth.

It is important to obtain more evidence on the theory of complementarity of needs in marital choices because free choice on the basis of romantic love is becoming institutionalized for all classes in industrialized societies. Psychological needs may override in-group marriage, which is associated with marital stability. We can have a better basis for understanding the stability or failure of marriages if we understand what affects choices at the psychological as well as the sociological level and how the balance in psychological needs may be disturbed if husbands and wives develop differently during the various stages of the life cycle.

Romantic love as a principle of marital choice may not turn out to be as irrational as is often claimed since a balance in the satisfaction of unconscious psychological needs is also important for the stability of marriages. As religious, familial, community, and legal sanctions lose their traditional effectiveness in stabilizing marriages, as marital happiness becomes more important for personal happiness, and as the marital tie becomes para-

mount in family relationships, the principle of mutual graitfi-
cation of needs at the deepest psychological levels becomes, in
fact, the essence of marital stability.

HUSBANDS AND WIVES

One major aspect of marital relationships that has varied considerably in human societies has been the amount of sharing or
segregation of activities and obligations that has been allowed
or prescribed by the culture. This, in turn, has varied with the
economic roles of men and women and the strength of the values
of patriarchalism and authoritarianism in various societies.

SHARING OR SEGREGATION. Generally, as with types of family
structure, the least technologically developed societies and the
most technologically developed societies have had similar patterns : marital sex role definitions have been less rigid and exclusive in hunting and gathering and in advanced industrialized
societies. In horticultural, herding, and agricultural societies, the
differentiation of marital roles according to sex tends to be more
pronounced.

The amount of sharing or segregation of homemaking or child
care activities in industrialized societies varies according to class
and according to length of marriage and the presence or absence
of children. The urban upper middle class is least traditional in
this respect, the lower middle class is intermediate, and the
working class, especially those who are closer to their rural
origins, is most traditional.

The early years of marriage, before the arrival of children,
and the retirement stage are characterized by the greatest amount
of joint husband-and-wife activity, within and outside the home,
for all classes. In later years, there may even be a slight role
reversal if the wife is younger, is employed, and continues to
work after the husband has retired. The retired husband usually
becomes more emotionally expressive. His relationships with
grandchildren, for example, in which he is not typically an authority figure in modern societies, are often characterized by
more warmth, indulgence, and spontaneity than he was able to
express toward his own children during their childhood. Older

wives, on the other hand, tend to become more openly assertive and less self-sacrificing, probably in response to the greater independence and freedom they experience when their children are grown.

But among all women who are not upper class, and in all contemporary societies for which we have information, employed married women continue to assume the major responsibility for housekeeping and child-rearing activities.[32] Working wives work longer hours and have far less leisure time than their husbands. This has been the experience of the great majority of women in agricultural as well as in industrial societies, regardless of where women have worked and the kind of work they have done.

Why are employed married women, most of whom work full time, not asking for, or insisting on, more help in the home from their husbands? A major reason probably is that they usually contribute less than half of the amount contributed by their husbands to family income. In all contemporary societies, capitalist or socialist, industrial or industrializing, women are concentrated in lower-level occupations and receive less pay for the same type of work. Middle- and working-class women may also feel a need to confirm their femininity by performing homemaking chores, especially if they are employed in occupations sex-typed for males. Or, they may feel guilt about working outside the home, if this is not an absolute necessity, economically.[33]

The child-rearing years are characterized by the greatest amount of role segregation. The wife is least likely to be gainfully employed, although this is changing rapidly, and is usually deeply involved in child care. The husband is invested in his work, the amount and degree of his commitment depending on the prestige of his job, his opportunities for advancement, and the extent to which he can utilize his ability, judgment, and initiative on the job. Time permitting, where the husband does participate in household activities that have been traditionally defined as feminine, he will feel less conflict if he is middle class than if he is working class.

The wife's dependence on the husband is highest during the child-rearing years, especially if she does not work. Previously negotiated, more equalitarian authority relations and household activities may shift back toward more traditional patterns during this stage of marriage. Certainly economic pressures increase, especially if the wife quits her job after the birth of a child. It is this period that is characterized by the greatest amount of marital role conflict for the middle-class, highly educated woman who has been encouraged to be independent and self-reliant in other areas of life.

Marital satisfaction, incidentally, at least as reported by wives, tends to parallel the pattern of joint or segregated activities throughout the years in marriages that remain intact. It is highest when joint activities are high: during the early years and, in the middle class, during the "empty nest" stage, after the children have left. The child-rearing years diminish joint activities and responsibilities in the husband-wife relationship and, given the modern values of sharing, reciprocity, and companionship in marriage, reported marital satisfaction declines.[34]

The sexual satisfaction of married women is also related to the degree of equality, interchangeability, and flexibility in marital roles. The sexual adjustment of women, more than that of men, is situational. It reflects the amount of mutuality in other spheres of marital life and it fluctuates more according to changing circumstances. In the lower working class, where marital roles are most segregated, wives are least responsive sexually. Changing circumstances—unemployment, for example—diminish the wife's sexual responsiveness more than the husband's potency, although both are affected by this crucial change in the husband's status.

Husbands are more likely to evaluate their marriages in terms of the sexual relationship. Wives, who continue to be more bound to the traditional morality, despite major political and economic changes in industrial societies, are less likely to value sex for the sake of sex. In the United States at present, women in all classes, except the most economically deprived, place companionship above economic support, sexual gratification, or the possibility of having children, as the prime value in marriage. College students who are about to be married usually emphasize this aspect and, also, communication. They hope to be able to express feelings, negative or positive, openly, directly, and for the purpose of increasing the honesty and the intimacy of the relationship. This is a modern orientation.

COMMUNICATION. Communication between husbands and wives was free and open in hunting and gathering societies. It becomes an important value in modern marriages because the effectiveness of talking things out is more recognized and accepted than it is in agricultural societies. Freudian psychology, the talking cure, has left its mark on the cultural heritage—in the United States particularly. The Freudian formula for diminishing conflict is to promote awareness of unacceptable, unconscious impulses. This diminishes guilt and the anxiety which is often a defense against anger and destructive impulses. Diminished anxiety improves communication.

The Freudian emphasis on insight and communication has filtered outward and downward from the urban, professional upper middle class, via the mass media, in disguised but recognizable ways. One has only to look at the man-woman relationship as depicted in the movies of the 1930s in this country to appreciate the changes that have occurred in human relationships in the past fifty-odd years. The modern viewer, particularly if under the age of thirty, reacts with impatience, if not irritation, to the coyness and to the comedy or tragedy of errors that is based on the inability of the hero and the heroine to be direct and honest with each other—to tell it like it is, in today's cliché.

Psychologically sophisticated husbands and wives are more aware and more accepting of destructive impulses, are better able to discuss and control these impulses, and are less likely to suffer the agonies and the anxieties of blindly defending against them. These patterns are most prevalent within the urban, professional upper middle class in industrial societies, but they represent a trend that is slowly spreading up and down the class structure and to older as well as younger husbands and wives.

Communication between husband and wife also improves in

modern societies because communication is freest between status equals. One doesn't joke with an authoritarian parent, teacher, or employer. The modern family, increasingly equalitarian, is more spontaneous, less repressed, and less inhibited in its parent-child, husband-wife relationships, Members are freer to communicate love, hate, dreams, fears, fantasies, and realities. The old adage that silence is golden was a symptom and a symbol of an authoritarian age.

Where relationships are formal and rooted in authority rather than love, inhibited communication is typical. The exchange of confidences and what sociologists call self-disclosure is a parent-child phenomenon in traditional societies; in modern societies, it is a husband-wife imperative.

POWER AND DEFERENCE. In the absence of force, the power of wives, in all societies and at all times, has varied according to their *control* over economic resources. To produce economic resources is not enough. The crucial variable is who determines how family resources are distributed or used. In contemporary societies, who makes the important decisions about whether or where to move, or go on vacation, or how to spend extra income—on new furniture or on sending the children to camp, for example? Routine household decisions, such as which bill to pay first, are usually left to wives. These decisions do not reflect power differences, since they do not involve differences of opinion, usually.

The amount of power wives have had in various societies is indicated by the freedom they have had to be sexually active before marriage, to choose their own marital partners, to obtain a divorce. Their relative power is usually reflected in folklore, technology, and ideology, although the glorification of women in some societies, as goddesses, for example, was usually in direct contrast to their actual power in the home and in the society.

Women in currently industrializing societies, especially in Africa, Southeast Asia, and the tribal areas of India, lose power with the conversion to cash crops and wage labor economies. In countries with labor surpluses, women are excluded from many available jobs, especially in urban areas. In postindustrial societies, employed wives experience an increase in power. But patriarchal traditions die hard.

Deference rituals such as bowing, kneeling, and the use of titles and polite forms of address symbolize differences in prestige and power in human relationships. These patterns tend to disappear in societies as the absolute authority of monarchs, popes, employers, and patriarchs declines and the prestige of citizens, workers, parishioners, women and children rises.

In all societies, the norms of togetherness in eating, sleeping, working, and playing and the extent of sharing material and psychic goods have reflected differences in power and prestige within the family.

In traditional societies, particularly those in which the status of women was low and the marital tie deemphasized, husbands and wives were often separated: they slept separately, ate separately, walked separately, and sat separately at public functions. Sex taboos—menstrual or postpartum, the latter sometimes lasting two or more years (since this was a major technique of birth control)—reinforced the norm of separateness. Public display of affection by look, gesture, speech, or touch was taboo. Wife-to-husband deference was expressed by a meek demeanor, soft and restrained speech, downcast eyes, speaking only when spoken to, sitting on lower, less comfortable chairs or at the foot rather than the head of the table, and eating the leftover and less choice portions of food.

The norms of chivalry that developed in the West—opening doors, or relinquishing seats for females, for example—are not deference patterns in this sense. They signify female fragility. As biological sex differences become less important in determining sex roles in industrial economies, chivalry declines.

DIVORCE. Divorce is another phenomenon that has reflected male-female status differences and control of economic resources in various societies.[35] In herding, horticultural, and agricultural societies women have had less freedom than men to initiate divorce. Patrilineal societies have had low divorce rates; matrilineal societies have had higher divorce rates. Regardless of whether or not societies have permitted divorce, additional sexual outlets (with concubines, mistresses, and prostitutes) have usually been available to wealthier married men. Polygyny was common in nonliterate societies; polyandry was rare.

Customs such as the payment of a bride price to the bride's family or the rendering of service by the groom to her family for varying lengths of time served two functions. They compensated the bride's family for the loss of a productive worker, particularly in horticultural societies. And they encouraged the stability of marriages, since the time spent in service was lost and the bride price not returnable in the event of divorce. The custom of providing a dowry to the groom or the groom's family arose among the upper strata in traditional societies where the bride did not perform major economic functions. In modern societies, these practices tend to disappear. The status of both marital partners becomes more equal and economic factors decline in importance where the extended family is not the economic productive unit.

Divorce rates also tend to rise. This fact is usually cited to argue that the family in modern societies is breaking down. The United States, which has by far the highest divorce rate in the world and where the divorce rate has increased at least tenfold within the past hundred years, is regarded by many analysts as a bellwether in the trend toward the disappearance of the family as a social form in urban, postindustrial societies.

A calm and unbiased look into world history and cross-cultural variations in divorce customs does not support the fears, or perhaps the wishes, of the prophets of disaster. In many nonliterate societies divorce rates were higher than in the contemporary United States. If we take into account all causes of nuclear family breakdown—death as well as desertion and divorce—we find, furthermore, that more families are remaining intact for longer periods of time than ever before.

Certain agricultural societies, such as Japan, Egypt, and Algeria in the late nineteenth century, have had higher divorce rates than in today's United States. Finally, there is no necessary and inevitable connection between level of industrialization and divorce rates—Japan, for example, has low divorce rates, at least at the present time.

The tendency, however, is for divorce rates to rise with the level of technological development. The reasons are obvious. The status of women is higher, and they have the possibility of obtaining self-supporting employment other than in domestic service. Men can buy necessary goods and services—clean laundry, cooked food, clothing, and shelter—from commercial establishments. Increased urbanization and geographic mobility diminish the effectiveness of family, community, and religious social controls and sanctions. Finally, the modern psychological orientations and higher expectations in marriage—for love, happiness, and mutual satisfaction—are more difficult to achieve than the traditional goals of economic cooperation and physical survival.

One reason that divorce rates in the United States are higher is because people rely more on their marriages for personal happiness than in other industrial societies. According to nationwide surveys, marital satisfaction is more important than satisfaction with work, income, health, friends, family life generally, leisure activities, and community for most men and women in the United States.[36] The spread of no-fault divorce laws to almost all states and the availability, more or less, of legal aid for the poor are also important factors.

Next to the death of a family member, divorce is the second most stressful life experience. Divorced individuals in modern societies are not absorbed into extended family structures. They experience varying degrees of loneliness, anomie, confusion, and depression. The culture contains few clear-cut norms defining the role of the divorced man or woman. Alcoholism and suicide rates rise. Old friends are lost, since they are expected to take sides, and the eligibility of the newly divorced person may be a threat to intact marriages. Divorced women usually have a more difficult time than men, especially economically.

And yet the majority of those who are divorced remarry. Humans cannot survive without love, and love (and hate) is virtually a family monopoly. Friends are shed more readily than family as individuals move up and down the class structure. In crises and emergencies, the nuclear family, if it has a choice, turns to the extended family first. Adolescents, according to the evidence of many surveys, are more influenced by family than by friends in the most important decisions of their lives, particularly in the educational and occupational spheres.

In the United States, most separations occur within the first three years of marriage, and more than half of all divorces occur within seven years of marriage. The divorce rate drops precipitously after that time. The recent increase in divorces in later years of marriage will probably decline, as will the divorce rate, generally. This happens as more people wait longer and have more experience (including sexual experience) with the opposite sex before making a commitment to marriage.

PARENTS AND CHILDREN

Child-rearing practices are either permissive, authoritarian, or somewhere in between. Permissive child rearing does not imply overindulgence or overprotection. This has been a popular vulgarization and distortion of the concept and practice of permissiveness, especially in the upper middle class in the United States, until recently.

The permissive parent-child relationship is one in which the child's needs and wishes are taken into account in the process of socialization. Parents do not set arbitrary feeding schedules for the newborn infant; the child's weight and hunger needs are taken into account. Decisions and demands made upon the child are flexible rather than absolute. The parents' comfort and convenience are not the foremost considerations in disciplining the child. Children are seen, heard, and, frequently, listened to.

Authoritarian parents demand absolute obedience and submission to external rules. Power is used openly, and physical punishment rather than explanation or reasoning is used to obtain unconditional obedience. The spontaneous display of affection as well as aggression within the family is curbed. The hostility that the child cannot express at home may be displaced onto subordinates, strangers, and out-groups in later life. The bully and the sadist are products of authoritarian homes.

Prejudice, where it is not a subcultural norm, is often a psychological result of authoritarian child-rearing practices.[37] Prejudice tends to decline in postindustrial societies because permissive child-rearing practices become more widespread. The need to project and displace repressed hostilities onto less powerful outsiders is diminished if the child can express aggression more freely within the home.

The early excesses of runaway permissiveness in child-rearing in this country have been curbed in recent times by common sense, supported by the findings of social science. It is pretty well established now that children identify with parents more strongly and are most likely to internalize parental values when parents are perceived as loving and supportive and when they temper their affection with reasonable and nonarbitrary rules.[38] Neither extremely permissive nor extremely authoritarian parents do as well in this respect. The new and current child-rearing formula in the United States, and the trend in all classes, is firmness, combined with affection and respect for the child's needs. (Compare the first and the latest editions of Dr. Benjamin Spock's *Baby and Child Care.*)

Permissive child-rearing practices are most common in hunting and gathering societies and in postindustrial societies, especially in the middle class. Agricultural societies, with their rigidly hierarchical authority structures, are characterized by authoritarian father-child relationships. Conflict is a typical by-product of differences in authority. Where these differences are extreme, conflict will often be extreme, even if it is suppressed, which it usually is, in agricultural societies. Women and children do not talk back to patriarchal husbands and fathers. For this reason, mother-child relationships in agricultural societies have usually been more warm, affectionate, and relaxed than father-child relationships.

As pointed out earlier, in matrilineal societies, where the mother's male relatives had more authority over a child than the father, father-son relationships were usually warm and

unrestrained. Affection rather than fear characterized these relationships, A modern parallel is found in kibbutz communities.
Parents have little authority over their children and are not
responsible for their discipline and custodial care. Most sources
report that the emotional tie between parent and child in these
communities is relatively unambivalent and unconflicted.

In newly industrializing societies, the father becomes more
permissive and more affectionate, especially in his relationships
with his sons, as he loses the economic basis of his absolute authority. In industrialized societies, personality traits such as intelligence, energy, interests, and other resources such as time,
education, and skills, become more important in family decision-
making and authority relationships, especially in the middle
classes. This occurs even as the pretense of male authority (Wait
till your father gets home!) persists.

The urgent necessity for economic cooperation from all members of the family declines in industrialized societies, and fathers become less authoritarian. What other factors promote
permissive parent-child relationships in modern societies?

Parents project their world views and their life circumstances
into their relationships with their children. If life is brutal, if
parents are rigidly controlled by powerful authorities, if strict
obedience and conformity to social demands is their lot, and if
there is little hope or expectation of changing circumstances for
their children, parents will bring up their children to obey strict
rules and regulations.

If authority is more diffuse, if cultural norms are vague, contradictory, constantly changing or even absent, if opportunities
and choices exist, especially in the occupational sphere, if the
future is unpredictable, if self-control, independence, resourcefulness, and flexibility are more adaptable than mechanical conformity to unchanging norms, parents will be more permissive.
Children in modern societies must make many independent decisions and choices. Uncertainty, unpredictability, and constant
change are everywhere.

The availability of opportunities affects values even in nonindustrialized societies. It is for this reason that many values in

family life that are regarded as modern were widespread in the United States before industrialization. The United States was a relatively open society from the beginning. The frontier, with its vast quantities of land and other natural resources, provided unparalleled possibilities for mobility and achievement.

Foreign travelers to the United States, from colonial times to the present, have commented on the lack of discipline and control in parent-child relationships in the United States. The spoiling and overindulgence of American children, their rudeness, and their refusal to be properly respectful and obedient to elders, are recurrent themes in travelers' accounts of American family life.

INTENTIONAL CHILDLESSNESS

In postindustrial societies, given certain changing conditions—economic pressures, contraceptive advances, legal abortion, the rising status of women, greater emphasis on personal happiness —husbands and wives are more likely to choose deliberately not to have children, or to have only one child. In mainland China, because of population pressures, the one-child family is now a powerfully sanctioned government edict.

In the United States, only about 5 percent of all married women deliberately do not have children.[39] This very small percentage is not expected to increase and, like the divorce rate, may very well decline in the years to come.

Married people who are intentionally childless are more likely to be first-born, urban, highly educated, and career-oriented. Usually, they are not religious. They married late or were previously married. They are less conventional. They are less traditional about sharing household chores. And they are more likely to come from homes where child rearing was unusually stresssful for their parents.

The decision not to have children is most often gradual. It begins with a series of postponements for a variety of reasons. It ends with the final realization, more often contested by the husband, that children would interfere too much with more important goals and interests.

Married couples who choose not to have children are now more open about their attitudes than in the past. But they are usually stigmatized as selfish or neurotic in most industrial societies, where children continue to be highly valued, although for different reasons than in the past.

OLDER FAMILIES

In the absence of severe economic and physical problems, older people (over age sixty-five), in marriages that remain intact, usually report greater marital and personal satisfaction than during earlier years. Longitudinal studies indicate that many older adults, like many young children, grow out of certain problems, to some extent.[40] Older people use more mature (more realistic) defense mechanisms. They are more likely to see the humor in a problem. They are less likely to become obsessed by a problem that cannot be resolved, to deny or repress the problem, or to fantasize impossible solutions to the problem.

Although people over 75 usually have one or more chronic, degenerative diseases, in contemporary societies more people are living longer than ever before in human history. In the United States today, the fastest growing age category is 75 and over.[41] People who are between 80 and 85, and those who are over 85, are increasing even faster, proportionately. Articles, books, courses, workshops, and seminars on the elderly are also multiplying. The stressful effects on family life of large increases among the disabled elderly are enormous, especially since they have fewer, geographically more dispersed children to take care of them than in the past.

In nonliterate societies, the right to die was a privilege of the elderly, the ill, and the exhausted; in technologically more advanced societies in the West, to die intentionally is illegal and immoral. In preindustrial Western societies, people who unsuccessfully attempted suicide were often put to death by the authorities, publicly and brutally. In contemporary societies, the majority of disabled old people are protected and are cared for at home, regardless of the level of technological development, class, and differences in government policy.[42] Feelings of obligation to the aged are universal.

In the United States, despite contrary images in the mass media, older, disabled family members are not abandoned, except in rare instances. They are not usually institutionalized unless or until other members of the family feel that they have no other choice—physically, psychologically, economically. Older disabled men are usually taken care of by their younger and somewhat healthier wives; older disabled women, usually widowed, are more likely to be taken care of by their children.[43] When there are no children, nieces and nephews usually take over. The upper-class frail, ill, and housebound elderly are taken care of by around-the-clock nurses and servants. Household space to accommodate elderly relatives and their paid caretakers is no problem.

The empty nest stage of family life is contracting at both ends in the United States. Largely for economic reasons, more than half of the young men in this country who are twenty-two to twenty-nine years of age are living at home.[44] Grandparents and great-grandparents are not coming home to their elderly or middle-age children in great numbers as yet, but if threatened Social Security cuts take place, the crowded, multigeneration households of the urban poor in the past may also return.

We have seen how technological development, scientific advances, and economic changes have affected family structure, functioning, values, roles, power, and problems in major types of societies. A closer look at typical ethnic and class variations in family life in the United States provides further illustration of changes and survivals in contemporary family life. Certain trends—the adoption of urban values, the increased employment of women in the nonfamily economy, greater freedom in sexual behavior and marital choice, higher expectations in the marital relationship, more permissive parent-child relationships, greater emotional involvement of fathers with their children, rising survival rates of the very old—occur in all industrialized societies. Similarities in these trends outweigh differences, despite unique historical circumstances and cultural heritages in specific societies.[45]

FIVE

American Variations:
Ethnic Contrasts

In the United States today, family relationships vary typically according to class, ethnic origin, and urban-rural residence. These locating factors are the major sources of subcultural differences in family life. Race and religion are also sources of difference, but race and religion tend to correspond to ethnic origin. Italian Americans are usually Catholic and white. African Americans are black and usually Protestant.

Ethnic Origin, Race, and Religion

Historically, ethnic groups (from the Greek *ethnos* meaning nation) came into existence within a particular society as a result of war, conquest, and colonization, or as a result of migration. The first ethnic groups were slaves in advanced horticultural societies.

Ethnic groups may be the original populations in a society, such as the Indian population (Native Americans) in the United States, who were conquered by invaders. Or, they may be relatively large numbers of people who have come into a society from a common geographic origin, an origin that may go back to the very distant historical past, as in the case of Jewish

Americans. The Jews were originally from the Middle East, but they have emigrated to the United States from a variety of countries over the years.

The important point here is that regardless of geographic origin and status within a particular society at any particular time, ethnic groups are associated with distinct subcultures—with values, norms, beliefs (including religious beliefs), customs, and skills—that distinguish these groups, in certain respects, from other ethnic groups in a society. When ethnic groups are physically or racially distinct, this also corresponds to geographic origin in Asia, Africa, or Europe. (The native populations of the Americas—North, South, and Central—are now believed to have originated in Asia.)

In the United States, compound nationality labels—African American, Mexican American, Japanese American—are beginning to replace "color" racial labels (black, brown, yellow) in an era of cultural pluralism, although there are objections to these labels also. Nevertheless, the concept of ethnic origin is less ambiguous and less loaded than the concept of race. In modern times, furthermore, the constant movement of populations, and the inevitable interbreeding that sooner or later occurs when different populations come into contact, blur racial categories and distinctions. It is often more realistic, more meaningful, and less confusing to classify a particular family as Puerto Rican American, than to attempt to categorize the family racially.

The United States Bureau of the Census classifies Spanish-speaking families as white. But the Indian ancestry of many Spanish-speaking families is more apparent than the African ancestry of many African Americans, who are classified as nonwhite by the Census Bureau.

Compound nationality labels also confuse and confound. Mexican Americans, for example, prefer to be known as Chicanos and use the term Anglos to refer to all non-Hispanic peoples, not just those who are of English origin. Some American blacks prefer identification by color, others by the concept of Afro-American, and still others prefer African American.

Here, I will be consistent, at least, in referring to ethnic groups by country of origin—except for Jewish Americans, where this is not possible.

Physical differences are more important than cultural differences in affecting relationships between ethnic groups. Physical differences are more obvious, they are far more resistant to change, and they are more readily used as a basis for prejudice, exclusion, and segregation.

Subcultural norms, values, beliefs, and customs affect family life and all other spheres of existence. Historically, as societies develop technologically, economic resources increase, and societies and ethnic groups within societies adopt urban values such as individualism, achievement, rationalism, equalitarianism, and tolerance. This occurs regardless of unique historical experiences and preexisting cultural values.

These values have been called middle-class American values or dominant American cultural values.[1] Actually, they are values that become more widespread in industrial societies, generally, depending on the extent of economic and educational opportunities and the strength of preexisting traditional values. In postindustrial societies, class overrides ethnic origin (including race and religion) and urban-rural residence in defining family roles.

The expanding, more educated middle classes in postindustrial societies are urban and national in their identifications, regardless of where they live. They are more likely to reject the traditional values of rural local communities or countries of origin. The distinctive family roles and values of rural families and diverse ethnic groups tend to disappear, slowly, as families and individuals rise in the class structure.

Highly educated upper-middle-class Catholics in the United States, regardless of specific country of origin, are more likely to practice birth control, and to approve of legal abortion, divorce, euthanasia, the ordination of women, and the right of priests who marry to remain in the Church.[2] Middle-class African American families, as mentioned in chapter 1, are more "middle class" in certain respects than their white counterparts. They have lower birth rates, more equalitarian family relationships, higher levels of achievement motivation, and are more likely to go to church and to join community clubs and associations.[3]

Power and wealth, and other resources that go with power and wealth, are extremely important in determining which societies and which ethnic groups adopt urban values and how fast they adopt them. This will become clear as we trace generational changes in the family lives of various ethnic groups in the United States today.

The United States contains an incredible number and variety of ethnic groups. The Soviet Union consists of fifteen Soviet Socialist Republics, dominated by the Russian Republic, which is culturally and physically most European in origin. The *Harvard Encyclopedia of American Ethnic Groups* describes over a hundred ethnic groups in the United States, ranging from Acadians to Zoroastrians (originally a Persian religious group, recently arrived in the United States, and numbering about two thousand people).

The United States provides an enormously rich source of data on changes in the family lives of people arriving at different times, from different classes, and from societies with different values and in different stages of technological development. The most heterogeneous society in the world is a natural experiment from which much can be learned about what affects rates of acculturation and assimilation of ethnic groups in human societies, generally.

Acculturation and Assimilation

The survival of traditional values such as familism, authoritarianism, fatalism, religiosity, and ethnocentrism will be stronger among some ethnic groups than others. What conditions speed up or slow down acculturation—the adoption of urban values and urban ways of thinking, feeling, and behaving among immigrant groups (and among migrants from rural areas)?

Probably the most important factor is the availability of educational and economic opportunities in the areas where ethnic groups settle. This, in turn, is related to time and to geography. People with few skills and little or no education who emigrated to the United States when unskilled labor was needed fared better than more recent immigrants. Newer immigrants, now mainly from Asia and Central and South America, are arriving at a time of widespread unemployment and the mechanization and automation out of existence of many manual jobs.

In West Germany, badly needed Turkish immigrant workers were welcomed at railroad stations with bouquets of flowers before the recessions of the 1970s and early 1980s. They are now being urged, sometimes violently, to return to Turkey. In the United States (and in Great Brtiain), more restrictive immigration policies have been enacted, and stronger efforts are being made to return illegal settlers to their homelands. Immigrants to the United States who settled in large cities in the past usually had better educational opportunities than those who settled in rural areas. The City University of New York, for example, provided unique opportunities for free higher education and professional training not only to the native born, but to vast numbers of immigrants, their children, and their children's children, from the mid-nineteenth century until the mid-1970s, when tuition was imposed for the first time.

Another factor that affects rates of acculturation is the degree of cultural and physical difference of the immigrant ethnic group from the dominant group. The dominant group in the United States, politically and economically, continues to be white, Protestant, and of English and Northern European origins.[4] English immigrants have acculturated faster than Irish immigrants. Race and language are the same, but Irish immigrants have been Catholic, usually, and more likely to come from rural areas.

Cuban Americans have acculturated faster than Puerto Rican or Mexican Americans. Language and religion are the same, but most Cuban immigrants, at the time of the Castro revolution in 1959, were middle class, urban, and educated. As members of the middle class in Cuba, most were physically more Spanish than Indian or African in ancestry.

Isolation or contact with the dominant group also speeds or slows down acculturation. Central or South American women who work as domestics in upper-middle or upper-class households in New York City acculturate faster than women who work in the garment center with other Hispanic women. Factory workers do not need to learn the language and they are not as exposed as domestic workers are to the values and norms of middle-class, educated, urban people.

The Amish, in Pennsylvania, isolate themselves as completely as possible from the wider society and have managed to maintain their traditions intact for generations. They run their own schools. They do not have electricity. And they avoid the consequences of electricity, which expand the working day with good light and enlarge the sphere of psychological identifications via radio, movies, and television.

The willingness of an ethnic group to acculturate can be quite as important, and sometimes more important, than acceptance by the dominant ethnic group. Like the Amish, French Canadians who have settled in Northern Maine have also isolated themselves and preserved their traditional culture. But unlike the Amish, they are also very close to their country of origin and they return to Quebec for frequent visits. This reinforces the traditional culture. Puerto Ricans living in New York City and Mexican Americans living in the border states are in a similar situation. The fact that Cuban immigrants cannot go home again is another reason for their faster rate of acculturation.

All these factors promote or discourage social mobility, and upward social mobility, especially from the working class into the middle class, tends to homogenize ethnic and rural-urban differences in family life. This process is underwritten by the efficiencies of automated technologies. Gross material differences in living standards decline. At the same time, other factors, such as higher general levels of education, widespread exposure to the mass media, and increased opportunities in societies with growing economies, also undermine traditional values.

Class as well as ethnic differences in values and norms diminish in modern times, more slowly in some societies than in others, more noticeably between the working and the middle class than between the middle class and the poor. But the trend is clear.

The final stage in the process of acculturation is assimilation, or the fusing of group identities into a single national identity.[5] This is the melting pot ideal of old, discredited now, but not yet dead. Assimilation, so defined, has not occurred in the United States except for Northern European Protestant immigrants to this country. We have a concept of Anglo Americans, but it is rarely used.

Nevertheless, and despite the current trend away from the goal of assimilation and toward increasing pride and emphasis on ethnic differences and cultural pluralism in America, the process of assimilation is very likely inevitable. Social mobility is the great leveler here.

Racial differences and barriers slow the process for some groups more than for others, as do religious differences. This will become clear as we discuss specific ethnic variations in family life in the United States along a three-generational time perspective. But whatever the starting point, wherever culturally and physically dissimilar groups have been in contact for any length of time, an interchange of values, behavior patterns, and genetic traits almost always occurs. This happens regardless of the inhibiting or delaying effect of ethnocentric attitudes and powerful negative sanctions.

Despite the leveling tendencies of mass production, mass consumption, mass education, and mass recreation in modern societies, family roles continue to vary typically on a scale from the traditional and rural to the modern and urban. Since, with time and acculturation, ethnic variations in family life tend to merge into class variations, an analysis of typical family relationships within various ethnic groups is a logical preliminary to a discussion of class differences in American family life.

Ethnic Variations

The recent emphasis on cultural pluralism and ethnic heritage in the United States seems to contradict the statement that ethnic groups tend to shed their distinctive family values as they become socially mobile. The celebration of national origins, however, does not represent an attempt to reestablish the traditional family values that more or less characterized almost all of these groups. Nor does it represent an attempt to reinstate or perpetuate the historic economic misery of these groups—a misery that current generations may not know about or remember. It represents, rather, a glorifying of distinctive ethnic art, language, dress, and food preferences for the purpose of promoting ancestral pride and a positive identity among those who have had little of either.

If we examine the contemporary family roles of various ethnic groups in this country, we can see illustrated the process of acculturation, as this has been accelerated or delayed, primarily by the availability of opportunity in the new environment, by the extent of discrimination, and by the degree of cultural and physical similarity or difference of the acculturating group from the dominant society. The last two factors, the degree of physical difference and the degree of discrimination, have usually varied together. A description of just a few of the extraordinary number of ethnic groups in the United States illustrates, how very different the experience of acculturation can be for different people.

AFRICAN AMERICAN FAMILIES

More has been written about African American families, probably, than about any other ethnic group. Since it would serve no purpose to repeat what is generally known, the emphasis here will be primarily on the traditional and urban values and how black families vary in this respect. It is meant to supplement more familiar approaches to understanding black family life, which have focused almost entirely on the black poor.

Probably the most significant factors affecting the family lives of American blacks are the lack of a strong patriarchal tradition and the concentration of a majority of black families at income levels that are grossly inadequate, by whatever standards are used to make this judgment. That black poverty is largely a result of racial discrimination, which is more severe for American blacks than for other, physically less identifiable groups, is indicated by Census Bureau data. African Americans have a significantly lower median income than families of Spanish-speaking ancestry, even though Hispanic Americans have a lower median level of education.[6]

The new opportunities that opened up for the black community in the 1960s, furthermore, benefited mainly upper-working-class and middle-class black families. These opportunities have declined sharply for both classes in recent years.

The consequences of low income for black family life are direct and clear. With the possible exception of Native Americans, African Americans have the highest death rates, the highest divorce rates, the highest illegitimacy rates, and the highest percentage of unmarried adults and female-headed households. All of these rates and percentages decline directly as family income increases.[7]

More than one half of the adult black population over eighteen years of age is unmarried, as compared to less than one third of the white population. Statistically, the probability of marriage is closely tied to income levels and to sex ratios. Survival rates for black males, as previously mentioned, are much lower than for black females, especially after the age of twenty. And black male survival rates are lower than the survival rates of whites of all ages and both sexes.

Most black singles are not single by choice, but because they cannot marry. Finding eligible marital partners is more difficult for black females; sustaining a stable marital relationship economically is more difficult for black males.[8]

Lower-working-class (poor) black families are traditional in certain respects. Familism (along the female line, particularly), superstition, religion, and fatalism are strong. But African Americans lack a powerful patriarchal tradition. This stems historically from the slaveholder's definition of the adult black male role as that of breeder and economic provider for the slaveholder and the slaveholder's family. It is reinforced currently by the greater difficulty that black males experience in fulfilling economic obligations for themselves, their wives, and their children.

The absence of a strong patriarchal tradition has positive consequences for black family life that are usually ignored or mislabeled by white researchers and commentators. Generally, black families are more equalitarian than white families, and middle-class black families are more equalitarian than any other family type.[9] In the past, this has been labeled black matriarchy by white male researchers, writing from the vantage point of a more patriarchal heritage.

Black husbands and fathers are also more emotionally available, warm, and affectionate to their wives and children, are less opposed to their wives' employment, and are more willing to share in child-rearing and homemaking activities. These distinctive variations in the husband-and-father role are in the direction of modern, urban patterns in family life—patterns such as role sharing, companionship, and psychological support.

These preexisting norms promote the adoption of other urban values, given enabling economic opportunities for the black male. Whites, in fact, are moving in the direction of age-old black family patterns—especially greater emotional expressiveness and communication, mutual sexual gratification, and declining role segregation in the husband-wife relationship.

The relative absence of patriarchalism bodes well for the realization of two other urban values—rationalism and achievement. Black women are more likely to take advantage of family-planning programs and legalized abortion than are Puerto Rican women, whose traditional husbands continue to define virility in terms of fertility. Black women are, generally, and from long experience, more practical, more resourceful, and more flexible than women who have been submerged within the patriarchal tradition for centuries.

From the end of the Civil War until recently, in the United States, black women have been far more likely than white women to work outside the home. In the middle class, they were also more likely to be college educated. Daughters in middle-class black families who did not want to work as domestics had few alternatives. As college graduates, usually from segregated colleges in the South, they could at least become schoolteachers. Black men had a somewhat wider range of occupations open to them and were less likely (and are still less likely) to attend college.

This is another reason for the greater prevalence of unmarried adults in the black community. In the past, college-educated black women often married less-educated men. Now, they do not, usually.

Black children, since they do not typically have authoritarian fathers, do not experience one of the psychological sources of low achievement motivation.[10] Greater economic opportunity combined with an early emphasis on independence, which is typical among black families, and the confident setting of high standards on the part of black mothers, should result in higher levels of achievement motivation in black children than in children of families where the father is more authoritarian. In fact, the evidence does indicate that middle-class black children have more intense achievement needs and higher levels of aspiration than their white counterparts. A higher proportion of blacks than whites, in the same family income bracket, are enrolled in college.[11]

Black wives and mothers who are poor want strong, supportive husbands as much as wives and mothers in any other ethnic group. Black husbands and fathers, in all classes, share these values, and when economic and educational opportunities permit, they live by them.

The possibility of achieving the psychological rewards that become more important in nuclear family relationships in industrialized societies is closely tied to the economic and educational resources available to the family, especially at the extremes. Since American black families at comparable levels of education receive less income than whites, the higher divorce rates of black families at all social class levels are at least partially understandable.

In many respects, however, black and white families become more alike as each succeeding urban generation continues to acculturate to modern values. This process is hindered less by subcultural values among American blacks than by racial discrimination and inadequate economic resources.

In recent years, as white families in the United States have experienced greater economic stress, marriage rates have declined and divorce rates, illegitimacy rates, and female-headed households have increased—even faster than among the black population.

MEXICAN AMERICAN FAMILIES

Mexican Americans are the second largest ethnic group in the United States.[12] Because of high (but declining) birth rates and continuing emigration, they are also the fastest growing ethnic group in the United States. They are concentrated mainly in the Southwestern states of Texas, Arizona, New Mexico, and California.

Since World War II, the isolation of Mexican Americans has been declining steadily. This occurred initially as many members of this ethnic group went off to war. Since then, their isolation has declined as the border states have become more and more industrialized and urbanized. Gradually, also, Mexican Americans have moved from Texas to California, from farm to city, and from field to factory. With this movement has come new contacts, new opportunities, new perspectives, and changes in family relationships that reflect the increasing adoption of urban values.

Because this particular ethnic group lives in a variety of geographic settings, it provides an excellent illustration of differences in the rate of acculturation of the same ethnic group in different environments. This rate has varied according to differences in discrimination and opportunities in different geographic areas. In San Antonio, for example, unlike Los Angeles where there has been less discrimination and more opportunity, Mexican Americans from the same class origins, who have been in the United States for the same length of time, have had much slower rates of acculturation and social mobility. Compared to their compatriots in Los Angeles, Mexican Americans in San

Antonio have lower median incomes, lower median levels of education, lower rates of intermarriage with Anglos, and are more likely to live in segregated barrios even if they are middle class. The contrast between Mexican Americans who live in Los Angeles and those who live in the smaller cities, towns, and rural areas of Texas is even greater.

Physical difference from the Anglo population continues to be a more significant factor in acculturation in rural areas. There, distinctions are still made by Mexican Americans and Anglos on the basis of degree of Indian and Spanish ancestry. In Los Angeles, the association between physical difference, income, and segregation declines, although it does not disappear, certainly, and the trend toward assimilation is more pronounced.

Familism is the strongest surviving traditional value among older Mexican American families, along with patriarchalism and machismo—the cultural ideal that equates masculinity with male dominance and sexual conquest.

There has been much controversy among researchers on the question of the extent of Mexican American patriarchalism and machismo in traditional Mexican society and among Mexican Americans in the United States today.[13] Part of the problem has been a confusion in defining concepts. If machismo is equated with male dominance or authoritarianism, but divorced of its sexual implications, then certainly its strength in agricultural societies and in industrial societies can be questioned by those who want to do so. Women, especially wives who are brighter and more resourceful than their husbands, have always been able to exert some degree of informal authority, especially within the home and in matters involving their children, even in the most patriarchal societies. The facade of male deference, honor, and respect sometimes conceals this fact. Male authority among traditional Mexican American families appears often to have been more symbic than real. In any case, younger, more educated Mexican Americans, especially those who live outside the barrios, in larger cities, do not even verbalize the cultural ideal of male dominance.

The most recent evidence on Mexican American families in

large cities indicates the effects of extensive acculturation. Extended family households are rare. Family visiting is declining in younger generations, even among the poor. The obligations of comadres and compadres are not taken seriously by younger people. Role segregation in the home is declining slightly, especially if the wife is gainfully employed, and younger husbands and wives are more likely to turn to each other than to the extended family for advice and support.

JAPANESE AMERICAN FAMILIES

Arriving from an overcrowded island with few natural resources, Japanese immigrants brought with them values emphasizing hard work, self-discipline, achievement, and education.[14] Despite racial discrimination, the median family income of Japanese Americans is now higher than the national average. This is explained by the fact that Japanese Americans are much more concentrated in urban areas, where wage and salary levels are higher, and are more likely to have two or more wage earners within the family.

The physical difference of Japanese Americans, as a basis of discrimination, persists. Highly educated Japanese American professionals are more likely to be underemployed (in jobs for which they are educationally overqualified) than whites. Japanese Americans also earn less in similar occupations, and are closer in this respect to American blacks.[15]

Unlike the black population, however, persisting traditional values emphasizing obedience and conformity appear to be more important than physical difference in slowing the advancement of Japanese Americans to the highest occupational levels in the United States. In Hawaii, where acceptance by the host society has been somewhat greater, Japanese acculturation has proceeded more rapidly. Values do not deter political and economic advancement for long, given real and effective opportunities. A majority of Japanese Americans in all generations, furthermore, unlike Chinese Americans, have lived in mixed or mostly non-Japanese American neighborhoods since the beginning of emigration to the United States.

The Issei generation, first-generation immigrants who were

born in Japan, arrived here some time between the end of the nineteenth century and 1924, when immigration from the Orient and Eastern Europe was sharply restricted by the Johnson Act. Second-generation Japanese Americans, the Nisei, born largely before 1940, experienced an unusual push into modernity not only by their parents' emphasis on education, but by the West Coast evacuations of Japanese Americans during World War II. Familistic values were weakened by the loss of confiscated family homes and businesses. This removed an important source of Issei control over their offspring. After the war many Nisei were forced to seek out independent, nonfamily occupational opportunities. They were scattered geographically to the East and Mid-West and were more speedily acculturated.

The third generation, the Sansei, born largely since World War II and now mainly in the adult occupational world, are the most totally acculturated of all. And yet certain subcultural differences in family roles apparently persist, even within the Sansei and the fourth generation (the Yonsei).[16]

In the Orient, the patriarchal tradition was more intensely crystalized than in the West. The deference and obedience of wife and children toward husband and father, and of younger generations toward elders, were blunted somewhat in practice. But patriarchalism was more extreme and more formalized in ritual, ceremony, religion, and law in the Orient than in Western societies.

The extended family form, the ancestral clan or house as the basic family unit, was far more important in the Orient as reality and as cultural ideal, for all social classes. Arranged marriages and emphasis on the family line and family honor were common even among the poor in Japan. The values of obedience, deference, duty, and responsibility were constantly reinforced by sanctions that promoted shame and guilt for the slightest deviation from established customs.

Research on Japanese American family life, especially in the past, has emphasized survivals of the traditional culture in husband-and-wife relationships and child-rearing practices. The pattern of male dominance has been more prevalent at all class levels than among ethnic groups of European origin. Child-rearing practices have been more likely to stress discipline, conformity, obedience, politeness, and emotional reserve (especially the suppression of aggression).

The traditional culture is reinforced by continuing emigration from Japan. But the weakening of traditional values and norms currently is indicated most dramatically by the high rate of Sansei intermarriage (as much as 50 percent) in geographic areas where Japanese Americans are less concentrated.

Initially, a majority of those who married out were women who apparently sought to escape surviving patterns of patriarchalism. But the rate of male out-marriage is also rising sharply now.

Japanese Americans have achieved higher median levels of education, income, and occupational prestige than other racial minority groups in the United States. They are not isolated, geographically or psychologically. Economic factors have been more effective than the intensity of traditional authoritarian values in slowing the rate of acculturation of Japanese Americans, to the extent that it has been slowed.[17]

JEWISH AMERICAN FAMILIES

A majority of Jewish American families trace their ancestry and surviving ethnic values to the small towns or shtetls of Eastern Europe.[18] Since Jews from the Eastern European Pale of Settlement (where they were confined by law) were not permitted to own land, they were a commercial people. Unlike peasant populations, they could achieve some degree of social mobility. Certain of the urban values, an emphasis on rationalism and achievement, were a significant feature of their cultural heritage prior to emigrating to the United States. Their rapid social mobility, relative to peasant immigrants to this country, is usually traced to these preexisting values and commercial skills. Other immigrant groups (the Levantine Greeks, for example) with a commercial heritage have also experienced more rapid occupational mobility in the United States.

The traditional Jewish religion fostered a devotion to sacred learning, searching analysis, and critical questioning. A life devoted to learning brought the highest status in the shtetl community. Education was far more important than income and wealth as a source of prestige. And wealth brought with it the divine commandment to help those who were less fortunate economically.

Familism was strong, but individual achievement was highly valued. Mothers strongly encouraged and rewarded competitive achievement in their children, starting at a very early age. Excelling the accomplishments of the father and the mother was a source of pride rather than envy to the parental generation, and great sacrifice toward this goal was not unusual. This was unlike the pattern among other traditional families in Europe, where a son's achievements might be viewed as a threat to the strongly patriarchal father. As an indication of the strength of familistic values, powerful sanctions were also used to regulate marriages, which were arranged for all, including the poor. The patriarchal tradition in shtetl society was weakened by the economic role of wives who frequently helped run small family businesses. Husbands often abdicated their breadwinning role, in part, to pursue the goal of religious learning.

Arriving in America, largely during the period of mass immigration that ended in 1924, most Jews settled in the great metropolitan centers, at first in the East and then gradually in the Midwest and West. Encountering occupational discrimination, they tended to concentrate in self-employed occupations and in the newer light industries.

From the first to the third generations, the acculturation patterns of American Jews, overwhelmingly urban and encountering a moderate and varying degree of discrimination, illustrate the close fit between their preexisting values and the opportunities that were available in the United States. But their acculturation experiences also reveal the persistence of certain ethnic values in family relationships.

Preexisting achievement, educational, and philanthropic values were transferred from the sacred to the secular by Jewish immigrants and their descendants. The academic and helping professions were highly valued as occupational goals, and an interest in reform politics was widespread. Occupational differences of first and second-generation Jewish and Italian groups in this country have reflected distinct differences in parental values and expectations within the two groups. These can be traced to their differing life circumstances and cultural heritage in Europe.

Education was neither valued nor necessary in southern Italian peasant society. Peasants did not need to know how to read and write in order to do their work, and even limited social mobility was rare. Fatalism (*que será será*) rather than an active mastery approach to the world was more appropriate to their life circumstances, which were grimly impoverished and not likely to change. These traditional values and the view of children as economic assets lingered longer among Italian emigrants to the United States. They were less willing than Jewish immigrants to sacrifice for the educational goals of their children and they were more likely to encourage their children to drop out of school and contribute to the economic needs of the household.

Equalitarianism, especially in parental and child relationships, has been strong in Jewish homes, as indicated by the greater tendency within this group to be permissive in child-rearing. The value of equalitarianism is also indicated by the apparent greater prevalence of the partner marital role within this ethnic group. This probably reflects, in part, the traditionally more active business role of Jewish women in the European shtetl.

Familism and ethnocentrism, on the other hand, have been more persistent among Jews than among most other immigrants. The intermarriage rate is lower than among Catholics and Protestants, although this rate is rising, especially among highly educated, more mobile, and more secularized male professionals. When compared with that in other ethnic groups of the same social class, the Jewish divorce rate is lower, and extended family ties, as measured by frequency of visiting and exchange of services among relatives, are stronger.[19]

Jewish Americans tend to marry later than non-Jews (about

two years), and they usually have fewer children (two or less). They are declining as a percentage of the total population in the United States (less than 3 percent). The Gallup Poll, when it breaks down public opinion responses into religious categories, no longer includes a Jewish category. There are too few Jewish respondents in the typical Gallup Poll nationwide sample of 1,500 adults.

The concept of the Jewish mother is currently popular in literary and academic circles. What does this concept mean and to whom does it apply? The Jewish mother is the traditional mother who looks to her children rather than to her husband for psychological gratification and empathy. The stereotype of the Jewish mother has been applied to Jewish women possibly because the syndrome is more characteristic of women in a subculture that emphasizes strong achievement motivation and intense involvement and identification with children.

Second-generation American Jewish sons and daughers have been disproportionately represented in the communication and entertainment industries. They have portrayed their manipulating, guilt-inducing mothers in novels, plays, movies, and in the academic literature. But they are not unique in their relationships with their mothers. Traditional women who do not have gratifying relationships with their husbands tend to invest in their children instead. And they expect a payoff, in psychological and material rewards, which in fact, until recently, they very often received.

In part, familism has been more persistent among Jews of all classes in succeeding generations in this country because of the concentration of first- and second-generation Jewish immigrants in self-employed, commercial, and professional occupations which tied them to local communities. Geographic immobility reinforced the traditional religious, familistic, and philanthropic values. Younger generations, now largely in the middle class, are more likely to be salaried employees in large corporations. They are more mobile and more subject to the acculturating influences of the wider society.

Despite continuing differences in family life, complete acculturation of American Jews to the modern, urban values is very likely inevitable in the long run, barring a severe economic and political crisis in which the Jews might once again become the target of displaced hostility by the frustrated and the desperate. Eventually, and ironically, the Jews will probably fulfill the vision of the mid-nineteenth-century German Jewish emigrants to this country. Social class will completely override ethnic tradition and the Jews will retain their separate identity if at all, as simply another religious denomination in the American firmament.

The key to ethnic family change in modern times should be clear by now. Acculturation to urban values depends ultimately on the physical and cultural baggage that immigrant groups bring with them. Even more important, it depends on the existence of real and effective economic and educational opportunity in the host society. Social mobility is the prize and class location is the major and prevailing factor in the persistence of traditional values or the adoption of modern values in contemporary American family life.

American Variations: Class Differences

Humans are evaluating animals. In all societies they have evaluated and ranked each other on a scale from superior to inferior. In most societies, furthermore, there is pretty general agreement about where people belong in this hierarchy.[1] According to the prevailing values of a society, people with similar amounts of prestige will be placed in layers or strata above or below each other on a rank order from high to low.

Historically, the ranked categories, layers, or strata that have differentiated people in terms of prestige have been called castes (if position is hereditary, unchangeable, and sanctioned by religion), estates (if position is sanctioned by law and extremely difficult to change), and classes (if position is theoretically open and achieved by individual talent and effort).

In hunting and gathering societies, age and sex were the major bases for categorizing individuals and for assigning overall prestige in the society. Age and sex were also the major determinants of the roles people played. Within the broad categories of male or female, and young or old, individuals differed in esteem. This derived from personal qualities such as strength, bravery, intelligence, resourcefulness, and temperament. But families did not differ in prestige, and all families played out their roles in very similar ways.

In horticultural and in agricultural societies, the bases for evaluating and ranking human beings expand to include wealth, power, and ancestry. The family becomes the social unit that is ranked, and family roles vary in certain typical ways according to the position or social status of the family in the overall society. Individuals are ranked according to family membership, and this rank does not change, typically, from birth to death.

In urban, industrialized societies, ancestry declines in importance, although it by no means becomes insignificant, and achievements and personal qualities become more significant in establishing the overall prestige that human beings enjoy.

Class membership is determined by income and wealth, education, and occupational prestige. Individuals are born with the social status attributed to their families. But the possibility of changing this status, and the economic, political, and psychological disabilities or rewards that go with it, is greater than in preindustrial societies.

In modern societies the effects of class on family roles decline somewhat as cultural and subcultural norms become less imperious. Individual differences in personality and in resources such as intelligence, skill, time, and energy become more significant in defining the scripts that family members act out.

But membership in a particular class continues to penetrate and color all life experiences. It affects not only the quality of life, but the length of life, on the average. It affects speech, dress, nutrition, living space, control over work situations, leisure time and leisure activities, comfort, safety, and health. It affects attitudes, values, behavior, self-confidence, self-esteem, morale, and the intensity of feelings of alienation, prejudice, psychological distress, and role conflict. Ultimately, personality traits are psychological in origin, but the extent and frequency of certain personality traits are affected by class location.

In the United States, the upper classes travel more, read more, have more education, vote more, have more friends and entertain them more, receive more mail, and join more organizations. They are less likely to divorce, separate, or desert each other. They relate to each other differently and they raise their children differently. They commit different kinds of crime and they are punished differently when they are caught.

One of the most important things sociologists can know about families or individuals is their location in the class structure. This is widely recognized, as indicated by the fact that journalists in this country often use the term "sociological" in refering to class factors.

Social scientific studies of the class structure in the United States date largely from the early years of the depression, another time of heightened class awareness. However, many of the pioneering studies treated the family only incidentally in their attempted profiles of class-bound worlds.

Recently, more knowledge has been accumulating on class differences in family roles, values, functioning, problems, and destinies. In the 1980s, in the United States, the family as well as the economy is viewed as an institution in crisis. Both are very topical areas of concern in the mass media and in scholarly research and publications.

A summary of all the available information on class and family life is beyond the limits of a short, general essay on the past, present, and future of the family. But it is possible to use the model of technological and scientific development and the shift to urban values as a basis for selecting, organizing, and interpreting some of the information that has been collected on class differences in contemporary family life, especially in the United States.

THE AMERICAN CLASS STRUCTURE

Except at the extremes of poverty and wealth, the American class structure is characterized by a vagueness and blurring of boundaries. Especially in the past, and at the middle levels, the value of equalitarianism and the realities of mass production and mass consumption have obscured the existence of class in America as objective fact and as a subjective state of consciousness.[2]

This has not been true of other economically stratified societies. In medieval Europe, for example, estates were rigidly demarcated and were symbolized, among other things, by dress. The type of dress worn by members of the various estates was often sanctioned by law; peasants were not permitted to wear silk. This rigidity in class patterns persists to some extent.

European workers are more likely than their American counterparts to wear their workers' caps and clothes to work. American workers do not usually wear identifying caps and, in any case, they are more likely to keep their work clothes in lockers. On the street they are often not readily distinguishable as working class, in either dress or demeanor. Their speech, less articulate and grammatical, may identify them as working class to those who listen, but it is not as distinguishing a mark as the cockney speech of working-class Londoners. In the United States, "sir" and "madam" are often used in jest, and not necessarily as a sign of deference or respect.

The value of equalitarianism and the relatively high standard of living in the United States have dulled the consciousness of class. Yet it has not eliminated the fact of class: the existence of objective, observable, and large measurable differences in prestige, power, and wealth that separate people from each other, intellectually, emotionally, and physically. Position in the class structure is still a crucial factor in determining valued friends and eligible marital partners.[3]

Americans have tended to deny the validity of class because class consciousness is not as strongly developed in this country as it is in others. The very term "class" is painful to many ears in the United States. In American sociology, concepts such as socioeconomic status, interest groups, democratic pluralism, and national elite have been more acceptable, and respectable, than concepts such as class, class conflict, and ruling class.

Why has the level of class consciousness been low in this country? Feelings of class solidarity and the extent of identification with others in similar class positions will not be strong in societies characterized by a strong set of common values that deemphasize the conflicting interests of different classes—national integrating ideologies such as fascism or socialism, for example. But this is not applicable to the United States, despite the existence of a democratic ideology that is accepted, ideally, by many Americans.

Awareness of class will also be less extreme where the possibility of moving out of one's class is accepted, desired, and believed in. This situation has certainly characterized the United States in the past. Individuals who identify with members of a higher class and who believe in the possibility of joining this class someday will feel little class solidarity.

On the other hand, blocked social mobility, that is recognized, and a higher general level of education in a society intensify feelings of class identity. Both promote awareness and understanding of class interests and how these are or are not being met. For these reasons, class consciousness and class solidarity have increased recently in the United States, especially within the lower and middle levels. The upper class has always had this kind of consciousness and understanding.

Occupation is the most valid indicator of class. Education, and income and wealth are the other major variables that determine class membership. The three usually go together, but sometimes they do not. Income alone can be very misleading in determining the class standing of individuals or families.

Skilled blue-collar workers—carpenters, electricians, plumbers, mechanics—usually earn more than lower-level white-collar workers such as civil servants, salespeople, secretaries, nurses, and schoolteachers. But skilled workers do not typically have certain attitudes and values that are associated with the middle class. Their family relationships, sexual behavior, reading habits, buying habits, club memberships, attitudes toward foreign affairs and other aspects of world outlook and daily life differ, typically.

Married skilled workers with children are less likely than white-collar parents to value higher education as an absolute good, although they are more likely now than in the past to encourage their children (daughters as well as sons) to go to college. Nevertheless, they will be more approving of concrete vocational fields such as teaching, accounting, or engineering than they will of the humanities and social sciences, where preparation for specific occupations is less obvious. If their child drops out of college, they will consider the time and money spent in college wasted. The middle-class parent is more likely to view whatever time is spent in college as a valuable growth experience.

Despite the cherished American value of equalitarianism, real differences remain, not only at the extremes of rich and poor, but among those who are in between. This brings us to another important point. Since it is the family that is usually classified as upper, middle, or working-class, where, then, do we place a family in which the husband is a factory worker and the wife is a secretary? Is the family working class or middle class?

In the past, the occupation, income, and education of the husband determined the class location of the family. But for purposes of explaining and predicting family values and behavior more accurately (how much role sharing and communication there will be, for example) we should locate families according to the more prestigious occupation, regardless of whether it is the husband's or the wife's occupation.[4] The head-of-the-household concept has disappeared from Census Bureau questionnaires and from popular discourse. It becomes obsolete when over half of the married women in the United States are gainfully employed. It is even more inappropriate when about one third of the women married to manual laborers are employed in middle-class occupations. These women, who identify with the middle class, are typically less traditional than working-class wives who are not employed.

Sociologists usually subdivide the three broad classes—upper, middle, and working—into upper and lower levels: the upper and lower divisions of the upper class (old and new money), the upper and lower middle class, and the upper and lower working class (the poor). These are not arbitrary categories. Despite the trend toward the adoption of urban values in all classes, typical and significant differences in family life persist within these six major segments of the population. These differences show up in large-scale research surveys and, even more dramatically, in smaller, depth-interview studies of particular family groups.

While there is considerable disagreement about where to establish class boundaries, the percentage of upper-class individuals in the United States today is approximately 2 percent (including the newly rich) and is relatively stable. The upper middle class consists of about 10 percent of the population. Until the recessions of the 1970s and 1980s this part of the population was growing rapidly. Expanding and rationally planned industrial economies require ever-greater numbers of experts to manage large business organizations. Industrialized societies also need increased numbers of expert professionals to meet the higher standards of services that citizens desire and expect.

About 40 percent of the population in the United States is lower middle class. In postindustrial societies, this segment of the society grows most rapidly as industries engaged in distributing, selling, and communicating expand. Even during the recurring recessions of recent years the classified ads have continued to offer numerous daily and Sunday enticements to clerk-typists, bookkeepers, salespersons, and gal/guy Fridays (formerly known as gal Fridays).

The rest of American society is working class, including the 15 percent to 20 percent who are lower working class, or poor. For decades, the working class has been contracting, slowly, as unskilled, semiskilled, and skilled manual occupations have been mechanized and automated out of existence. In recent years, in the United States, the ranks of the working class have increased very slightly, as college-educated males (and sometimes females) take nonunionized manual jobs because they are unable to find jobs that require college degrees and are appropriate for college graduates.[5]

My sketch of family life in the various classes in the United States has been pulled together from dozens of research studies by sociologists and other social scientists. I will focus on typical or statistically most frequent patterns. But it is important to remember that in a constantly changing and increasingly mobile society there are many exceptions and there is much overlapping in the behavior and values that will be described.

It is also important to notice that among younger generations, especially, similarities in values are increasing for all classes. This is occurring despite the hardening of the economic differences between the classes and the recent decline in upward social mobility—especially among white males.

Another interesting point to note is that in spite of vast differences in money and the things money can buy, there are certain similarities in the family lives of the hereditary very rich and the very poor. For different reasons, familism and the extended family are strongest and the birth rate is highest at the top and at the bottom of the class structure. Practically everything else that can be directly measured or observed—age at first marriage, marriage rates, illegitimacy rates, divorce rates, female-headed households, family violence—goes up or down, directly, as one goes up or down the class structure.

The two levels of the upper class in the United States, upper and lower, or old and new, are distinguished according to the age of family wealth. Wealth, like good wine, increases in value with age. The old upper class has inherited its wealth from ancestors. The new upper class is first-generation rich, and sometimes famous.

OLD UPPER-CLASS FAMILIES

Since upper-class individuals do not answer questionnaires, empirical studies of this class in the United States are very limited in number. Those that are available, furthermore, contain little information about upper-class family life. Anecdotal, journalistic accounts are not necessarily representative of all upper-class families and are likely to be biased. It is difficult for middle-class journalists or social scientists to write with detachment about a segment of society whose wealth and circumstances are often beyond imagining. Accounts of this class have also been written by those who are in it, insiders who are natural participant observers and who write about what they know. But these accounts also suffer from bias—the bias of the deeply involved rather than the bias of the awed, the envious, or the critical.[6]

What, then, do we know about this class that social scientists, journalists, and members might agree about? Fortunately, we are concerned with family roles and relationships, a far less controversial topic than the political and economic behavior of the hereditary wealthy and a topic about which there is more agreement.

As with the working class, the old upper class divides into the traditional and the modern, in values, behavior, and world outlook. This is largely associated with age and generation. The traditional old upper class has as its models Anglo-Saxon Protestant ancestors who established the family fortune—in land ownership before the Civil War and in business and fluid capital since then. In the traditional old upper class, the values of familism, patriarchalism, and ethnocentrism are basic in family relationships. Other values, often identified with the Protestant ethic, are also widespread—values such as frugality, sobriety, emotional reserve, physical endurance, impulse control, and the constructive use of leisure time. The work ethic is strong, whether it is channeled into gainful employment or into community service.

The great emphasis that is placed on genealogy and family lineage is reflected in naming practices such as the use of surnames of earlier branches of the family, or the use of the mother's family name as given or middle names. Family solidarity is reinforced by frequent rituals and ceremonies—debutante balls, formal engagements, large weddings, baptisms, Thanksgiving and Christmas gatherings of the clan. It is not unusual to see older adolescents traveling in Europe and elsewhere with their parents or other relatives. This phenomenon is rare in the middle class, and not only for financial reasons. The extended family is a binding reality in this class, cemented by economic dependence and the control by the older generation of vast economic resources. Nepotism is a duty, not only to the individual, but to the family line. Those family members who control the family fortune feel strongly obligated to pass on the wealth, intact at least and increased if possible. The family black sheep and ne'er-do-well are not only tolerated, but family members will go to great lengths to protect them for the sake of the family reputation.

Ethnocentrism is strong, but it is the kind of ethnocentrism that is based not on fear or lack of information about out-groups, but on the desire to preserve the family from taint by the middle classes or by minority group members. To this end upper-class families try to isolate themselves and their children by developing their own exclusive clubs, resorts, and schools. The value of ethnocentrism has also been symbolized in the traditional upper class in the past by loyalty and deep involvement in local community affairs by families whose localism was grounded in land ownership in the South or business enterprises in the Northeast.

In the traditional hereditary upper class, marriages are no longer arranged, but great pressure is exerted on the young, sometimes subtly, but often not so subtiy, to marry within the group. Largely because of the slight tendency of upper-class males to marry down, and also because of the surplus of females in all classes, women in the upper class have a more difficult time obtaining marital partners. Their field of eligible males is highly restricted. For this reason and others, such as the greater difficulty in obtaining divorce freely because of more complicated family finances, the average age at marriage tends to be higher for the upper class generally.

The double standard is strong among older, traditional members of the upper class. Because marital alliances, particularly in the past, were undertaken often to fulfill familistic obligations, upper-class males frequently maintained mistresses to fulfill the erotic needs that may not have been gratified in their marriages.

Nuclear family relationships in the traditional upper class have been characterized by formality, ritual, and emotional reserve. The authority of the husband and father is not a facade, preserved as a sop to cultural dictate; it is an effective reality. Separation, a symptom of extreme differences in authority within the family, has also been a characteristic of the traditional upper class. This is indicated by the custom of maintaining separate bedrooms for husband and wife and by long separations from children, who are sent to boarding schools or who remain in the continuous care of servants whether the parents are at home or are traveling.

The husband-and-wife relationship is characterized by a clear and distinct separation in roles. The wife functions as hostess and companion, particularly on formal occasions, and the husband typically engages in business or public service activities. A large number of upper-class males in the United States, incidentally, earn salaries in gainful employment, an indication of the persistence of the work ethic in this class.

Parent-child conflict is muted in the traditional upper class, as it is in the upper class generally, traditional or modern, old or new, by the presence of nurses, governesses, housekeepers, and other retainers who are actually involved in the day-to-day custodial care and disciplining of the children. The mother, however, acts as the ultimate arbiter in conflicts between children and servants, if she happens to be at home.

The traditional, hereditary upper class is changing, as are all classes in rapidly changing America, and the major reasons for change are pretty much the same. Technological advances affect all classes, however differently in detail, as do increased mobility, changing opportunity structures, higher levels of education, and other social conditions that undermine remaining traditional values. When large corporations, requiring skilled managers, absorb the family businesses of the hereditary rich into national and international corporations, the scion of the old family may be retained in what was formerly the family business, if he is talented. He may also be retained if his name on the corporation masthead promotes solidarity, as constitutional monarchs are retained in Europe as a symbol of solidarity or past glory. But this is not typical. Local community roots are weakened for this class, as for others, and for the upper class, geographic mobility, international in scope, becomes a more significant type of mobility than in other classes.

The rise of the meritocracy and the decline of nepotism infringe on the ability of the old upper class to maintain its social exclusiveness. Prestigious schools and colleges expand their recruitment under pressures of an equalitarianism stemming from a need for a wider base of talent to keep complex technologies and economies operating and from social movements that are ultimately responding to this need. The newly rich and the near-rich aristocracy of talent push on and into old upper-class havens and retreats slowly but more effectively than in the past. The modern, more mobile hereditary upper class becomes cosmopolitan and international, more equalitarian and less ethnocentric.

The breaking of local geographic ties that occurs with the decline of family businesses has also been enhanced since World War II by the invention of high-speed jet transport (hence the term Jet Set). The dinner party network has become worldwide as has the entourage of friends, functionaries, and servants. Although familism persists, it is much modified by the circumstances of broader horizons and the greater opportunity for the children of the rich, also, to strike out on their own in nonfamily-controlled occupations.

Family relationships among the younger generations are closer and warmer. Husbands and wives are less likely to maintain separate bedrooms, and are more intimately involved with their smaller numbers of children. Prince Charles of Great Britain remained with Princess Diana during her labor, was present in the delivery room when his son was born, and whisked mother and child home from the hospital within twenty-four hours after the delivery. The child will not be placed in the separate nursery wing of Kensington Palace, but will be housed in the same wing as his parents.

These patterns have traveled upward from the highly educated professional upper middle classes. An emphasis on parent-child bonding, especially between the father and his newborn infant, has been going on for some time within the upper middle classes. The concept and idea of bonding were formulated initially by British psychoanalysts.[7]

NEW UPPER-CLASS FAMILIES

In the past, the new upper-class, self-made men and women who had climbed usually from middle-class origins to the very top positions in business, government, and the professions would have continued to be defined as middle class. They would have served the upper class, but they would not have been granted the right to socialize and intermarry with the hereditary wealthy. In industrialized societies, however, the criteria of overall prestige are weighed somewhat differently. While hereditary wealth and family lineage are important, skill and talent, particularly of the kind that has resulted in national or international fame, become very highly valued. The new elite of talent in the United States, often of minority group origins, are international jetsetters and conspicuous consumers of an order that is qualitatively different from that of their former middle-class friends and associates whom they have left behind.

Thorstein Veblen, an American sociologist who achieved a degree of notoriety among social scientists during the early part of the twentieth century for his satirical and often bitter analyses of American business enterprise, the American class structure, and American institutions of higher learning, coined the phrase "conspicuous consumption" to refer to expenditures in excess of what is needed for physical comfort. Veblen noted that people engage in this kind of spending because: "In order to gain and hold the esteem of men, it is not sufficient merely to possess wealth or power. The wealth or power must be put in evidence, for esteem is awarded only on evidence."[8] The new upper class, because of its more insecure status, is more likely than the old upper class to engage in conspicuous consumption. They have great wealth—and they flaunt it.

The new upper class values achievement and hard work highly since these are the basis of their claim for recognition and acceptance. Gracious living, the way of life of the old upper class, is difficult for these successful men and women to emulate. Wives may be better able than husbands to adapt to the demands of the new status since the companion role is one they may have performed before their husbands achieved fame. Where the wife is unable to make this transition, a divorce may result. The mass media publicize divorces of celebrities from the women they married when they were very young. However, the actual frequency of these divorces is not very high outside the entertainment field.

Family relationships in the new upper class reflect in part their middle-class origins and also the changed circumstances of the family. Marital relationships are more equalitarian, less formal and reserved, and somewhat less stable than those of the old upper class. The two classes are merging in these respects, and also with respect to parent-child relationships, which are more spontaneous, more permissive, and more emotionally intense and involved.

A controversy that has exercised a number of observers is whether the new upper class is responsible for the changes which have been occurring within the younger, more modern, hereditary upper-class families, or whether the newly arrived families will, with time, acculturate to the traditional patterns of the old upper class. It seems most likely that both are responding to the changed conditions, economic and ideological, of modern times and that the traditional values will continue their decline. The new elite of talent are not likely to embrace patterns that are dying out in the old upper class, and the old upper class is changing, not because they are imitating their new associates, but because their objective life circumstances have also changed.

In modern times, talented celebrities are invited to eat dinner with their ''betters,'' whereas in former times, they entertained during or after dinner. The sons and daughters of the new elite, born to wealth and educated in exclusive preparatory schools, often marry the sons and daughters of the old upper class. The circulation of elites, in the case of marriage, remains largely within the category of the very wealthy, old and new.

UPPER-MIDDLE-CLASS FAMILIES

Upper-middle-class families in the United States and elsewhere are the epitome and the vanguard of much that is modern in contemporary family life. Because it is close to the causes and consequences of social change, the emphasis in this class is on the new—the latest in ideas, in consumption patterns, and in human relationships.

Upper-middle-class men and women are highly successful business executives, public servants, professionals, and entertainers who are near but not at the top of various occupational and income hierarchies in government, business, the professions, and recreation. They have careers, not jobs, and, at least within the present middle-aged depression-born generation, they are highly invested in these careers and in the work ethic. They are usually not alienated at work, since they do not experience the blocked mobility that results from a lack of formal education.

At the higher levels of the status game, many are called but few are chosen. Exceptional talent, hard work, and drive, however, can conceivably result in national recognition and achieved upper-class status, for at least some members of this social class. Upper-middle-class employees also have a great deal of freedom on the job, since the higher the prestige of an occupation, the greater is the degree of autonomy at work.

Upper-middle-class families are highly mobile, along all three of the dimensions of mobility—social, psychological, and geographic. The relatively isolated nuclear family is more likely to be found within this class (and the new upper class), although it is probably not typical, even here. While husband-wife and parent-child relationships tend to be equalitarian, the husband's authority within the family stems more from achieved resources than from cultural definition.

To describe the family as equalitarian does not mean that each partner has absolutely equal authority in all decisions about what to do, where to go, whom to see, and how to behave. If this were the case, decision-making would often be stalemated. A more accurate description of family authority patterns in what are described as equalitarian households is that power, influence, and authority are situational and vary according to what is being decided and who is more invested in the outcome. Since men, for example, are the major breadwinners in a majority of two-income homes, they generally make the decision as to where the family will live and whether they will move in response to a new job opportunity.

While the husband's authority is high, it is not arbitrary. Many decisions are based on discussion and mutual accommodation. If the wife has more skill, interest, or investment in a particular area of decision-making, her arguments are likely to prevail. If she does not have a job and has more time at her disposal, she will perform the preliminary tasks that lead to a decision in such areas as finding an apartment or choosing a house, selecting furniture, and investigating travel possibilities, for example. The husband participates in the final decision, even if it is not in an area that interests him most. His opinion carries more or less weight, depending upon his skills, preference, or interest in whatever is being decided. But his opinion carries more weight, generally, than the opinions of husbands in lower-middle-class and working-class families.

The two-career husband-and-wife relationship is quite frequent in the urban upper-middle class, particularly among professionals. The sharing of homemaking obligations, however, is usually more limited than in the lower-middle class, less because of cultural sex role definitions than because of the demands of the husband's career. The wife may delegate homemaking chores, in part, to paid help, although she usually continues to perform many of the traditional functions in the home. She also tends to regard her marital role as her primary status in life. Regardless of the prestige of the wife's occupation, and even if it is higher than that of the husband's occupation, the wife will not become dominant in the household unless she outearns her husband. This parallels the situation in the upper working class, where the wife may have a white-collar job but does not outearn her husband and does not, therefore, become dominant.

Communication, in the absence of psychopathology, is free, intimate, and intensive between all members of upper-middle-class families. This is a highly educated class, typically, and as such, family members have the verbal tools and the intellectual orientation that promote introspection and concern with personal development and individual freedom. For this reason and because of the greater personal freedom that parents experience in their own lives, permissive child-rearing practices are most prevalent in this class.

Rationalism is highly valued in the upper middle class, but

irrationalism is better understood and, therefore, more feared. Faith in the expert is almost supreme, and the preoccupation with the latest discovery, the newest scientific technique, and the current formula for more successful child rearing, improved marital relationships, and more beautiful homes and gardens is endless.

Since many upper-middle-class families have been socially mobile, the past is usually not venerated. This is indicated by home furnishings that are typically avant garde and, income permitting, handmade and of original design. Those members of this class who identify with the upper class will furnish their homes with antiques—family heirlooms that have lost their original home, purchased by those who long for an ancestral home and the venerable past they do not have.

Conspicuous consumption is usually high in mobile or marginal families who have the money to validate their ambiguous or changed status by material possessions—diamonds, furs, designer clothes, luxury cars and homes. The upper middle class, especially successful business people, are in the forefront of this kind of consumption behavior, limited only by their means or by the expedient necessity not to upstage their superiors, if they are employed in large corporations. Professionals have their academic degrees to validate their status and are, for that reason, somewhat less likely to be conspicuous consumers.

The artistic, creative, and intellectual segment of the upper middle class attempts to avoid placement within the class structure and obvious identification with class symbols. Yet they also have evolved typical and identifiable life patterns. They may live in working-class neighborhoods or warehouse districts, but they furnish their homes in typical ways, at any particular time. They place the strongest emphasis on the urban values in their ideal and actual family relationships.

LOWER-MIDDLE-CLASS FAMILIES

Respectability, conformity, and petty striving have been popular labels used by social scientists in attempts to profile this particular class in American society. This too is changing. Studies of the lower middle class now tend to be more discriminating, less biased, and more sympathetic.[9] Respectability, for example, may still be a very basic value in this class, but from all evidence, the group sex movement (swinging), although small in numbers, has drawn many of its recruits from this stratum.[10] The upper middle class does not usually have the time to engage in organized group sex activities and in the constant pursuit of new partner couples that is required for successful participation in the movement. The working class is largely still too traditional and repressed in the area of sexual behavior to take part in this movement.

Even in this kind of breaking out of conventional practices, however, the traditional value of fidelity is preserved, and the modern value of equality between the sexes is proclaimed by lower-middle-class married swingers. In group sex activities, married couples participate together or not at all. Elaborate precautions are taken to ensure that relationships with new couples are limited strictly to sex, thus providing less threat to the marriages of participants.

In general, however, and despite glaring but infrequent exceptions, the standard of respectability is still quite binding for the great majority of families in this class. Lower-level white-collar workers are the backbone of the nation, not only as members, but as active supporters of patriotic, civic, and religious organizations. Lower-middle-class parents and children pack the churches, Boy Scout and Girl Scout organizations, the Kiwanis and Lions clubs, and veterans organizations.

This class is in between the working class and the upper middle class in the adoption of certain modern values. The emphasis on instilling achievement motivation in their children is quite high, for example, boosted by more objective availability of opportunity than in the working class. But the lower middle class has never had the affluence that promoted the overindulgence of children in many upper-middle-class families after World War II. Child-rearing practices are less authoritarian than in the working class. Physical punishment is not as frequently used as a technique for disciplining children as it is in the working class.

Permissiveness, however, is tempered by stricter limits and by more emphasis on the rights of the parent than is typical in the upper middle class.

Unlike the working class, whose models are usually within the same class, the lower middle class identifies upward and is somewhat more concerned with status validation and striving. They are not usually conspicuous consumers. Thrift and saving are still highly valued despite the enticements of a credit-card economy. While they are prevented from rising in the class structure because of limited education, they strive to help their children move into the upper middle class and will often make extreme sacrifices for this goal.

Many lower-middle-class families now live in tract suburbs that are ethnically, but not racially, varied and are relatively homogeneous with respect to age and income. They are not usually as lonely or isolated as the geographically mobile working class. Visiting as couples in the evening or coffee klatching during the day, and the cooperative exchange of baby-sitting and other services, provide the equivalent of extended family activities and mutual aid for many.

Inflation, high mortgage interest rates, the soaring prices of automobiles and gasoline, and increased traffic congestion have led to significant changes among younger generations of the lower middle class (and the working class). The flight to the suburbs continues, but individual home ownership has declined in favor of apartments, condominiums, cooperatives, and attached housing. Husbands and wives are now far more likely to have jobs in the suburbs than in central cities.

The amount of joint activity and sharing of obligations within the home is high in this class. Traditional sex role definitions are less rigid than in the working class, and the husband is usually more available than in the upper middle class to share in household and child-rearing activities. The wife often maintains the fiction of male dominance, but joint decisions and consultation with the husband on mundane decisions are more frequent than in the working class.

While they are not in the forefront of change in family roles and values, and while traditional values such as ethnocentrism are more widespread, the children of this stratum of American society are next in line to experience many of the changes first introduced by the upper middle class. With a higher general level of education, greater upward social mobility, and greater economic resources, the differences in acculturation to modern values all but disappear. But these differences are significant, and they continue to divide the upper and lower levels of the largest and fastest growing segment of the American class structure in very real ways.

UPPER-WORKING-CLASS FAMILIES

Working-class occupations are those in which individuals work with things, primarily—tools, equipment, machines—rather than with knowledge and communication skills.[11] Secretaries work with machines, but symbols and ideas are essential to their work since they must know spelling, grammar, and the elements of style. Sales people use persuasive ideas and a knowledge of their product in the performance of their jobs. Physicians use equipment of all kinds, but their work is grounded on a large body of theory and knowledge about the human body and the human psyche.

The upper and lower working classes are distinguished, among other things, by the circumstances of their employment—by type of job, the level of skill and knowledge required, the pay, and the steadiness and security of employment. The lower working class is unskilled, unemployed, underemployed, or irregularly employed. The upper working class is more likely to be steadily employed in semiskilled jobs, requiring a few days of on-the-job training, or in skilled jobs requiring vocational training, lengthy apprenticeships, or fairly extensive on-the-job-training.

Semiskilled and skilled workers are most likely to be unionized. They have higher and steadier incomes than unskilled workers, and more security and self-esteem. While survival is not as perilous as it is among the poor, the upper working class has less autonomy and less control over their lives, on and off the job, than the middle class. Their alternatives in the face of catastrophe—unemployment, severe illness, dislocation by urban renewal—are fewer and less adequate than in the middle class. Their limited education, lack of savings, and more traditional values often hinder rational accommodation to the blows, uncertainties, and rapid changes of modern life.

The percentage of high-school dropouts is high among skilled and semiskilled workers, but not as high as it is in the lower working class. Wives often have more education than their husbands, since females are less likely than males to drop out of high school. For this reason, if they work, they may have more prestigious white-collar jobs. The husband usually earns more, however, and authority patterns within the home, superficially at least, seem to follow the traditional patriarchal pattern.

The blue-collar worker puts forth the image of toughness, courage, unsentimentality, and command, and his wife supports his self-proclaimed status as boss and ultimate authority in the household. Both husband and wife verbalize the traditional values and sex role definitions, and they believe that what they verbalize is what actually exists.

But here, also, ideal and reality often do not coincide. The working-class wife, in fact, usually has more authority than the middle-class wife in managing the budget, the home, the children, and relationships with the extended family and her husband. Effective authority within the family reflects the community status of the husband and his personal resources, as well as subcultural definitions and expectations. This is evident in the working class, as elsewhere, despite the stronger hold of the traditional values in this class.

In the working class, the husband abdicates in many areas of decision-making that involve the home and the children. When, sporadically, he does assert his will, more often he does so in a coercive way. Hence, the working-class wife views her husband as dominant and controlling, despite her very real authority in day-to-day family activities.

Other traditional values are real as well as apparent, especially among the older generations. Familism, for example, is a meaningful aspect of daily existence and is reflected in frequent

visiting and exchange of services. The extended family continues to serve interests and emotional needs to a greater extent
than do experts, friends, clubs, or formal organizations.
An emphasis on achievement is discouraged by realistic economic and educational barriers. Individualistic achievement,
furthermore, usually means estrangement from family, neighborhood, and peers. The fruits of rationalism are not readily
apparent to those who have few real alternatives: luck, chance,
the breaks are more persuasive explanations for evaluating individual destinies as well as life itself.

Religious beliefs are strong, especially among older wives and
daughters, but churchgoing is less frequent than in the middle
class. Churchgoing does not serve the purpose of status validation. It is also less frequent than in the middle class because the
joining of clubs and organizations, generally, is less frequent in
the upper working class. Memberships are usually limited to labor unions and patriotic organizations where participation is
often marginal.

Ethnocentrism is strong, reinforced by lower levels of education, less mobility, and, in large cities, by more frequent hostile
contacts with impoverished racial minority groups. The middle
classes are more insulated from the poor and have more power
and more money to resist invasions of their neighborhoods.

Upper-working-class authoritarianism in child rearing is less
strong in the United States than among similarly located families in England, Italy, Germany, the Soviet Union, and other
countries that have been surveyed. But the emphasis is still primarily on obedience rather than independence.

Materialism is a value that has taken hold, but the accumulation of material goods has a different meaning than it has in
the middle class. Working-class families are not conspicuous
consumers. They cannot afford it and, furthermore, there is no
need for it. The husband's level of achievement is obvious. He
is not doing the bureaucratic crawl in a large firm, nor is he
taking risks, as a self-employed entrepreneur, that may lead to
riches and fame.

Because most manual jobs, like most lower-level white-collar jobs, are dull, routine, and dead end, permitting little use of independent judgment, resourcefulness, or control over the work situation, work tends to be devalued in this class, relative to family and leisure activities. Work is a job, not a career; the paycheck is the sanction for going on. And the paycheck is used for compensatory rather than conspicuous consumption.[12] Buying, usually on credit, provides temporary relief from feelings of boredom, frustration, and deprivation.

Older working-class wives embrace the traditional wife-and-mother role more unquestioningly than middle-class wives. If they work, they do so largely for economic reasons. They are more likely than middle-class women to claim they would not work if they did not have to, but most now claim they would continue to work for psychological reasons, such as loneliness or boredom. Household work is less efficiently performed than in the middle class. Household chores usually expand to consume the time available to perform them. Employed wives, in all classes, with much less time, spend less time on the same chores. Working-class wives, furthermore, are unlikely to hire household help.

On personality tests, older working-class women have appeared more passive, insecure, nurturing, dependent, and emotionally volatile than middle-class women. In the middle class, feelings of inferiority are less pronounced, and personal freedom, independence, and privacy are more valued. A higher level of education is a very important underlying reason for these basic differences as well as differences in the way female children have been socialized in the two classes.

The traditional values permeate all family relationships in the older generations of the working class. The self-sacrificing orientation of the mother is evidenced daily and in hundreds of ways. She derives more pleasure from buying for her children than for herself. She values and stresses family solidarity and mutual responsibility above individual goals and needs when the two are in conflict. Her world is bound, defined, and limited to family concerns and interests.

In her maternal role, she emphasizes respectability and obedience more, creativity and self-reliance less. With more children to control, she has less time to reason, spell out general principles, or to turn affection off and on as a means of exercising that control. A threat, followed up by a slap, is more effective in the short run. Since she is less ambivalently self-sacrificing, and is less questioning of traditional child-rearing techniques, she feels less guilt about using physical punishment than do middle-class women.

Sex roles are also more traditionally defined and more sharply segregated in the working class. Husbands and wives share few common interests outside the children and few common friends and recreational persuits. Husbands are more likely to confide in male relatives, if they confide in anyone. Wives also confide in same-sex relatives: mothers, sisters, and daughters. Cross-sex relationships are suspect because they are viewed as inevitably sexual in motivation—a situation more pronounced in, but certainly not exclusive to, the working class.

Surviving traditional values of male superiority and emotional reserve restrict communication. For this reason, possible constructive compromise, or negotiation are more difficult to achieve. A relationship in which one member feels fearful and inferior inhibits free communication. The tendency to turn to relatives for advice usually reinforces a fatalistic resignation: make the best of it; it is fate; God's will; woman's lot.

Given the modern values in marriage—companionship, intimacy, deep and intensive communication, and mutual emotional support—the subculturally prescribed psychological separation of husband and wife and the greater economic stresses they experience result in higher divorce rates than in the middle class. Divorces among the higher classes in our society are more publicized, but they are, in fact, less frequent.

The emphasis on traditional definitions of masculinity also restricts the possibility of mutual sexual enjoyment. Tenderness and concern for the wife's response will be rare if sexual gratification is viewed as a male prerogative. Foreplay, positional variations—any variation in technique or procedure other than the male on top, genital sex patterns—are viewed as perversions.

The double standard, permitting sexual freedom to males but not to females, is still quite strong in the working class. Husbands, however, are less likely to engage in extramarital affairs during the later years of marriage than middle-class husbands. Here, again, the reasons probably have to do with the lesser economic resources of working-class men. With age, the money and power of higher status males can buy what youth and physical attractiveness no longer can.

The foregoing profile applies to the majority of older, white working-class families in this country and also to more recent working-class migrants from rural areas and immigrants from other countries. But change is constant in modern societies and change is a never-ending challenge to sociological generalizations. We do not despair, however, because outdated sociology is good history. These family patterns are past history rather than present reality for many white manual workers in the United States.

Sociologists recognize this fact in their distinction between the traditional and the modern working class. This distinction often parallels age and generation. The typical differences in marital and parental roles are usually associated with the length of urban residence of the family, beginning with the initial immigration or migration of a grandparent or parent from a rural area outside the United States or within it. The generational time span for acculturation to urban values is accelerated or delayed by such factors as physical difference, class origins, the availability of education and occupational opportunities, the degree of discrimination, and the compatibility of the cultural traditions of the area of origin with urban values.

Modern working-class families are generally younger, have a higher level of education (high school graduation; perhaps some additional training in community colleges), and have been geographically mobile (into working-class suburbs, uually). They are more like the middle class in their greater emphasis on values such as equalitarianism, achievement, and individualism in family life.

With geographic mobility, the extended family is not so significant as it was in the past, and loyalties and commitments shift to the nuclear family. The separate friends and separate interests of husband and wife are shed to some extent. Friends are visited in common and instead of, or in addition to, relatives.

Sex role stereotyping within the family also declines: husbands and wives share homemaking obligations more, and sons and daughters are treated more alike.[13] Communication is freer and less strained, promoted by the greater verbal facility and insight that accompanies a higher level of education and by decreased authoritarianism in fact as well as in form. Wives are more assertive and report higher self-esteem.

The increased mutuality in the husband-wife relationship is reflected in greater sexual satisfaction and greater marital satisfaction. Sexual fulfillment for both partners is desired and accepted as the standard. Variations in sexual techniques are attempted, and sexual preferences are more freely discussed and accommodated.

The wife is less passive, less dependent, less fearful, and less self-sacrificing. She expects and receives more respect from husband and children. Her home territory shifts from the kitchen to the family room or the living room. If she works, her husband is less likely to feel threatened by her employment than in traditional working-class families.

The husband is less rigid about traditional definitions of masculinity. He shows more warmth and affection to sons as well as to daughters. He helps market, clear off, wash up, and straighten out. He may even walk the baby in the park on the weekend, if he is not moonlighting.

Modern working-class families are transitional rather than fully modern in values and behavior. As such, they experience the stresses that transition often brings, but they have fewer of the economic safeguards and releases available to middle-class families.[14] Loneliness, isolation, boredom and despair are more frequent. The loss of the extended family as a daily interacting unit is less compensated by organizational memberships and extensive friendship networks. Recently, in London, a large number of young, housebound, working-class mothers with small children, newly separated from their extended families, have been jumping to their death from flats on the top floors of high-rise public housing projects.

The job is a less gratifying outlet in the working class. There is less money available to buy household or other kinds of help, and there is less money to buy commercial pleasures and diversions. Television looms large—as it does in all working-class homes—a low-cost and effortless source of ready-made fantasy, instant amusement, and substitute living.

When they walk down the street in their new neighborhoods, modern working-class family members are less likely to know the faces in the crowd. And the crowd has thinned out considerably in their cleaner, quieter, less violent, and somehow less exhilarating suburban worlds.

LOWER-WORKING-CLASS FAMILIES

The traditional rural values, however modified in emphasis and behavior by particular ethnic groups, are strongest within the unskilled working class in the United States. The poor are the most recently uprooted from agricultural environments and rural ways of life.

Fatalism, superstition, ethnocentrism, authoritarianism, and familism are strong. Urban values are visible to this segment of the population, but objective life circumstances often prevent their adoption. Achievement motivation, for example, is not a monopoly of the middle class. Young children of all classes have high aspirations. The children of the poor, however, lose these aspirations, gradually and almost inevitably, in the process of growing up in the United States.[15]

Many of the statistical indicators of personal and familial misery are stronger in this segment of American society than in any other—the incidence, for example, of husband, wife, and child abuse, murder, rape, incest, desertion, and physical and mental illness.[16] The family unit is torn apart, primarily, by objective and unremitting economic stress. The effective domi nance of the wife and mother is strongest in this class, despite the appearance of male dominance. The husband is least able to legitimate his authority in the home by means of personal or economic assets. Unable to get adequate, secure employment, he is likely to escape the field and become part of the drifting underclass of temporary employees in agriculture, in hotels, laundries, kitchens, basements, and nonunionized factories and hospitals.

Courtship and marriage are not romanticized and idealized in the lower working class. The decision to marry is often casual, the result of a fatalistic acceptance of the inevitable, particularly if the girl becomes pregnant. Teenage marriages, precipitated by pregnancy, are common. A choice of partners within the same neighborhood is also common because geographic mobility is relatively restricted in this class. The young cannot afford to travel, and they do not go off to college. They are not usually offered jobs in faraway places.

Husband and wife are often emotionally estranged and isolated, separated by suffering and unfulfilled expectations. Sex is mutually exploitative, used more consciously and deliberately than in other classes to support the economic needs of the female and the narcissistic ego needs of the male. Communication is halting and sporadic, reflecting cultural traditions and accumulated anger and frustration. Overt display of affection is rare in the absence of sentiment and optimism. The husband defines the marital relationship in terms of the gratification of his physical needs. The wife accepts this, but longs for more. Since the husband-wife relationship tends to be characterized by emotional frustration and isolation, and since the wife has few outside interests, the lower-working-class woman views her primary status in life as that of mother rather than wife. The mother-child relationship is the strongest and most intimate family tie in this class, as it tends to be, generally, in traditional societies.

Female-headed households, regardless of ethnic origin, are frequent in urban slum areas, since the husband is often an economic burden and the wife may be better able to obtain and hold a job. Welfare policies in some states that specify the absence of an adult male in the home as a condition for obtaining government funds reinforce this pattern. The desire for love, companionship, children, and economic support, which cannot be gratified any other way, often leads the lower-working-class woman into a fatalistic acceptance of a succession of temporary male partners, who provide a shadowy semblance of the cultural ideal.

A few social scientists, and many spokesmen for the poor, have defended this pattern as an appropriate and highly adaptive response to life circumstances. They have accused critics of arbitrarily imposing their own middle-class values on the poor, who do not share these values. But the poor do share these values. Female-headed households are not preferred, and overwhelming misery, despair, guilt, and frustration are common features of this kind of existence. The deserted mother and child and the seemingly irresponsible male settle for less. They have been defeated in their initial efforts to live by values that are modern and urban and are middle-class only incidentally because this class can achieve them more readily economically.[17]

Child-rearing practices among the poor also reflect life circumstances and the opportunity structure. The discipline of children is most harsh, most severe, and most inconsistent in this class, emphasizing strict situational obedience, and values such as neatness and cleanliness that are taken for granted in other classes. Where chaos is a real possibility, order and discipline will be emphasized more. Where basic physical deprivation is constant, child rearing focuses on the physical. Slum mothers (rural and urban) have less time to worry about their children's motivations, deeper feelings, and psychological development. As in traditional agricultural societies, physical survival is an overriding value.

Work experiences color family relationships. Engaged in occupations that are routine and under direct supervision, requiring few communication skills and with little possibility to exercise autonomy and independent judgment, the poor do not encourage these traits in their children. It is not that they do not want to ; they are exposed to urban values and they would act them out if they could. The slum mother nags her child to do well in school. The child perceives the undertone of hopelessness, however, and this undertone will remain until objective circumstances change and opportunity is available and is perceived as such by this class.

Poor families have been portrayed as perpetuating poverty because traditional values of the subculture of poverty—fatalism, particularly—are ill suited to the adoption of urban values in an urban environment. The controversy over which comes first, economic conditions or subcultural values, is like other dichotomies—heredity and environment, free will and determinism—that have exercised intellectuals and academicians in the past. This particular controversy is somewhat easier to investigate and resolve, however.

Where rational and, above all, adequate efforts have been made to improve opportunities for the poor, these efforts have worked. To take one example, Head Start programs that provide compensatory education for children of the poor are more effective when they start with three-year-old children rather than with four-year-old children.[18] Children who participate in these programs are less likely to repeat grades or to need more costly special education classes when they are older. Parents become more involved with their children's educational experiences, and the children's self-esteem and IQ scores improve. As young adults, these children are more likely to be in college or to be steadily employed in skilled jobs than are children from the same neighborhood schools who did not have Head Start training.

Poverty remains a problem in the United States because to eradicate poverty would require a basic restructuring of the economic system in the United States, largely at the expense of defense industries and the hereditary upper class. The poor, furthermore, serve important functions for the maintainance of American society.[19]

The poor ensure that the dirtiest work in the society gets done. They are a source of enormous profit to businesses that employ them, off the books, at far less than the minimum wage. They provide a market for inferior goods—used cars, bad housing, outdated bread, milk, and meat—and clients and patients for poorly trained or profiteering doctors, dentists, and lawyers. They provide jobs for legions of service workers such as police, prison attendants, probation officers, and social workers. They raise the status of the nonpoor, relatively, and serve as horrible examples to the upper working and middle classes in a highly competitive society. They provide a buffer for other classes from environmental threat and the public intrusions of new highways and urban renewal projects.

The poor and their multiple personal and familial problems will remain with us in the United States as long as unemployment continues to be equated with laziness and poverty with sin and immorality. They will remain with us as long as a small number of hereditary wealthy directors of the largest corporations in the United States continue to effectively dominate government policy, openly, and not so openly.[20]

ROLE CONFLICT AND CLASS

In industrialized societies, family roles not only change in content very rapidly, but another phenomenon, role conflict, becomes constant, universal, and more intense.[21] In each of the major social classes, families experience somewhat unique variations in the type and intensity of role conflict.

Roles, as pointed out in chapter 1, are explicit or implicit guides or blueprints for thought, emotion, and behavior that spell out what the individual can or cannot, should or should not, and must or must not do as a occupant of a particular status. In modern societies, the content of roles, especially values, attitudes, beliefs, and norms, is constantly changing, and the number of roles is constantly expanding.

Individuals experience role conflict—the feeling of being frustrated or torn in opposite directions by unfulfilled expectations or contradictory or impossible demands—when they do not have the emotional or economic resources to enact a role (the unemployed lower-working-class male who cannot support his family), when incompatible demands are simultaneously required within the same role (parents who must discipline children but at the same time be loving and affectionate to their children) ; when individuals are torn by incompatible demands of various roles (the employed wife and mother) ; or when role conceptions and expectations are not mutual (the husband who wants a full-time homemaker wife but is married to a woman who wants a professional career).

The culturally defined content of roles, and even more important, the means or techniques for enacting roles, are constantly changing in industrialized societies. Humans are barely equal to the challenge of constantly multiplying roles and role obligations and the many contradictions built into these changing roles. The tendency for people to expect more from each other than is possible also increases.

Families in all classes experience the strain of role conflict for different reasons. In the working class, a major source of role conflict is the frequent lack of economic resources to fulfill role obligations. The survival of traditional values in circumstances where they are no longer appropriate is another serious problem in this class. The new values in marriage, such as companionship and intimate sharing of psychological experiences, are incompatible with traditional sex role definitions, still strong among older members of this class, that prescribe separateness of interests and activities of husband and wife.

In the middle class, economic problems are less pressing, family members are less unquestioningly accepting of tradition, and are more experimental in their approach to fulfilling their role obligations. Here other reasons for role conflict are more prevalent. In the upper middle class, for example, motherhood is often experienced as a crisis. The college-educated young woman, independent and accustomed to a great deal of freedom and varied experiences, may find the demands of unrelieved motherhood and the restrictions of twenty-four-hour-a-day total responsibility for another human being incompatible with her previous socialization experiences and values and with her personality.

Among successful professionals, sixty- to eighty-hour work weeks are not uncommon. The overlapping demands of various roles is probably the most frequent source of role conflict in this segment of the population. The emotional requirements of the husband-and-father role are difficult to fulfill, not because of surviving traditional definitions of masculinity, but because the time and energy required to pursue a career successfully may leave little time for fulfilling family obligations. Working-class men who moonlight have the same conflict.

In the upper class, familism and the frequent, prolonged economic dependence of adult sons and daughters, even into middle age and beyond, or until the death of the family patriarch or matriarch, is incompatible with the modern values of individualism and independence. In this class, as in the working class, the persistence of traditional values in the face of changed circumstances subverts the mutuality in expectations that promote smooth family functioning.

The companion role, which is common for women in this class, requires that a woman remain an interesting and sexually stimulating companion throughout her life. This may be difficult to achieve, given the lengthened life span, the rather abrupt aging of women after menopause, and the lack of a gainful occupational base as a source of interest, involvement, and topics of conversation. Community service activities, which utilized the personal skills of higher-status women in the past, are increasingly taken over by professionals and by the welfare state in technologically developed societies. Middle-class women in the empty nest stage, with leisure time and no inclination to work, or with inadequate or outdated skills for obtaining employment, face the same problem.

Merging Trends in Family Life

Recently, Theodore Caplow and his associates repeated a classic community study of Muncie, Indiana, originally carried out in the 1920s.[22] Their work has provided further evidence of a merging in family values and behavior over the years, especially between the upper-working and the middle classes. In the 1970s, unlike the 1920s, middle-class wives were almost as likely to be employed as working-class wives. The huge increase in employed married women was the single greatest change in family life during this period. Employed wives in both classes, typically, earned less than half of the family income and had an average of two hours a day less leisure time than their husbands.

Compared with the 1920s, middle-class wives were much less likely to have paid household help in the 1970s. This, plus other symptoms of declining purchasing power, indicate a hardening of the class structure at the middle levels as well as at the top and bottom. There was less social mobility between the generations in the 1970s than in the 1920s.

Generally, family life was more open and more valued. Generational conflicts were less severe and family solidarity had increased. Nuclear families were not isolated. Close relatives were visited more often than close friends. Citizens were optimistic about their personal and family futures, but were pessimistic about nuclear war, the economic decline of the United States, inflation, environmental pollution, and the quality of life.

Muncie, Indiana, is not typical of the vast array of communities, towns, cities, suburbs, and exurbs in the United States. However, the conclusions of this study are supported by other, larger-scale survey research studies of family life here and in European countries.

Before turning to the question of the future of the family in industrial societies, a brief review of the major and continuing overall trends in marital relationships and parent-child relationships, for all classes, all ethnic groups, and for rural as well as urban families in the United States may be useful. These trends, it is important to remember, are emerging in all industrialized societies in the West. They are particularly characteristic of American society for certain historical and ideological reasons, but also because until recently the United States has had the most advanced technology, by far, of any country in the world.

Societies with high levels of technological development change rapidly and require highly educated, psychologically flexible, and mobile populations. The higher levels of education and the decline in extended family and community control characteristic of modern societies promote a greater tendency to think critically and to use rational means for achieving goals, a decrease in ethnocentrism, and an increase in tolerance of human differences. Child-rearing practices become less authoritarian, reflecting the necessity to produce men and women who can adapt to rapid social change and to the possibilities of many more choices and alternatives in occupations and ways of life. Individualism, particularly in its components of self-discipline and resourcefulness, is more adaptive than the ability to take orders and to conform unquestioningly to situational norms in modern societies. When norms are constantly changing, ambiguous, contradictory, or even absent, general principles as guides to behavior become more realistic and appropriate than specific rules and regulations.

Declining authoritarianism in child rearing by parents who have more flexibility and more choices and alternatives in their own lives results in children who are more tolerant of outgroups, more honest and psychologically introspective, less sexually repressed, and less hostile. At the same time, the greater availability of educational and occupational opportunity (at least until the recent recessions), the greater need for drive and talent, and the decline of nepotism tend to promote emphasis on achievement in child rearing in all classes, all ethnic groups, and in all regions and locales—urban, urbanizing, and rural.

Marital relationships also reflect these changed conditions and values. Since married men and women have more options, they are guided less by ideals of duty, obligation, loyalty, self-sacrifice, and arbitrary cultural norms in their family lives. The current standards are companionship, free and open communication, mutual gratification—sexual and psychological—and mutual growth. These patterns are underwritten by the greater leisure and abundance experienced by more people in industrialized societies, despite economic setbacks at times. While the trends in marital relationships, child-rearing practices, and social character are most pronounced in the upper middle class, the new values and role conceptions are diffusing upward and downward. All families, in varying degrees, are exposed to the demands and the effects of modern technology and developments in scientific knowledge.

SEVEN

Today and Tomorrow

Alternatives to the traditional nuclear family have become more popular in recent times. Those that involve more than two sexual partners—group marriages, sexually "open" marriages, communes that do not restrict or regulate sexual activity—have low survival rates (one or two years, usually).[1] Long-term participation becomes too stressful, psychologically.

Throughout history, humans have required stability and security more than they have required variety in their emotional attachments. In human relationships, security and freedom are incompatible needs, and in modern times, freedom becomes just another word for loneliness. Loneliness was rare in nonliterate and in preindustrial societies, as a concept and as a human experience.

The actual prevalence of alternatives to traditional family groups, such as singles, the living together of unmarried couples (heterosexual and homosexual), sexually open marriages, and communes, is small. Less than 3 percent of the households in the United States consist of two unmarried people of the opposite sex.[2] And because of the vagaries of Census Bureau questionnaires, this includes mothers and sons, fathers and daughters, employers and opposite-sex live-in servants, and owners or renters with opposite-sex boarders.

Publicity about alternative forms has been far out of proportion to their actual extent in the United States. This is probably because these alternatives now involve a greater number of middle-class people. Singles, attached to family groups, usually, and living together without the benefit of a marriage contract, also known as common-law marriages, have long been prevalent among the poor in economically stratified societies.

Communes are substitutes for family groups.[3] They provide support services such as economic sharing, emotional support, and physical care, especially during illness, that were usually provided by families in traditional societies. Recruits have been mainly unmarried individuals or single parents, mothers, usually, and their children.

Religious communes have had higher survival rates because they are more rigidly structured and have a more compelling, integrating ideology. Faith reinforces commitment and conformity. But communes, in the United States at least, are not likely to become widespread, as temporary or permanent substitutes for family groups. Even communes with the loosest structure invade privacy and submerge individualism—two values that, from all evidence, are stronger than ever in the United States.[4]

Other apparant alternatives to the nuclear family, such as singles or unmarried couples who live together, are not regarded by most participants as lifetime alternatives. Singles have grown in number and in prominence in recent years, but in the United States, less than 10 percent of the population is likely to remain single permanently (as compared to less than 5 percent a generation ago).[5]

What has actually increased is the number of young people of marriageable age and a delay in the age at first marriage. This delay is related, in part, to the changing status and roles of women, especially in the middle class. More women are pursuing demanding careers and are not interrupting their careers to marry and have children as in the past.

Other factors that have delayed marriage are economic insecurity, greater sexual liberalism, especially among middle-class women (underwritten by the revolution in birth control techniques), and the fact that there are more women than men of marriageable age in most contemporary societies. Actually, the delay in age at first marriage is a return to earlier patterns when, for economic reasons, people married later because they could not afford to marry earlier, if at all.

The living-together relationship is usually a temporary relationship, especially for people under thirty-five.[6] Older people in these relationships may be divorced and unwilling to try again. For most younger people, living together represents an extension of the dating relationship made possible by better birth control techniques and more liberal sexual attitudes. Another factor that has promoted living-together relationships is the extended period of adolescence in industrial societies, since training for adult occupations takes so much longer. Higher expectations in marriage, the increased divorce rate, and economic decline and uncertainty have also promoted a fear of commitment to marriage at an early age.

Living-together relationships are not trial marriages. Most younger participants do not know whether or not they will marry their partners eventually. Surprisingly, those who do marry are as likely to divorce as couples who do not live together before marrying. The legal sanction of a marriage certificate changes expectations. The dating game is over, and conflicts surface that were previously ignored or suppressed.

The number of people in living-together relationships in the United States appears to be leveling off and may decline in the near future. More women, apparently, are beginning to view this particular alternative as exploitative rather than liberated. Younger women also reduce their options for marrying if they spend years in a relationship that breaks up. There are fewer partners available at a later age, unless they marry men who are younger than they are. This, incidentally, is happening more often now.

One nontraditional form that has increased tremendously in recent years and from all evidence will continue to increase, at least for a while, is the single-parent household, This situation, also, is usually temporary, especially in the middle class. Three quarters of the single parents in the United States marry, or remarry, eventually.[7] Stepparent families, also known as blended or reconstituted families, have become a popular topic of research and public concern in recent years.

The greatly increased number of stepparent families reflects the dramatic increase in the divorce rate. It also indicates persistence of a desire by most people who have a choice to live in stable, sexually monogamous groups.

THE PERSISTENCE OF THE NUCLEAR FAMILY

In times of severe economic and political crisis, the moral deterioration of the family is a common lament, and the death of the family is a favorite prediction of sages and seers. The contemporary family is in deep trouble, in some respects. This is indicated by the fact that many serious people, among them artists, academicians, and leaders of women's movement groups, are currently raising the question of the continued necessity of a nuclear family, based as it is on exclusive, enduring husband-wife and parent-child relationships.

The nuclear family will not only persist, it will be stronger than ever in times to come. We live in an age of rising psychological as well as economic expectations. The family as an institution will not disappear if people expect more of it and are more willing to express and to act on their dissatisfactions. This is more likely to preserve than to destroy the institution of marriage, which is the basis of the nuclear family. Nontraditional forms—homosexual marriages, living-together relationships, communes—will also continue because of the increased tolerance of individual choice among more educated, less ethnocentric, more permissively reared people.

Relationships in contemporary nuclear families are often too intense. Help with the two nonproductive generations, the very young and the very old, is frequently inadequate. Role conflicts, especially those stemming from insufficient economic resources and changing and incompatible values and role expectations, are widespread. But ultimately for biological reasons, and more immediately for psychological reasons, the pairing husband-wife relationship and the exclusive parent-child relationship will endure.

The biologically grounded continuous, nonseasonal sex drive of humans and the lengthy period of physical and emotional dependence of the human young underlie this prediction. No society has existed or can exist without norms regulating the continuous sex drive of human beings. Sexual conflict, rivalry, and jealousy must be at least minimally controlled in order to protect the very dependent young and ensure the cooperation that becomes increasingly imperative in highly specialized and increasingly interdependent technologically developed societies.

It is quite possible to dull the human need for enduring love and affection, to deny or repress this need, to sublimate it, or to convert it into opposite kinds of needs, such as hate and sadism. But this is accomplished at great psychic cost to the individual and, often, to the society. The cost may take the form of anxiety, guilt, and depression, or a compulsive need for achievement, power, and recognition. This may promote creativity and productivity, but it can also result in brutality, murder, and carnage.

The satisfaction of emotional needs, furthermore, underlies and to an important extent affects the physical and intellectual growth of infants and children. Studies of the effects on ill or orphaned children of separation from parents—the slowing of growth, the retardation of intelligence, and even premature death—date back to the 1920s. This is not to argue against day care centers, which will undoubtedly become universal as the employment of women in the nonfamily economy becomes universal in postindustrial societies. It is an argument against the elimination of stable love objects for infants and children which can be guaranteed only by the preservation of the institution of the family. No society has ever been able to delegate completely the task of providing for the emotional needs of all infants and children to substitute nonfamily groups because it is not possible to do so.

The basic difficulty in attempting to delegate the satisfaction of emotional needs on a large scale to specialized groups outside the family and household in densely populated societies is that this would have to be carried out in bureaucratic settings. And bureaucracy is repressive to the emotions. The family is the only area of life in industrialized societies that is not bureaucratized. All other major institutions—the government, the economy, education, religion—have been transformed by the creeping and inevitable spread of bureaucracy. Most people, with the exception of the very old (those who are not institutionalized), the very young, a shrinking category of the self-employed, and a rapidly diminishing number of nonemployed wives, spend a major part of their lives in bureaucratic settings.

The highest values in bureaucratically managed organizations are efficiency and predictability. The basic orientation in social relationships is impersonal. Human emotional needs are irrelevant and detrimental to good bureaucratic functioning, since emotions interfere with the goals of efficiency and predictability. It is doubtful that the basic function of the family in providing for the emotional needs of infants and children could be adequately carried out even by well-trained, well-paid, deeply committed teachers and nurses. These individuals might be very service-oriented, but they would be likely to change jobs in a mobile society. And they would limit their emotional involvement with their clients, by definition of themselves as professionals.

Social science has found some answers to the problem of how to provide more adequately for the emotional needs of children in institutional settings. It is now known that children do better in hospitals and nurseries if one nurse is assigned to a specific number of children than if all nurses are assigned indiscriminately to take care of all the children. While this practice approaches the exclusive one-to-one parent-child relationship, it does not duplicate it and it cannot replace it.

Other sources of stable, emotional support, especially for children, are increasingly unavailable in postindustrial societies. The servant class is disappearing and grandmothers are almost as likely to be employed as mothers.

Marriage and the nuclear family will continue as basic institutions in human societies, functioning imperfectly and inefficiently, and sometimes destructively, but persevering because it is not possible to offer anything more workable to provide for the basic emotional needs of human beings—young or old.

PRIVATE PROBLEMS AND PUBLIC POLICY

In industrial societies, governments assume more responsibility for services previously provided by the family. Usually, societies that label themselves socialist assume more of this responsibility and redistribute wealth and income more equally. Capitalist societies spend less and redistribute less.

The United States spends less than most capitalist European countries on income redistribution and on public services. But the concentration of vast quantities of wealth within less than 2 percent of the population is very similar in almost all Western industrial societies, and in nonsocialist industrializing societies as well.

Japan, on the other hand, has evolved an economic system that is unique. Japan has the lowest unemployment rate of any capitalist country in the world. It has the smallest earning differential between management and workers. It has the most equal income distribution of all capitalist industrialized nations. And yet the Japanese government spends even less on social services than the United States government.

Business firms in Japan provide services to individuals and families that ease economic and psychological stress. Companies are not run solely for the enrichment of shareholders. They provide a wide range of services for employees—health care, housing, low-interest loans, and other forms of financial help. They ease conflicts between family and work obligations with flexible work schedules, paid maternity leaves, and free day care facilities at workplaces.

Workers are rarely laid off. Only a small proportion, less than one third, are sheltered by guaranteed lifetime employment contracts. Both these and other workers are transferred by economically troubled companies to growing industries in a diversified economy, or they are loaned to the government for public works projects. The market economy in Japan is not based primarily on individual greed, but on collective sharing, cooperation, and planning. There is more than one way to resolve the problems of economic inequality and insecurity that shatter families and destroy people.

In the United States, recurring recessions, persisting inflation, rising unemployment rates, and the coming of age of the very large post-World War II baby boom generation (overeducated or undereducated, underemployed or unemployed, pessimistic, if not despairing), have had direct, measurable, and stressful consequences for the family lives of most people. Additional stress stemming from the spread of crisis and malaise in middle age, and the prolongation of life of the physically and economically dependent aged, especially those who are over eighty-five, has had similar effects.

Despite smaller numbers of children, the purchasing power of families has declined significantly. Married women, working class or middle class, with or without children, no longer have a choice between gainful employment and full-time homemaking. Except among the upper 2 percent of the population in the United States, it now takes two incomes, or more, to support a family comfortably, or even adequately. Neither the United States government nor the business sector provides enough support services for people and their families.[8]

The empty nest stage of family life, when children have grown up and departed and parents report less conflict and greater marital satisfaction, is contracting in the United States. Grown children are staying home longer, or are coming home in large numbers, unable to find employment, unable to pay high rents, mortgages, school or car loans, or simply because they need psychological support.

Experimental multi-adult family or substitute family groups are declining, but single-person, single-parent, stepparent, and one-child or no-child households are multiplying. Rates of functional illiteracy continue to increase. Rates of child abuse and child homicide, juvenile delinquency, adolescent suicide, especially among males aged sixteen to twenty-four, and teenage pregnancy are rising sharply. Drug abuse is widespread, although it appears to be leveling off at the moment.

New clichés, such as less is more, will not solve old problems. The poor, who are always with us in the United States, are poorer. The rich are very much richer. The New Deal and the Great Society programs, never adequate as solutions to boom and bust, monopoly capitalist economics (World War II rescued the New Deal, but a limited war in Vietnam and the rising cost of oil and other raw materials could not keep the Great Society going) are now obsolete historical slogans. Programs to decrease inequality in the United States have been decimated by policymakers and by the top leaders of business and industry who influence them, motivated by a shortsighted and mighty greed and by an obsessive drive for power, devoid of empathy or understanding.

The reforms necessary to maintain family life at economically and psychologically more tolerable levels in the United States and elsewhere are neither obscure nor impossible. A curtailment and redistribution of the vast amount of unearned income of the old upper class, especially from trusts, rents, and dividends, would provide more than enough funds to help the truly needy, the less needy, and the middle class. It would provide ample funds for planned, coordinated, national and international programs to match people with jobs and housing and to eliminate poverty and unemployment.

In the United States, a redistribution of the unearned income of the upper 2 percent of the population by the government could feed the hungry, shelter the homeless, provide the necessary funds for free health care for all, free higher education, student stipends, complete support for the aged, family allowances for children, and free day care and educational facilities for infants and preschool children, beginning at birth.

Long-range government planning and control over the business sector could promote productivity and rebuilding rather than profiteering and raiding, especially in basic industries. This, in turn, could easily underwrite a shorter work week and more job sharing between the employed and the unemployed, the overworked and the underworked, women and men. With a shorter work week, employed husbands and wives would have more time to spend with each other and with their children. The forty-hour work week is an anachronism, technologically and morally. Hunters and gatherers had the equivalent of a three-day work week, typically.[9] Why can't we?

Never before has the economic value of an ounce of prevention been so high. New York State spends twenty times more on foster home placement than it spends on income maintenance for intact nuclear families. It costs incomparably less to train people for necessary work, especially in the public sector—to repair, build, or rebuild roads, housing, bridges, sewers—than to maintain people in prisons and mental hospitals.

The burden and the obligation of reducing inequality and providing necessary public services for families and for all citizens is not likely to be shared to any appreciable extent by the business sector in the United States, as it is in Japan. The extreme emphasis on individualism and individual accumulation and success subverts the altruistic impulse. It could happen here. The predictions of social scientists have often been wrong, especially in the short run. But it is not very likely.

FAMILIES IN THE FUTURE

We have seen that certain changes in family values and roles become more prevalent, in all classes, in industrialized societies. We can predict that these trends will continue, and families and societies will continue, if the greed for wealth and power by dominant classes in most nonsocialist, industrial and industrializing societies is checked in time.

The family, however changed in form and functions, will survive, if human societies survive. Sexual activity, before and within marriage, will continue to be freer and more gratifying. Marital choice will continue to be freer, especially for women, as differences in the economic resources of men and women continue to decline. Family relationships, within and between generations, will continue to be closer as urban-rural differences, sex differences, and generational differences in power and in economic and educational resources continue to diminish.

Perhaps the major change in family life in postindustrial societies, as the twentieth century draws to an end, will not be the universal employment of all able-bodied women—rich, poor, young, middle-aged, older, single, married, divorced. It will be the greater loving involvement of men, with their fathers, with their wives, with their children, and, therefore, with other human beings.

Only then will the endless greed for power and wealth, war, and other evils associated with extreme economic inequality disappear from the earth. Only then will we return to the way things were for 99 percent of human history, before technological advance created an economic surplus that was not shared by all. And only then will humans once again be able to live with less envy, hate, and fear.

Love does not thrive where poverty dwells. We must nurture it with decent living conditions for all—everywhere, and soon. The truly rich will not share enough of their wealth, willingly enough. They, too, need help, in whatever form this will come, short of revolution in industrial societies. Revolution has not succeeded in these societies. Central governments are too well equipped with surveillance and destructive technologies.

Power and love are incompatible and irreconcilable needs. The present balance of terror will be eliminated only by humane and humanizing long-range, worldwide economic planning and reforms.

We live in hope because we dare not do otherwise. Knowledge does not buy power, just as money does not buy happiness. But it helps. We now know more than we have ever known about the sources and consequences of human destructiveness within individuals, families, and societies, at all times, and in all places. The next step is to act—rationally, soon, and before the world stops.

Notes

1. THE SOCIOLOGICAL MANDATE

1. See William H. Masters and Virginia E. Johnson, *Human Sexual Response* (Boston: Little, Brown, 1966), and *The Pleasure Bond: A New Look at Sexuality and Commitment* (Boston: Little, Brown, 1975).

2. David Knox and Kenneth Wilson, "The Differences Between Having One and Two Children," *The Family Coordinator* (1978), 27:23–25.

3. Joann Vanek, "Time Spent in Housework," *Scientific American* (November 1974), pp. 116–20.

4. See Orville G. Brim and Jerome Kagan, eds., *Constancy and Change in Human Development* (Cambridge, Mass.: Harvard University Press, 1980); and A. B. Doyle, "Infant Development in Day Care," *Developmental Psychology* (1975), 11:665–66.

5. See Jacques Donzelot, *The Policing of Families*, Robert Hurley, tr. (New York: Pantheon Books, 1979); and Betty Yorburg, *Utopia and Reality* (New York: Columbia University Press, 1969), pp. 20–21, 97–110.

6. U.S. Bureau of the Census, *Statistical Abstract of the United States: 1980* (Washington, D.C.: GPO, 1980), p. 471.

7. Kenneth Keniston and the Carnegie Council on Children, *All Our Children: The American Family Under Pressure* (New York: Harcourt Brace Jovanovich, 1977).

8. See Robert Coles' five volume *Children of Crisis* series, published by Atlantic–Little Brown (Boston) during the years 1967 to 1980.

9. Urie Bronfenbrenner, *The Ecology of Human Development: Experiments by Nature and Design* (Cambridge, Mass.: Harvard University Press, 1979).

10. Much of this type of research is reported in journals addressed primarily to family therapists. An example is *Family Process*.

11. See Richard Hofstadter, *Social Darwinism and American Thought* (Boston: Beacon Press, 1955), for a discussion of the historical role of this model in the ideological battles between proponents of the welfare state and proponents of rugged individualism.

12. See Frederick Engels, *The Origin of the Family, Private Property, and the State* (Chicago: Charles H. Kerr, 1902). *The Woman Question* (New York: International Publishers, 1951) contains excerpts from the writings on the family by Karl Marx, Frederick Engels, V. I. Lenin, and Joseph Stalin.

13. Robert K. Merton has provided one of the clearest statements of this model in *Social Theory and Social Structure* (Glencoe, Ill.: Free Press, 1957), pp. 19–84.

14. For a good general source on family theory see Wesley R. Burr, Reuben Hill, F. Ivan Nye, and Ira L. Reiss, eds., *Contemporary Theories About the Family* (New York: Free Press, 1979), vols. 1 and 2. See also Jerold Heiss, "Family Theory—20 Years Later," *Contemporary Sociology* (1980), 8:201–4.

15. Arthur R. Jensen, "How Much Can We Boost I.Q. and Scholastic Achievement?" *Harvard Educational Review* (Winter 1969), 39:1*–123.

16. Quoted in Lee Edson, "Jensenism, N., The Theory That I.Q. Is Largely Determined by the Genes," New York *Times Sunday Magazine*, August 31, 1969, pp. 10–11.

17. See Arthur R. Jensen, "Reducing the Heredity-Environment Uncertainty," *Harvard Educational Review Reprint Series* (1969), 2:212.

18. See Daniel G. Freedman, *Human Sociobiology* (New York: Free Press, 1979).

19. Charles J. Lumsden and Edward O. Wilson, *Genes, Mind, and Culture: The Coevolutionary Process* (Cambridge, Mass.: Harvard University Press, 1981).

20. See Gerhard and Jean Lenski, *Human Societies* (4th ed.; New York: McGraw-Hill, 1982); Joan Huber, "Toward a Socio-technological Theory of the Women's Movement," *Social Problems* (1976), 23:371–88; Betty Yorburg, *Sexual Identity* (New York: Wiley, 1974); and Robert Winch and Associates, *Familial Organization* (New York: Free Press, 1977).

21. See Gerhard Lenski, "History and Social Change," *American Journal of Sociology* (1976), 82:549–64.

22. Robert W. Winch, *The Modern Family* (3d ed.; New York: Holt, Rinehart and Winston, 1971), p. 29.

23. Kingsley Davis and Wilbert E. Moore, "Some Principles of Stratification," *American Sociological Review* (1945), 10:243. See also Talcott Parsons, "A Revised Analytical Approach to the Theory of Social Stratification," in Parsons, *Essays in Sociological Theory* (Glencoe, Ill.: Free Press, 1954), pp. 386–439.

24. William Goode, *The Family* (Englewood Cliffs, N.J.: Prentice-Hall, 1964), p. 21. For an updated discussion of illegitimacy by the author, which focuses more on family than on societal needs and concerns, see the second edition of this book (Prentice-Hall, 1982), pp 41 12.

25. *Ibid.*, p, 24

26. A notable exception is in the work of Emile Durkheim, a nineteenth-

century founder of modern functionalism. See Emile Durkheim (1893), *The Division of Labor in Society*, George Simpson, tr. (New York: Macmillan, 1933).

27. See Talcott Parsons, *The Evolution of Societies* (Englewood Cliffs, N.J.: Prentice-Hall, 1977).

28. Suzanne Keller attempts to correct for the omission of power in the functionalist model in *Beyond the Ruling Class* (New York: Random House, 1963).

29. Examples of efforts in this direction are Gerhard Lenski, *Power and Privilege* (New York: McGraw-Hill, 1966); Pierre L. Van Den Berghe, "Dialectic and Functionalism: Toward a Theoretical Synthesis," *American Sociological Review* (1964), 28:695–705; and Peter M. Blau, ed., *Approaches to the Study of Social Structure* (New York: Free Press, 1975), especially the article by Seymour Martin Lipset.

30. See Martin A. Nettleship, R. Dalegivens, and Anderson Nettleship, eds., *War: Its Causes and Correlates* (The Hague: Mouton Publishers, 1975; distributed by Aldine-Atherton, Chicago.), especially the articles by Marilyn Keyes Roper and Rose Oldfield Hayes, who trace the first organized wars between neighboring societies to conflicts over surplus trade items.

31. Herbert Spencer (1873), *The Study of Sociology* (Ann Arbor: University of Michigan Press, 1961), pp. 341–42.

32. Jesse R. Pitts, "The Structural-Functional Approach," in Harold T. Christensen, *Handbook of Marriage and the Family* (Chicago: Rand McNally, 1964), p. 76.

33. Engels, *The Origin of the Family*, pp. 60, 89.

34. *Ibid.*, pp. 70, 71.

35. *Ibid.*, pp. 98–100.

36. See Joan Aldous, "From Dual-Earner to Dual-Career Families and Back Again," *Journal of Family Issues* (1981), 2:115–25.

37. See William J. Goode, *World Revolution and Family Patterns* (New York: Free Press, 1963).

38. A pioneering study documenting the relationship between economic resources and authority is Robert O. Blood, Jr., and Donald M. Wolfe, *Husbands and Wives: The Dynamics of Married Living* (New York: Free Press, 1960). See also Ronald E. Cromwell and David H. Olson, eds., *Power in Families* (New York: Wiley, 1975); and Gerald W. McDonald, "Family Power: The Assessment of a Decade of Theory and Research, 1970–1979," *Journal of Marriage and the Family* (1980), 42:841–54.

39. See Hyman Rodman, "Marital Power and the Theory of Resources in Cultural Context," *Journal of Comparative Family Studies* (1972), 3:50–67.

40. Merton, *Social Theory and Social Structure*, pp. 5–6.

41. A pioneering approach to this level of analysis can be found in Gerald Handel, "Psychological Study of Whole Families," *Psychological Bulletin* (1965), 63:19–41. This approach is illustrated in Gerald Handel, ed., *The Psy-*

chosocial Interior of the Family (Chicago: Aldine, 1967; rev. ed., 1972).

42. Emile Durkheim (1897), *Suicide,* John A. Spaulding and George Simpson, trs. (Glencoe, Ill.: Free Press, 1951).

43. See Arlie Russell Hochschild, "Emotion Work, Feeling Rules, and Social Structure," *American Journal of Sociology* (1979), 85:551–75.

44. For short but comprehensive reviews of recent trends and prospects in sociological research on the family, see the articles by Felix M. Berardo, Reuben Hill, Greer Litton Fox, and Jacqueline P. Wiseman, and a comment on these articles by Joan Aldous, in *Journal of Marriage and the Family* (1981), 43:249–70.

45. Examples of this type of research are Chaya S. Piotrokowski, *Work and the Family System: A Naturalistic Study of Working-Class and Lower-Middle-Class Families* (New York: Free Press, 1978); and Lillian B. Rubin, *Worlds of Pain: Life in the Working-Class Family* (New York: Basic Books, 1976).

46. Melvin L. Kohn, *Class and Conformity: A Study in Values* (2d ed.; Chicago: University of Chicago Press, 1977). See also Godfrey J. Ellis, Gary R. Lee, and Larry R. Petersen, "Supervision and Conformity: A Cross-Cultural Analysis of Parental Socializaton Values," *American Journal of Sociology,* (1978), 84:386–403

47. See John Scanzoni, "Contemporary Marriage Types," *Journal of Family Issues* (1980), 1:125–40.

48. Charles F. Westoff, "Coital Frequency and Contraception" *Family Planning Perspectives* (1974), 6:136–41.

49. Margaret M. Paloma, Brian F. Pendleton, and T. Neal Garland, "Reconsidering the Dual-Career Marriage," *Journal of Family Issues* (1981), 2:205–14; and Suzanne Model, "Housework by Husbands," *Journal of Family Issues* (1981), 2:225–37.

50. Richard A. Berk and Sarah Fenstermaker Berk, *Labor and Leisure at Home: Content and Organization of the Household Day* (Beverly Hills, Calif.: Sage, 1979).

51. Daniel Patrick Moynahan, *The Negro Family: The Case for National Action* (Washington, D.C.: GPO, 1965).

52. Lee Rainwater, "Crucible of Identity: The Lower Class Negro Family," *Daedalus,* (1966), 95:258–64.

53. Jerold Heiss, *The Case of the Black Family: A Sociological Inquiry* (New York: Columbia University Press, 1975); and Charles V. Willie, *A New Look at Black Families* (Bayside, N.Y.: General Hall, 1976).

54. See Eugene Genovese, *Roll, Jordan, Roll* (New York: Pantheon Books, 1974).

55. Herbert Gutman, *The Black Family in Slavery and Freedom: 1750–1925* (New York: Pantheon Books, 1976).

56. Frank F. Furstenberg, Jr., Theodore Hershberg, and John Modell, "The Origins of the Female-headed Black Family: The Impact of the Urban Experience," *Journal of Interdisciplinary History* (1975), 5:211–33.

57. Vern Bengston and Edythe DeTerre, "Aging and Family Relations," *Marriage and Family Review* (1980), 3:40–51.

58. See Ethel Shanas, "Social Myth as Hypothesis: The Case of the Family Relations of Old People," *The Gerontologist* (1979), 19:3–9.

59. Lois M. Tamir and Toni C. Antonnucci, "Self-Perception, Motivation, and Social Support Through the Family Life Course," *Journal of Marriage and the Family* (1981), 43:151–60; and Norma Haan and D. Day, "A Longitudinal Study of Change and Sameness in Personality Development: Adolescence to Later Adulthood," *International Journal of Human Development* (1974), 5:11–39.

60. See David Sudnow, *Passing On: The Social Organization of Dying* (Englewood Cliffs, N.J.: Prentice-Hall, 1967); and Thomas Powers, "Learning to Die," in Peter J. Rose, ed., *Socialization and the Life Cycle* (New York: St. Martin's Press, 1980), pp. 378–92.

2. THE BIOLOGICAL BASE

1. For a more detailed discussion of nuclear and extended families, and families who are in between, see Betty Yorburg, "The Nuclear and the Extended Family: An Area of Conceptual Confusion," *Journal of Comparative Family Studies* (1975), 6:1–14.

2. A fascinating and nonideological account of human evolution can be found in Peter J. Wilson, *Man, the Promising Primate: The Conditions of Human Evolution* (New Haven: Yale University Press, 1981).

3. The landmark work of Harry F. Harlow and his associates provided dramatic evidence of the effect of isolation and maternal deprivation on instinctual behavior in monkeys. See Harry F. Harlow and Margaret K. Harlow, "Social Deprivation in Monkeys," *Scientific American* (1962), 5:136–46. See also Jack P. Hailman, "How an Instinct Is Learned," *Scientific American* (1969), 12:98–106, which describes similar findings in experiments with sea gull chicks.

4. See James Ramey, "Experimental Family Forms—The Family of the Future," *Marriage and Family Review* (1978), 1:1–9.

5. Margaret Mead reported on one such society, the Mundugumor, in *Sex and Temperament in Three Primitive Societies* (New York: William Morrow, 1935), pp. 129–71.

6. See Kingsley Davis, "Extreme Social Isolation of a Child," *American Journal of Sociology* (1940), 45:554–65; and Kingsley Davis, "Final Note on a Case of Extreme Isolation," *American Journal of Sociology* (1947), 52:432–37. For a more recent example see Susan R. Curtiss, *Genie: A Linguistic Study of a Modern Day "Wildchild"* (New York: Academic Press, 1977).

7. See Daniel J. Levinson, *The Seasons of a Man's Life* (New York: Knopf, 1978).

8. Philippe Aries, *Centuries of Childhood* (New York: Vintage Books, 1962).

9. Herbert Goldhamer and Albert Marshall, *Psychosis and Civilization* (Glencoe, Ill.: Free Press, 1953).

10. Leo Srole et al., *Mental Health in the Metropolis* (New York: McGraw-Hill, 1962); and Leo Srole and Anita Fischer, *Mental Health in the Metropolis: The Mid-Town Manhattan Study* (rev. ed.; New York: New York University Press, 1978).

11. The classic and pioneering study in this field is August Hollingshead and Frederick C. Redlich, *Social Class and Mental Illness* (New York: Wiley, 1958).

12. See Lloyd DeMause, *The History of Childhood* (New York: Psychohistory Press, 1974).

13. For an excellent anthropological account of education in major types of societies, see George D. Spindler, *Education and Culture* (New York: Holt, Rinehart, and Winston, 1963).

14. See Leslie E. Zegiob and Rex Forehand, "Maternal Interactive Behavior as a Function of Race, Socioeconomic Status, and Sex of the Child," *Child Development* (1975), 46:564–68.

15. J. McVicker Hunt has been a major proponent of the concept of critical periods in learning capabilities. For a recent review of work in this area, see J. McVicker Hunt, "Psychological Development: Early Experience," *Annual Review of Psychology* (1979), 30:103–43. See also, Burton L. White, *The First Three Years of Life* (Englewood Cliffs, NJ.: Prentice-Hall, 1975).

16. See Samuel Bowles and Herbert Gintis, *Schooling in Capitalist America* (New York: Basic Books, 1976); and Christopher Jencks, *Who Gets Ahead: The Determinants of Economic Success in America* (New York: Basic Books, 1979).

17. Karl T. Alexander, Martha Cook, and Edward T. McDill, "Curriculum Tracking and Educational Stratification: Some Further Evidence," *American Sociological Review* (1978), 43:47–66.

18. Lionel S. Lewis and Richard A. Wanner, "Private Schooling and the Status Attainment Process," *Sociology of Education* (1979), 52:99–112.

19. On biological changes during adolescence, a good reference work is Herant A. Katchadourian, *The Biology of Adolescence* (San Francisco: Freeman, 1977).

20. Margaret Mead, *Coming of Age in Samoa* (New York: William Morrow, 1928)

21. William J. Goode, "The Theoretical Importance of Love," *American Sociological Review* (1959), 24:38. See also Bernard I. Murstein, *Love, Sex, and Marriage Through the Ages* (New York: Springer, 1974).

22. Reported in the New York *Times*, December 6, 1980, p. 1.

23. Two widely cited psychoanalytic sources on this topic are Peter Blos, *On Adolescence: A Psychoanalytic Interpretation* (New York: Free Press, 1962), and Erik H. Erikson, *Identity: Youth and Crisis* (New York: Norton, 1968).

24. For a recent review of this research, see Joseph Adelson, "Adolescence and the Generation Gap," *Psychology Today* (1979), 12:33–37.

25. A good source on aging written specifically from a sociological perspective is Diana K. Harris and William E. Cole, *The Sociology of Aging* (Boston: Houghton Mifflin, 1980). See also Robert C. Atchley, *The Social Forces in Later Life: An Introduction to Social Gerontology* (3d ed.; Belmont; Calif.: Wadsworth, 1980).

26. The classic and still unsurpassed study of the aged in nonliterate societies is Leo W. Simons, *The Role of the Aged in Primitive Society* (New Haven: Yale University Press, 1945).

27. William D. Crano and Joel Aronoff, "A Cross-Cultural Study of Expressive and Instrumental Role Complementarity in the Family," *American Sociological Review* (1978), 43:463–71.

28. For a more detailed review of research data on this controversial issue see Betty Yorburg, *Sexual Identity: Sex Roles and Social Change* (New York: Wiley, 1974), ch. 2. For an evolutionary perspective on this topic, see Sarah Bloffer Hrdy, *The Woman That Never Evolved* (Cambridge, Mass.: Harvard University Press, 1981).

29. See Arnold H. Buss and Richard A. Plovin, *A Temperament Theory of Personality Development* (New York: Wiley, 1975).

30. Richard Green and John Money, *Transexualism and Sex Reassignment* (Baltimore: Johns Hopkins University Press, 1969). See also, John Money and Anke A. Enrhardt, *Man and Woman Boy and Girl* (Baltimore: Johns Hopkins University Press, 1972).

31. Mary Jane Sherfey, *The Nature and Evolution of Female Sexuality* (New York: Random House, 1972).

32. See Clellan S. Ford and Frank A. Beach, *Patterns of Sexual Behavior* (New York: Harper and Row, 1951); and Frank A. Beach, ed., *Human Sexuality in Four Perspectives* (Baltimore: John Hopkins University Press, 1977).

33. Konrad Lorenz, *On Aggression* (New York: Harcourt, Brace and World, 1966); Robert Ardrey, *African Genesis* (New York: Atheneum, 1961), and *The Territorial Imperative* (New York: Atheneum, 1966).

34. For a revew of the evidence on the genetic basis of human aggression by a variety of experts from different fields, see Ashley Montagu, ed., *Man and Aggression* (2d ed.; New York: Oxford University Press, 1973).

35. See the classic and original work on this topic by John Dollard and his associates, *Frustration and Aggression* (New Haven: Yale University Press, 1935).

36. David McClelland, *Power: The Inner Experience* (New York: Irvington, 1975).

37. See C. R. Jeffery, ed., *Biology and Crime* (Beverly Hills, Calif.: Sage, 1979).

38. Ashley Montagu, *The Natural Superiority of Women* (New York: Macmillan, 1968).

39. Lolagene Coombs, "Preferences for Sex of Children Among U.S. Couples," *Family Planning Perspectives* (1977), 9:259–65.

3. TYPES OF HUMAN SOCIETIES

1. See the previously mentioned article by Gerhard Lenski, "History and Social Change," *American Journal of Sociology* (1976), 82:549–64, for an elaboration of this point.

2. The work of V. Gordon Childe on technological development is still relevant to much of this discussion. See *Man Makes Himself* (New York: Mentor, 1951) and *What Happened in History* (Baltimore: Penguin Books, 1964). Another valuable source is Gideon Sjoberg, *The Preindustrial City: Past and Present* (Glencoe, Ill.: Free Press, 1960). See also Gerhard Lenski and Jean Lenski, *Human Societies* (4th ed.: New York: McGraw-Hill, 1982) and Marvin Harris, *Culture, People, Nature* (3d ed.; New York: Thomas Y. Crowell, 1980).

3. See Emile Durkheim (1902), *The Elementary Forms of the Religious Life*, J. W. Swain, tr. (Glencoe, Ill.: Free Press, 1948).

4. Guy E. Swanson, *The Birth of Gods: The Origin of Primitive Beliefs* (Ann Arbor: University of Michigan Press, 1960), ch. 3.

5. See Max Weber (1922), *The Sociology of Religion*, Ephriam Fischoff, tr. and ed. (Boston: Beacon Press, 1963), ch. 2.

6. See Robert Redfield, *Peasant Societies and Culture* (Chicago: University of Chicago Press, 1956).

7. See Gerhard Lenski, *Power and Privilege* (New York: McGraw-Hill, 1966), pp. 267–70.

8. See Max Weber (1904), *The Protestant Ethic and the Spirit of Capitalism* (New York: Mentor, 1947). Weber gives greater weight to values than to economics in explaining the Industrial Revolution.

9. See Alain Touraine, *The Post-Industrial Society* (New York: Random House, 1971); and Daniel Bell, *The Coming of Post-Industrial Society: A Venture in Social Forecasting* (New York: Basic Books, 1973).

10. For a highly original and thoughtful essay on this topic see Murray Melbin, "Night as Frontier," *American Sociological Review* (1978), 43:3–22.

11. Two classic social scientific statements of the changing nature of social relationships in urban, industrial societies are: Ferdinand Toennies (1887), *Community and Society*, Charles P. Loomis, tr. and ed. (East Lansing: Michigan State University Press, 1957); and Georg Simmel (1900), "The Metropolis and Mental Life," in *The Sociology of Georg Simmel*, Kurt H. Wolff, tr. and ed. (Glencoe, Ill.: Free Press, 1950), pp. 409–24.

12. For documentation of changes in these values in six different, currently industrializing societies, see Alex Inkeles and David H. Smith, *Becoming Modern* (Cambridge, Mass.: Harvard University Press, 1974).

13. National Center for Education Statistics, *The Condition of Education* (Washington, D.C.: GPO, 1981), pp. 147, 157.

14. Focusing specifically on Brazil, Bernard C. Rosen has documented the spread of achievement motivation and other urban values in developing countries and the consequences of these changing values for family life. See Bernard C. Rosen, *The Industrial Connection: Achievement and the Family in Developing Societies* (New York: Aldine, 1982).

4. VARIETIES OF FAMILY LIFE

1. William J. Goode, *World Revolution and Family Patterns* (New York: Free Press, 1963), p. 25, and *The Family* (2d ed., Englewood Cliffs, N.J.: Prentice-Hall, 1982), p. 187.

2. Meyer F. Nimkoff and Russell Middleton, "Types of Family and Types of Economy," *American Journal of Sociology* (1960), 66:215–25; and Robert F. Winch and Associates, *Familial Organization* (New York: Free Press, 1977).

3. Peter Laslett and Richard Wall, eds., *Household and Family in Past Time* (Cambridge: Cambridge University Press, 1972); and Peter Laslett, "Characteristics of the Western Family Considered Over Time," *Journal of Family History* (1977), 2:89–115.

4. See Betty Yorburg, "The Nuclear and the Extended Family: An Area of Conceptual Confusion," *Journal of Comparative Family Studies* (1975), 6:1–14; and Jean-Louis Flandrin, *Families in Former Times: Kinship, Household and Sexuality* (New York: Cambridge University Press, 1979).

5. Gary R. Lee, "Marital Structure and Economic Systems," *Journal of Marriage and the Family* (1979), 41:701–14.

6. See Rae Lesser Blumberg, *Stratification: Socioeconomic and Sexual Inequality* (Dubuque, Iowa: William C. Brown, 1978).

7. See Neil Smelser, *Social Change in the Industrial Revolution* (Chicago: University of Chicago Press, 1959).

8. For a superb account of transitional patterns in an industrializing society, see Oscar Lewis, *Five Families* (New York: Basic Books, 1959).

9. See Michael Young and Peter Willmott, *Family and Kinship in East London* (Baltimore: Penguin Books, 1962).

10. Herbert Gans, *The Urban Villagers* (New York rev. ed., 1982), describes the effects of urban renewal on Italian extended families in the West End of Boston. See also, Andrew Rolle, *The Italian Americans: Troubled Roots* (New York: Macmillan, 1980).

11. See Theodore Caplow and Bruce A. Chadwick, "Inequality and Life Styles in Middletown, 1920–1978," *Social Science Quarterly* (1979), 6:367–86.

12. Frank F. Furstenberg, Jr., "Industrialization and the American Fam-

ily: A Look Backward,'' *American Sociological Review* (1966), 31:326–37; and Michael Gordon, ed., *The American Family in Social-Historical Perspective* (2d ed.; New York: St. Martin's Press, 1978).

13. See the special issue on the Japanese family, *Journal of Comparative Family Studies*, Vol. 12, Fall 1981.

14. For contemporary cross-national data on this topic, see the special issue on the one-parent family, *Journal of Comparative Family Studies*, Vol. 11, Winter 1980.

15. See Rae Lesser Blumberg and Maria-Pilar Garcia, ''The Political Economy of the Mother-Child Family: A Cross-Societal View,'' in Luis Lenero-Otero, ed., *Beyond the Nuclear Family Model* (Beverly Hills: Sage, 1977), pp. 99–164.

16. Suzanne M. Bianchi and Reynolds Farley, ''Racial Differences in Family Living Arrangements and Economic Well-Being: An Analysis of Recent Trends,'' *Journal of Marriage and the Family* (1979), 41:537–52.

17. See Peter Laslett, Karla Oosterveen, and Richard Smith, eds., *Bastardy and Its Comparative History* (Cambridge, Mass.: Harvard University Press, 1980), especially the article by John Knodel and Stephen Hochstadt.

18. For a critique of the French study, see John Bongaarts, ''Infertility after Age 30: A False Alarm,'' *Family Planning Perspectives* (March/April 1982), 14:75–78.

19. See Paul C. Glick, ''Remarriage: Some Recent Changes and Variations,'' *Journal of Family Issues* (1980), 1:455–78.

20. See Betty Yorburg, *Utopia and Reality: A Collective Portrait of American Socialists* (New York: Columbia University Press, 1969).

21. Ronald C. Kessler and James A. McRae, Jr., ''The Effect of Wives' Employment,'' *American Sociological Review* (1982), 47:216–27.

22. Arthur W. Calhoun, *A Social History of the American Family* (Glendale, Calif.: Arthur H. Clark, 1917), Vol. 1, p. 120.

23. E. A. Wrigley, *Population and History* (London: University Library, 1969).

24. Georgia Dullea, ''Female Circumcision a Topic at United Nations Parley,'' New York *Times*, July 18, 1980, B4.

25. See Murray A. Strauss, Richard J. Gelles, and Suzanne K. Steinmetz, *Behind Closed Doors: Violence in the American Family* (New York: Doubleday/Anchor, 1979).

26. Richard Von Krafft-Ebbing (1882), *Psychopathia Sexualis* (New York: Putnam, 1965); Havelock Ellis (1897), *Studies in the Psychology of Sex* (6 vols.; Philadelphia: F. A. Davis, 1905–15; and Sigmund Freud (1905), ''Three Essays on the Theory of Sexuality,'' in *The Standard Edition of the Complete Psychological Works of Sigmund Freud*, James Strachey, tr. and ed. (24 vols.; London: Hogarth, 1953–66), Vol. 7, 125–243.

27. Richard R. Clayton and Janet L. Bokemeier, ''Premarital Sex in the Seventies,'' *Journal of Marriage and the Family* (1980), 42:759–75.

28. Sigmund Freud (1921), "Group Psychology and the Analysis of the Ego," in *The Standard Edition of the Complete Psychological Works of Sigmund Freud*, James Strachey, tr. and ed. (24 vols.; London: Hogarth, 1953–66), Vol. 18, pp. 69–143.

29. Sigmund Freud (1914), "On Narcissism: An Introduction," in *The Standard Edition of the Complete . . . Works*, Vol. 14, p. 87.

30. Robert F. Winch, *Mate Selection: A Study of Complementary Needs* (New York: Harper and Row, 1958.

31. See Benjamin I. Murstein, *Who Will Marry Whom? Theories and Research in Marital Choice* (New York: Springer, 1976).

32. See Michael Paul Sacks, "Unchanging Times: A Comparison of the Everyday Life of Soviet Men and Women Between 1923–1966," *Journal of Marriage and the Family* (1977), 39:793–805; and Sheila B. Kamerman, "Work and Family in Industrialized Societies," *Signs* (1979), 4:932–50.

33. See Joan Aldous, "From Dual-Earner to Dual-Career Families and Back Again," *Journal of Family Issues* (1981), 2:115–25.

34. Norval D. Glenn and Sara McLanahan, "Children and Marital Happiness: A Further Specification of the Relationship," *Journal of Marriage and the Family* (1982), 44:63–72.

35. Willie Pearson, Jr., and Lewellyn Hendrix, "Divorce and the Status of Women," *Journal of Marriage and the Family* (1979), 41:375–85.

36. Norval D. Glenn and Charles N. Weaver, "The Contribution of Marital Happiness to Global Happiness," *Journal of Marriage and the Family* (1981), 43:161–68.

37. The original and pathbreaking research on this topic in the United States can be found in Theodore W. Adorno et al., *The Authoritarian Personality* (New York: Wiley, 1950).

38. See Diana Baumrind, "Reciprocal Rights and Obligations in Parent-Child Relations," *Journal of Social Issues* (1978), 34:179–95.

39. Research on this topic is sparse and based on small, self-selected samples, but see J. E. Veevers, "Voluntary Childlessness: A Review of Issues and Evidence," *Marriage and Family Review* (1979, 2:1–26; and Sharon Houseknecht, "Voluntary Childlessness in the 1980's: A Significant Increase?" *Marriage and Family Review* (1982), 5:51–69.

40. See, for example, George E. Vaillant, *Adaptation to Life* (Boston: Little, Brown, 1977).

41. *Statistical Notes* (Washington, D.C.: National Clearinghouse on Aging). Administration on Aging, Department of Health, Education, and Welfare Publication no. 80-20175, April 1980.

42. See Sheila B. Kamerman, "Community Services for the Aged: The View from Eight Countries," *The Gerontologist* (1976), 16:529–37.

43. Ethel Shanas, *National Survey of the Elderly: Report to Administration on Aging* (Washington, D.C.: Department of Health and Human Services, 1979).

44. U.S. Bureau of the Census, "Marital Status and Living Arrangements: March, 1980," *Current Population Reports* Series P-20, No. 365, 1981.

45. For a good collection of papers on historical changes in family life, see John Demos and Sarane Spence Boocock, eds., *Turning Points: Historical and Sociological Essays on the Family* (Chicago: University of Chicago Press, 1978).

5. AMERICAN VARIATIONS: ETHNIC CONTRASTS

1. See Robin M. Williams, Jr., *American Society: A Sociological Interpretation* (3d ed.; New York: Knopf, 1970).

2. Andrew M. Greeley, *Crisis in the Church: A Study of American Religion* (Chicago: Thomas More Press, 1979).

3. See the previously cited sources in chap. 1. For data on differences between middle-class black married and single people, see Robert Staples, *The World of Black Singles* (Westport, Conn.: Greenwood Press, 1981).

4. Wade Clark Roof, "Socioeconomic Differentials Among Socioreligious Groups in the United States," *Social Forces* (1979), 58:280–89.

5. For a more detailed discussion of the problems of assimilation in human societies, see Milton M. Gordon, *Human Nature, Class, and Ethnicity* (New York: Oxford University Press, 1978).

6. U.S. Bureau of the Census, *Statistical Abstract of the United States 1980* (Washington, D.C.: GPO, 1980), p. 460.

7. See U.S. Bureau of the Census, *The Social and Economic Status of the Black Population in the United States: An Historical Overview 1790–1978*, Series P-23, No. 80 (Washington, D.C.: GPO, 1979).

8. For an in-depth case study of the economic stresses and resulting marital difficulties of black males, see Elliot Liebow, *Talley's Corner* (Boston: Little, Brown, 1967).

9. Charles V. Willie and Susan L. Greenblatt, "Four 'Classic' Studies of Power Relationships in Black Families: A Review and Look to the Future," *Journal of Marriage and the Family* (1978), 40:691–94.

10. On the topic of child rearing within black families, see Karen W. Bartz and Elaine S. LeVine, "Childrearing by Black Parents: A Description and Comparison to Anglo and Chicano Parents," *Journal of Marriage and the Family* (1978), 40:709–19.

11. See Carnegie Council on Policy Studies in Higher Education, *Three Thousand Futures: The Next 20 Years in Higher Education* (San Francisco: Jossey-Bass, 1979).

12. For a short but comprehensive summary of research information on Mexican Americans, see Joan W. Moore and Harry Pachón, *Mexican Americans* (Englewood Cliffs, N.J.: Prentice-Hall, 1976).

13. See Alfred Mirandé "The Chicano Family: A Reanalysis of Conflicting Views, *Journal of Marriage and The Family* (1977), 39:747–56.

14. See Harry J. L. Kitano, *Japanese Americans: Evolution of a Subculture* (2d ed.; Englewood Cliffs, N.J.: Prentice-Hall, 1976). See also Kitano's article in the *Harvard Encyclopedia of American Ethnic Groups*, Stephan Thernstrom, ed. (Cambridge, Mass.: Harvard University Press, 1980), pp. 561–71.

15. Eric Woodrum, "An Assessment of Japanese American Assimilation, Pluralism, and Subordination," *American Journal of Sociology* (1981), 87:157–69.

16. See John Connor, *Tradition and Change in Three Generations of Japanese Americans* (Chicago: Nelson-Hall, 1977).

17. For documentation of this point, see Edna Bonacich and John Modell, *The Economic Basis of Ethnic Solidarity: Small Business in the Japanese American Community* (Berkeley, Calif.: University of California Press, 1980).

18. A classic account of shtetl culture can be found in Mark Zborowski and Elizabeth Herzog, *Life Is with People* (New York: International Universities Press, 1951).

19. See Marshall Sklare, ed., *Understanding American Jewry* (New Brunswick, N.J.: Transaction Books, 1982); and Bernard Lazerwitz and Michael Harrison, "American Jewish Denominations: A Social and Religious Profile," *American Sociological Review* (1979), 44:656–666.

6. AMERICAN VARIATIONS: CLASS DIFFERENCES

1. For data on similarities in occupational prestige in sixty societies, ranging in level of technology from industrializing to postindustrial, see Donald J. Treiman, *Occupational Prestige in Comparative Perspective* (New York: Academic Press, 1977).

2. A good general source on this topic is Daniel Rossides, *The American Class System* (Boston: Houghton Mifflin, 1976); see also Lee Rainwater and Richard Coleman, *Social Standing in America* (New York: Basic Books, 1978). For a conflict perspective, see Charles H. Anderson, *The Political Economy of Social Class* (Englewood Cliffs, N.J.: Prentice-Hall, 1974).

3. Friends who are most highly valued tend to be of slightly higher status, in fact. See Edward O. Laumann, *Prestige and Association in an Urban Community* (Indianapolis: Bobbs-Merrill, 1966); and Edward Shils, "Deference," in John A. Jackson, ed., *Social Stratification: Sociological Studies* (Cambridge: Cambridge University Press, 1968), pp. 104–32.

4. See Marie R. Haug, "Social Class Measurement and Women's Occupational Roles," *Social Forces* (1973), 52:85–98; Stephen L. Nock and Peter H. Rossi, "Household Types and Social Standing," *Social Forces* (1978), 57:325–45; and Valerie Kincaid Oppenheimer, "The Sociology of Women's Economic Role in the Family," *American Sociological Review* (1977), 42:387–406.

5. See National Center for Educational Statistics, *The Condition of Education* (Washington, D.C., 1981), p. 221.

6. An exception is the work of E. Digby Baltzell who was born into this

class but who is also a trained sociologist. See E. Digby Baltzell (1964), *The Protestant Establishment* (New York: Octagon, 1981), and *Puritan Boston and Quaker Philadelphia* (New York: Free Press, 1980).

7. See John Bowlby, *The Making and Breaking of Affectional Bonds* (London: Tavistock Publications, 1979).

8. Thorstein Veblen (1899; 1912), *The Theory of the Leisure Class* (New York: Mentor, 1953), p. 42.

9. A pathbreaking study of this kind was done by Herbert Gans, *The Levittowners* (New York: Pantheon Books, 1967). See also Chaya S. Piotrokowski, *Work and the Family System: A Naturalistic Study of Working-Class and Lower-Middle-Class Families* (New York: Free Press, 1978).

10. Studies of swingers have been based on small samples, but see Brian G. Gilmartin, *The Gilmartin Report* (Secaucus, N.J.: Citadel Press, 1978).

11. Two well-known interview studies of traditional upper working-class family life are Lee Rainwater, Richard P. Coleman, and Gerald Handel, *Working Man's Wife* (Chicago: Oceana, 1959), and Mirra Kamarovsky, *Blue-Collar Marriage* (New York: Random House, 1964). See also Edgar E. Le-Masters, *Blue Collar Aristocrats* (Madison: University of Wisconsin Press, 1975).

12. This applies also to the poor. See David Caplovitz, *Making Ends Meet* (Beverly Hills, Calif.: Sage, 1979).

13. A good description of recent trends and changes in the values and behavior of working-class women can be found in Janet Zollinger Giele, *Women and the Future* (New York: Free Press, 1978).

14. The great importance of economic safeguards is documented in a comparison between younger working-class and professional families in a depth-interview study by Lillian Rubin, *Worlds of Pain: Life in the Working-Class Family* (New York: Basic Books, 1976).

15. The effects of economic inequality on children are documented by Richard H. de Lone in *Small Futures* (New York: Harcourt Brace Jovanovich, 1979).

16. On the relationship between economic conditions and family violence see Richard J. Gelles, *Family Violence* (Beverly Hills, Calif.: Sage, 1979).

17. The best evidence for this point is found in community studies that attempt to portray the life of the poor in depth. See Oscar Lewis, *Five Families* (New York: Basic Books, 1959); Harry M. Caudill, *Night Comes to the Cumberland* (Boston: Atlantic-Little Brown, 1963); Elliot Liebow, *Talley's Corner* (Boston: Beacon, 1967); Gerald D. Suttles, *The Social Order of the Slum* (Chicago: University of Chicago Press, 1968); and Ulf Hannerz, *Soulside* (New York: Columbia University Press, 1969).

18. Consortium of Longitudinal Studies, "The Persistence of Pre-School Effects: A National Collaborative Study," *Young Children* (1978), 33:65–71.

19. On this point see Herbert Gans, *More Equality* (New York: Pantheon Books, 1973).

20. To cite just one of an accumulating number of research studies in sup-

port of this statement, see Michael Useem, "The Social Organization of the American Business Elite and Participation of Corporation Directors in the Governance of American Institutions," *American Sociological Review* (1979), 44:553–72. See also G. William Domhoff, *The Powers That Be: Processes of Ruling Class Domination in America* (New York: Vintage, 1979).

21. Sociologists sometimes use the term "role strain" to refer to what I have defined as role conflict. See, for example, William J. Goode, "A Theory of Role Strain," *American Sociological Review* (1960), 25:483–96; and Mirra Kamarovsky, "Cultural Contradictions and Problems in Role Analysis," *American Sociological Review* (1974), 38:649–62.

22. Theodore Caplow et al., *Middletown Families: Fifty Years of Change and Continuity* (Minneapolis: University of Minnesota Press, 1982). The original study was published in 1929. See Robert Lynd and Helen Merrell Lynd, *Middletown: A Study in American Culture* (New York: Harcourt and Brace, 1959).

7. TODAY AND TOMORROW

1. For a review of research evidence on this point see Larry L. Constantine, "Multilateral Relations Revisited: Group Marriage in Extended Perspective," in Benjamin I. Murstein, ed., *Exploring Intimate Life Styles* (New York: Springer, 1978), pp. 131–47; and James Ramey, "Experimental Family Forms—The Family of the Future," *Marriage and Family Review* (January–February 1978), 1:1–9.

2. U.S. Bureau of the Census, "Marital Status and Living Arrangements: March 1980," *Current Population Reports,* Series P-20, No. 365, 1981.

3. See Benjamin Zablocki, *Alienation and Charisma: A Study of Contemporary American Communes* (New York: Free Press, 1980) for a research report on sixty urban communes.

4. This is indicated, directly or indirectly, in repeated nationwide polls up to the present time. See Daniel Yankelovich, *New Rules: Searching for Self-Fulfillment in a World Turned Upside Down* (New York: Random House, 1981).

5. Paul C. Glick, "The Future of the American Family," Current Population Reports, Bureau of the Census, Special Studies. Series P-23, No. 78 (Washington, D.C.: GPO, 1979).

6. For a comprehensive review of research on living-together relationships see Paul C. Glick and Graham P. Spanier, "Married and Unmarried Cohabitation in the United States," *Journal of Marriage and the Family* (1980), 48:19–30.

7. See Glick, "The Future of the American Family."

8. See Sheila B. Kamerman, *Parenting in an Unresponsive Society: Managing Work and Family* (New York: Macmillan, 1980), and Sheila B. Kamerman and Alfred J. Kahn, *Family Policy: Government and Families in Fourteen Countries* (New York: Columbia University Press, 1978).

9. See Marshall Sahlins, *Stone Age Economics* (Chicago: Aldine, 1972).

Index